DON'T SAY YES
WHEN YOU WANT TO SAY NO

DON'T SAY YES WHEN YOU WANT TO SAY NO

HOW ASSERTIVENESS TRAINING CAN CHANGE YOUR LIFE

by

HERBERT FENSTERHEIM, Ph.D.

*Clinical Associate Professor of Psychology in Psychiatry,
Cornell University Medical College and
Head, Behavior Therapy Treatment and Study,
The New York Hospital, Payne Whitney Clinic*

and

JEAN BAER

DAVID McKAY COMPANY, INC.
New York

For Harry and Rose

Library of Congress Cataloging in Publication Data

Fensterheim, Herbert, 1921–
    Don't say yes when you want to say no.

    Bibliography: p.
    1. Assertiveness (Psychology) 2. Behavior modification. I. Baer, Jean L.,
1926–   joint author. II. Title.
BF575.A85F46   158'.1   74-25720
ISBN 0-679-50513-X

Contents

Author's Note

The material presented in this book stems from thirty years of scientific and clinical work, the first twenty spent in the traditional psychoanalytic approach and the remainder in behavior therapy. In both areas there are so many professors, colleagues, students (and patients) to acknowledge that I cannot list them all.

I would like to express my gratitude to Dr. Richard N. Kohl, professor of psychiatry, Cornell University Medical College and medical director, Payne Whitney Psychiatric Clinic of The New York Hospital, for encouraging and facilitating the formation of my Behavior Therapy Training Program and clinic at Payne Whitney.

I am also indebted to Dr. Helen S. Kaplan, clinical associate professor of psychiatry at Cornell University Medical College and head of the Sex Therapy and Education Program at the Payne Whitney Clinic—not just for her creative thinking in the area of sexual behavior and the professional stimulation she has given me in re-evaluating my approaches to treatment of patients but for many years of friendship. The late Dr. Gregory Razran, former chairman of the department of psychology at Queens College, was particularly helpful in leading me to greater understanding of the principles of Pavlov and their adaptation to psychotherapeutic treatment. He and his wife also provided the Florida retreat in which Jean and I began writing this book.

As I point out in this book, Assertiveness Training is not a simplistic concept, relying on gimmicky techniques. Carried out properly, AT involves considerations of neurophysiology, the individual's relationship with others within the social context, and the individual's general psychological organization. My own thinking in this area has been influenced by Andrew Salter, the New York psychologist who is generally regarded as the father of modern behavior therapy and whose highly original work within the field has won national and international recognition.

I would also like to say special words of thanks to Dr. Arnold Lazarus, professor of psychology and director of the Psy.D. Program in Clinical Psychology at the Graduate School of Applied and Professional Psychology of Rutgers University; Dr. Richard B. Stuart, professor, department of psychiatry, University of British Columbia and president, Association for the Advancement of Behavior Therapy; and Dr. Joseph Wolpe, head of the Behavior Therapy Unit, in the Department of Psychiatry, at Temple University School of Medicine. Through their publications plus correspondence and open discussions with them, they have contributed much to my own professional development in the Assertiveness Training area.

My heartfelt thanks go to Eleanor Rawson, our editor at David McKay Co., for her really loving interest and her concern about every word in this manuscript.

Above all, I would like to express my appreciation to my wife and co-author, whose challenging reportorial questions and insistance on "Don't give me theories—tell me how people can use them" forced me to clarify much of my own thinking. She has been truly a full collaborator in this book.

Herbert Fensterheim, Ph.D.

About the Collaboration That Produced This Book

Dr. Herbert Fensterheim, the senior author of *Don't Say Yes When You Want to Say No*, received his M.A. in psychology from Columbia University and his Ph.D. from New York University. He spent twenty years as an analytically oriented therapist before becoming one of the first clinicians involved with behavior therapy. Currently in private practice in Manhattan, he is Clinical Associate Professor of Psychology in Psychiatry, Cornell University Medical College and head, Behavior Treatment and Study, Payne Whitney Clinic, The New York Hospital. He has taught psychology at undergraduate, graduate and post-doctoral levels at leading universities and medical colleges. In addition he has written almost 100 professional papers, co-edited two professional books on behavior therapy, and is the author of *Help Without Psychoanalysis*. A recognized leader in Assertiveness Training, Dr. Fensterheim has given many talks to and workshops for the professional community at meetings of such groups as the American Psychological Association and the American Group Psychotherapy Association, thus enabling other therapists to learn the technique and teach it to patients.

Jean Baer, Dr. Fensterheim's collaborator (and in private life his wife) has written extensively on contemporary problems. Her previous books are *Follow Me!*, *The Single Girl Goes to Town*, and *The Second Wife*. She is a frequent contributor to *The Christian Science Monitor* and the major women's magazines. She has worked for the Mutual Broadcasting Company, the U.S. Information Agency, and spent many years as senior editor and special projects director of *Seventeen* magazine.

The substance and most details of the case histories presented in these pages are authentic. But the material has been greatly condensed to save the reader's time; and names and incidents have been disguised with great care to protect the privacy of patients.

Chapter 1 – Part 1

"It Worked for Me—
It Can Work
for You"

by

JEAN BAER

When I got married at the advanced age of forty, everyone said, "What a lucky girl you are."

I was. I married a man who is smart, sexy, sincere, considerate and looks vaguely like Yul Brynner. That was what I thought important at the time. But I didn't know how really lucky I was. My husband, Dr. Herbert Fensterheim, a clinical psychologist, specializes in behavior therapy of which one of the most important forms is Assertiveness Training (AT).

To the average person I would seem the last person to need any form of AT. I cope. In my working life I deal with difficulties and deadlines every minute. But the average person wouldn't know that I had spent eighteen years in the same job, expecting every day to get fired. Furthermore, I didn't dream of switching jobs. Where would I get another? I reasoned. Who would want me? And what would I be minus my glamor job? My answer, "Nothing"—this negative reaction despite the fact that through the years I had won a number of awards for performance.

In my personal life I was an equally timid soul. I loved it because all my friends turned to me in time of trouble. "You're the girl who comes with the chicken soup" they called me, even in pre-Portnoy's mother days. And I did. When they were bedded down with flu, there was I at their bedsides with that homemade soup. When I was sick, no one came to visit me. It never occurred to me to make the demand. Furthermore, any request, whether to go shopping or give a dinner party so that a single friend could have somewhere to invite a "new man," brought an affirmative response from me. I was always telling last minute white lies because I couldn't carry out my yes-promises.

Then, two years after my marriage, everything changed. One day on a Corsica beach, I burst into tears just like a Chekov heroine. Herb asked, "Can I help?" and my whole Pandora's box of problems burst open. I gave voice to all my fears: "There's a new regime at the office. I'll be the first to get fired." . . . "I've spent two years researching a book about Paris, 1900, but unless I leave you and move to Paris for a year, I can't write it. Anyway the subject is too hard for me." . . . "My friends are always making demands of me" . . . "My family picks on me" . . . "Sometimes you pick on me."

Herb listened to the torrent of words and then, with the same calm manner I'm sure he displays to disturbed patients, said, "You come on looking assertive, but you've lost control. You've stopped thinking where you want to go, and you've confused a whole set of goals. You've confused the goal of being liked with the goal of being respected. You've lost sight of sub-goals. You either do the ultimate or throw out what you've done. Let's establish some goals. What do you want to do with your life?"

I said, "I want to change my job, write another book, and have some peace. I'm tired of feeling picked on."

Re job, Herb counseled, "You've sat there for eighteen years, never asserting yourself, and all it has gotten you is work. How about taking a chance? With a new regime, you may be fired unless you think up something new to do. What could you do?" I knew what I could do. Immediately after our return to the United States, I sent a memo to my boss, outlining how my talents could be used in a different job. I got the promotion and a raise. Furthermore, I was one of five of the "old regime" who survived.

Re my French book, Herb made a statement which I cling to now every time I get depressed. He said, "Maybe you can't write it now, but it can be a long-time goal. Develop it. Maybe you'll eventually write it. But there are other steps you can take before you get to it. It isn't a choice between the French book and nothing." I immediately started working on a nonhistorical piece of nonfiction—one that could be done in New York—which emerged as *The Second Wife.*

Re friends and family, he had this to say. "You're so caught up in this need for being liked that you sacrifice your own self-respect. You could at least learn to handle put-downs in a way that makes you respect yourself. Now when friends and family criticize you, you just feel hurt and keep quiet, which is silent acquiescence which makes you hate yourself. A simple statement like 'I don't like what you've said,' will change the whole picture. And maybe, eventually, you'll learn to turn criticism back on them, and they'll stop doing it." Suddenly I realized I might be a female version of Caspar Milquetoast, but I didn't have to stay one.

As a result of this advice in just two years:

I changed my job to a far more glamorous and challenging one within the same firm at a 25 percent increase in pay.

Recently, another new regime took over, disbanded my department in an economy measure, and I actually did get fired. Did I feel like a "nothing"? Not at all. I welcomed the chance to try the free-lance way of life. Furthermore, within six weeks I had lined up writing assignments that exceeded my yearly salary. To my husband, I commented, "Everyone is making me offers. I thought without a job, I wouldn't have an identity." His answer: "You were the only one who thought so."

I have learned how to answer my so-called friends who put me down with such remarks as, "Anybody could write the books you write—you just sit down and do them, that's all." I progressed from "How can you speak to me like that?" to an assertive "Jealous?"

I have learned to say no to unreasonable requests. When my stepmother asks me (the only one of her female children and nieces who works full-time) to take care of her dog, I don't answer in the affirmative and then suffer for three months, while she vacations in California. I say, "I wish I could, but I can't." And then I hear her answer, "It's really better for Brownie to be in a kennel."

I can tell my husband the simple sentence, "I just don't want to do that."

I know that it is better to speak up than not speak up at all.

I have a series of goals and sub-goals. Five years from now I *will* write that French book!

As a result of my husband's lecture that day on the Corsican beach and the Assertiveness Training he has given me since, my whole life has changed from obsessive dithering to effective action. I know where I'm going. And all because I learned that the key to the happy, nonneurotic life is one little word—assertion.

It worked for me.

It can work for you.

In this book we will tell you how.

Part II
You Can Learn to Be Normal— Not Neurotic

Human beings want a life of dignity and self-fulfillment. Yet living leaves scars that distract us from these goals. Society teaches us to act in ways incompatible with these aims.

As a result, the world contains many people who don't recognize their own strengths or who have learned to act in inferior ways because they believe themselves to be inferior. They find it impossible to express emotions like anger or tenderness; sometimes they don't even feel them. They kowtow to the wishes of others and hold their own desires inside themselves. Because they possess no control of their own lives, they become increasingly unsure. They accept the state of *unassertiveness*.

In psychological terms, we say these people have *Inhibitory Personalities*. They have a thousand reasons for not acting, ten thousand reasons to fend off closeness. Low on self-sufficiency, they live their lives by the rules and whims of others. They do not know who they are, what they feel, what they want.

In contrast, people with *Excitatory Personalities* do *not* fear their feelings. Frightened neither of closeness nor combat, they act out of strength. The excitatory man knows who he is, what he wants. He is *assertive*.

Often a victim of unassertiveness does not recognize it as an emotional problem. From passivity and fear he or she justifies it with excuses: "If I speak up to my husband, he'll be mad at me" . . . "If I refuse to do that, she won't like me" . . . "My boss will fire me if I ask for a raise"

. . . "Why bother to try? I'm bound to fail." Unquestionably, these people suffer the sad and severe consequences of their unassertiveness: lack of personal growth and success, undeveloped relationships, mental anguish, and psychosomatic symptoms that range from fatigue and migraines to ulcers and impotence.

You learn this behavior with its unfortunate consequences. And even though it represents a neurotic lifetime pattern, you can unlearn it.

You can find the answers to your problems in a new scientific technique known as Assertiveness Training, through which by *changing your actions, you change your attitudes and feelings about yourself.* Assertiveness Training (which from now on we will call AT) takes as a premise: you have *learned* unsatisfactory forms of behavior, which have made you an unhappy, inhibited person, fearful of rejections, close relations, and standing up to others. AT aims at teaching you directly the arts of deeper communication with others, an active approach to life and self-mastery. *Just as you have trained yourself (or been trained) to be neurotic, you can teach yourself to be normal.*

BEHAVIOR THERAPY AND ASSERTIVENESS TRAINING

For more than a century, scientists have performed thousands upon thousands of experiments as they studied many forms of behavior, in the process learning that behavior is *lawful;* it follows certain rules. They gained the knowledge that under certain conditions behaviors can be changed and that these laws of behavioral change can have a practical application to the human problems of human beings.

Some twenty-five years ago this behavioral knowledge was first applied in clinical treatment with the introduction of behavior therapy, a radical (from the Latin *radix* meaning root) new technique with the premise that *what you do influences who you are and how you feel about yourself.* By changing the *symptoms* of neurotic behavior, you change you.

Until the emergence of behavior therapy (which from now on we will call BT), behavior per se possessed little importance in therapeutic treatment. Until two and a half decades ago, all treatment methods stemmed from Freud and accepted the idea that people are basically helpless until they gain knowledge of the conflicts, forces, and fantasies that reside in the unconscious and the childhood traumas that generated them. Psychoanalytically oriented therapists say it is who you are in the unconscious that influences what you do. Your behavior merely reflects your unconscious.

BT reversed this traditional stand. While psychoanalysis asks, "Why are you this way?" BT queries, "What can we do to change you *now*?" BT takes the individual's problem as it exists in the present, identifies the specific behaviors that must be changed to resolve his difficulties, and systematically attempts to change these behaviors, relying mainly, but not exclusively, on methods derived from the psychology of learning and conditioning and focusing the analysis on observable behaviors, accessible to counting or measuring, rather than on unconscious processes, drives, or conflicts. If a desired change does not take place, the behavior therapist assumes *he* is doing something wrong, re-evaluates and revises his approach until he obtains the desired results.

BT is not in direct conflict with Freud, Jung, or Horney. It maintains that the past is irrelevant to changing people and holds that people need not be passive and helpless in the face of cosmic unconsciousness.

BT feels that if you have learned a set of phobias in certain situations (whether impersonal, like riding in planes, or interpersonal, like fear of rejection), you can change your behavior so that you respond without fear. BT holds that you can get rid of unwanted habits, like overeating and obsessive thinking of put-down thoughts, and replace them with desired habits. BT says you can free yourself of tension, supplanting this state with one of calmness.

In this book, we will treat all of these behaviors, but the major emphasis will be on *the skills of relating to people and the world around you.* We call this area of BT Assertiveness Training.

THE ASSERTIVE PERSONALITY

According to *Webster's Third International Dictionary*, the verb "assert" means "to state or affirm positively, assuredly, plainly, or strongly."

In therapeutic terms, this provides only a limited explanation. The truly assertive person possesses four characteristics:

He feels free to *reveal himself.* Through words and actions he makes the statement, "This is me. This is what I feel, think, and want."

He can *communicate* with people on all levels—with strangers, friends, family. This communication is always open, direct, honest, and appropriate.

He has an *active orientation* to life. He goes after what he wants. In contrast to the passive person who waits for things to happen, he attempts to *make* things happen.

He acts in a way *he himself respects.* Aware that he cannot always win, he accepts his limitations. However, he always strives to make the good try so that win, lose, or draw, he maintains his self-respect.

In actuality, assertive behavior is the goal of *all* therapists. When achieved, it leads to a feeling of movement and a more exciting existence because of closer and deeper personal relations.

Because of a series of confusing environmental and conditioning factors, assertion has become a national problem.

Parents, teachers, clergymen, and businessmen have unwittingly conspired to produce a nation of timid souls. In early years, many mothers and fathers censor the child who decides to speak up for his rights and thus, hinder the child's assertion of self. Teachers reward the student who does not question the educational system and deal sternly with those who buck it. In most cases the church fosters the idea of humility and sacrifice rather than standing up for self. Many an employee learns early in his career that if he "speaks up," he is not likely to receive a raise or promotion and may even lose his job. Adopted at the office, this attitude carries over to home and social life.

On the other hand, people learn that to get ahead it is often acceptable, even necessary, to step on others. As Leo Durocher said, "Nice guys finish last." If you take this confusing cultural heritage seriously, almost every action and interaction becomes fraught with uncertainty.

Inappropriate learning may interfere with appropriate assertion. *You become conditioned to certain fears.* These may be social fears, like the fear of being disliked or rejected, or internal fears, like fears of anxiety, expression of anger, feeling tender. When you fear certain situations, you tend to avoid the circumstances that produce them, thus inhibiting assertive behavior and placing your life beyond your active control. For example, a sixteen-year-old girl, with a temporary case of acne, lacks partners at a high school dance. At seventeen, her complexion clear, she goes off to college, but the pain of the wallflower incident affects her whole life. She remains aloof from any close experience should something like it happen again.

Many people have an erroneous concept of assertion, confusing it with aggression and telling themselves "aggression is always bad." They fail to distinguish between being liked and being respected. *They mistake the essential difference between being selfish in the bad sense and selfish in the good sense* (the kind that made Walt Whitman write, "One's-Self I sing, a simple separate person").

Some people lack assertion because they have not acquired the skill through experience and practice. Bypassed by others with no more talent, they remain in the same job for years because they don't understand the method of getting promotions. Others cannot withstand insults or put-downs because they don't know some of the responses with which to counter such behavior (we will present these in Chapter IV). Others say yes to requests when they don't want to give an affirmative response, doing this because they have never learned the art of saying no.

In AT, the therapist functions as a teacher, with the aim of helping the patient to understand what is wrong with his life-style and how to change it. Attaching little importance to the unconscious, AT stresses two factors: (1) identification of the target behaviors that need changing, whether fear of closeness or lack of skills needed on the job; (2) the planning with the patient of a systematic program to achieve the life results he wants.

THE THEORETICAL BACKGROUND
OF ASSERTIVENESS TRAINING

To understand the theoretical basis of Assertiveness Training, you must comprehend the learning theories of Ivan Pavlov.

In the United States, the Russian physiologist is best known for his early twentieth-century experiment with the dog, meat, and bell. He demonstrated that behavior (in this case, salivation) brought on in the presence of one stimulus (food) could be brought on by another stimulus (the bell) if the second was paired with the food (meat powder). Eventually, the bell alone causes the dog to salivate. This new *learned* reflex is called a *conditioned reflex*. This famous experiment has given people a false impression of Pavlovian psychology, so that they think of it as a limited mechanical application to the conceptions of human behavior.

Actually, Pavlov set out to determine the characteristics of the nervous system that make it possible for animals and people to behave adaptively to changing conditions in the environment.

In his biological formulations, he discovered that the nervous system had two aspects:

(1) There is an *inherited* part of the nervous system. The evolutionary process has caused the nervous system to be structured in such a way that certain stimuli generate certain responses. Thus, at the stimulus of food, the dog responds with salivation because eons of evolution have made this an integral part of his nervous system. The same thing happens when the eye pupil changes in response to light.

Human nervous systems also contain certain characteristics which influence personalities. Psychologists call this "temperament." These are biological forces that affect sensitivity to stimuli, general level of energy, and tendency to certain moods, like depression and aggressiveness. This inherited temperament makes some people react more quickly and intensely than others. But because temperamental characteristics are built into the nervous system does not mean they cannot be affected, modified, and changed by life experiences.

(2) A person must live in an active relationship with his environment and respond to changes in the outside world with changes in his nervous system. As the situation changes, you learn to change. This is what Pavlov meant by a *conditioned reflex.*

Major among Pavlov's findings were his concepts of excitatory and inhibiting forces and their interplay.

Excitation is the brain process, which heightens activity and facilitates the formation of new conditioned responses.

Inhibition is a dampening process, which decreases activity and new learning.

Since the time of Pavlov, three theoreticians—Andrew Salter, Dr. Joseph Wolpe, and Dr. Arnold Lazarus—have developed various concepts of Assertiveness Training which stem, directly or indirectly, from the Pavlovian perspective.

Andrew Salter, a leading New York psychologist who founded modern behavior therapy, uses Pavlovian conceptions of excitation and inhibition as the basis for the treatment of nervous disorders. When excitatory forces dominate, people are action-oriented and emotionally free. They meet life on their own terms. The domination of inhibitory forces produces bewildered and beset people, who suffer from "constipation of the emotions." Low on self-sufficiency, they are always doing things they do not want to do. For psychological health, there must be a proper balance of excitatory and inhibitory processes in the brain. According to Andrew Salter, the neurotic always suffers from an excess of inhibition.

Therapy serves to build and strengthen the excitatory processes, creating a new balance, where they can dominate the brain functioning. This is achieved by having the patient deliberately act in an excitatory manner. His actions increase the extent of the excitation in the cerebral cortex until a new spontaneous balance occurs between excitation and inhibition, and the new behavior becomes a "natural" part of the person. Thus, at first there is a change in behavior, which in turn changes the biology of the brain, which in turn influences the entire psychology and personality of the patient. Salter describes the excitatory person as "direct. He responds outwardly to his environment. . . . He makes rapid decisions and likes responsibility. Above all, the excitatory person is free of anxiety. He is truly happy."

Dr. Joseph Wolpe, professor of psychiatry and director of the behavior therapy unit at Temple University School of Medicine, defines assertive behavior as "the proper expression of any emotion other than anxiety towards another person." By reason of your interpersonal fears, you may be unable to complain about poor service in a restaurant, contradict friends with whom you disagree, get up and leave a social situation that has become boring, chastise a subordinate, or express affection, appreciation, or praise. Dr. Wolpe's aim is to reduce the interpersonal anxieties and fears that keep you from doing these things. He does this through the clinical application of his "reciprocal inhibition principle," which has become one of the cornerstones of behavior therapy. The principle states, "If a response inhibitory of anxiety can be made to occur in the presence of anxiety-evoking stimuli, it will weaken the bond between these stimuli and the anxiety."

Thus, in AT therapeutic treatment, Dr. Wolpe teaches his patients to respond to social situations with anger, affection, or any other emotion that inhibits or counters anxiety. In AT sessions, Dr. Wolpe has the patient simulate the tension-provoking situations with role playing. He then trains the patient to express feelings *other than anxiety* during the role-playing. Each time the patient performs a scene successfully, he weakens the bond between the social stimuli and the anxiety response, until the anxiety completely disappears. As the patient learns to do this, he carries over the training to the life situation, and his behavior becomes more assertive.

From the sociopsychological approach, Dr. Arnold Lazarus, professor of psychology and director of the Psy. D. program in clinical psychology at the Graduate School of Applied and Professional Psychology of Rutgers University, stresses "emotional freedom" as the "recognition and appropriate expression of each and every affective state." Knowing what you feel is not enough, you must express it and express it appropriately. Assertive behavior emerges as that aspect of "emotional freedom" that concerns standing up for your rights. This involves (1) knowing your rights; (2) doing something about it; (3) doing this within the framework of striving for emotional freedom.

The person who fails to stand up for his rights has little freedom, feels uncomfortable and afraid, and, in his hunger for freedom, may sometimes turn "vicious" with inappropriate outbursts. For such people, Assertiveness Training consists of teaching them to know their legitimate rights, how to stand up for them and prevent them from being usurped. Dr. Lazarus also believes that part of recognition of your rights involves the recognition of, and respect for, the rights of others.

Whatever the theory and individual method of therapy, AT offers two assumptions:

1. *What you do serves as the basis for your self-concept.* The more you stand up for yourself and act in a manner you respect, the higher will be your self-esteem.

Hence my basic equation:

$$\text{Assertion} = \text{Self-esteem}$$

Actually this formula derives from one advanced by William James who offered the equation:

$$\text{Self-esteem} = \frac{\text{Success}}{\text{Pretensions}}$$

The James formulation contains two parts. The first concerns the doing of what you have to do in order to achieve *success* and involves the acquisition of work and social skills necessary for this purpose. The *pretension* part concerns your goals (what it is at which you would like to succeed) and involves choice and decision, for James realized that people may possess many unrealistic and conflicting goals and that achievement of one goal must be at the cost of suppression of another. He advised that the "seeker of his truest, strongest, deepest self must review this list (of possible goals) and carefully pick out the one on which to stake his salvation."

Essentially James meant that you can fulfill yourself only by accepting certain limitations and your self-esteem is equal to the degree to which you succeed in that fulfillment. A number of theoreticians have since elaborated on that point, and it serves as a cornerstone of the psychoanalytic theory advanced by Karen Horney.

However, since James's era, the world has grown more complex and cynical. Due to factors beyond your control, you can do everything right and still fail to achieve "success." In AT, the goal has switched from the end product (the success) to *the process* (how you act in your attempt to achieve success), and the behaviors involved in these attempts constitute those we call "assertive." The very act of selecting a goal says: "This is me. This is what I want." The act of moving toward a goal requires an active orientation, mastery of life situations and self. More personal goals demand open communication with others. The extent to which you assert yourself determines the level of your self-esteem.

The difference between the James formula and my AT equation lies in the emphasis on actual success. The AT formula maintains that as long as you act assertively, you maintain your self-esteem. You may fail and feel disappointed and frustrated, but your core of self-respect remains. You can use this concept as a criterion for assertive behavior. *If you have doubts whether a specific act was assertive, ask yourself whether it increased your self-respect even slightly. If it did, it was assertive. If not, it was unassertive.*

2. *Behaviors don't exist in isolation, but interact with each other, forming patterns we call the psychological organization.* At different points in our lives, the behaviors have different thrusts:

The Psychological Organization

Childhood. The child has his parents as the base of his security. When childhood dependence proves successful, the child has the strength and the security to restructure his psychological organization, and so move on to adolescence. Some people can't do it. They go through life maintaining the goals and habits of childhood, making parents of all people and, in ways—sometimes obvious, sometimes subtle—acting the part of the demanding child. These sad souls search for the "good parent" in the form of spouse or friend, who will comfort their distresses and provide the unqualified love a mother gives an infant. They want to be loved for what they are (regardless of what that is) rather than for what they do.

This demand cannot be met, and such people go through life hurt and disappointed.

Adolescence. The adolescent forms a new behavioral organization in which his goal becomes one of gaining security from peers rather than his parents. His safety stems from being part of a group and securing group acceptance and approval. Some people never outgrow this. Belonging to the group remains the foundation of security. Such a person never outgrows adolescence. He remains an inhibitory person because he never attains his own identity apart from the group, always worries about what others will think, and determines his own behavior by the thoughts of others, for others' negative thoughts may lead to group rejection.

Adulthood. As adolescence ends, a change takes place. The adult does not need the group for security. Instead his life may center around a small number of people—a few close friends, a friend of the opposite sex. Eventually, this base narrows and the base of security centers around one specific person. At this point, deeper, more permanent relations develop, one of which may lead to marriage. The close relationship with another person serves as a source for finding and expressing one's real individuality, both within the relationship and in life in general. Some therapists regard this as the pinnacle.

The complete individual. Other therapists believe that still another organizational step is necessary, involving a shift in the security gained from another human being to security based on self-respect. This has its roots based in the feeling, "I know my wants and values, but I am always willing to reexamine and change them. I want to feel deeply, act strongly, relate closely to others and yet always feel mastery of myself."

To achieve the state of the complete individual, you must realize that *if you change one behavior, you change a whole series of related behaviors.* As you learn new skills and change your actions, you can change your feelings and the entire pattern of your psychological organization. In this way, Assertiveness Training can produce a whole new life-style.

CASE

When thirty-seven-year-old, twice-divorced Seth Elwyn, a

civil engineer, first came to me, he said, "Help! I'm dating a girl whom I'd like to marry, but I'm afraid I'll fail again." Seth represented the perfect example of the unassertive man. Growing up in a female-dominated household consisting of a strong mother, five sisters, and a "quiet, retiring" father, who played "no role in my life," he had learned a pattern of compliant behavior. As an adult, he rarely asked for anything for himself. In his job, he agreed to whatever unreasonable demands his boss made, and there were many. At twenty-two, he married "a shrew." Seth recalled: "She picked on me and I just went along with it. After two years she walked out." When he acquired wife number two, she also began to exploit him unmercifully. After working a fifty-hour week at the office, plus overtime at home, Seth vacuumed the floors and did the grocery shopping, even though this wife did not work. She, too, walked out, saying "I've tried to provoke you to get signs of life, but I can't do it. No matter what anyone does to you, you never get angry and fight back."

This last taunt was true. Seth had never learned to express anger. As a result, he developed a fear of anger that, as fears do, led to avoidance behavior. His need to avoid anger was so great that he couldn't even allow himself the subjective experience of it. This had the consequence of not allowing him to recognize situations where people exploited or demeaned him. Because he didn't take notice of the situations, he could not assert himself. So people pushed him around and lost respect for him.

After seeing Seth for individual sessions of Assertiveness Training, I decided upon group therapy with two treatment goals: (1) to teach him how to express anger; (2) to train him to recognize exploitative and put-down situations and to learn how to stand up for himself in these situations. During the weekly group sessions, Seth role-played the angry man in imagined circumstances as well as in past and present situations from his own life. As he learned the skill, his fear of anger diminished, and he no longer needed to inhibit his angry feelings. At every group session, one member would either make an unreasonable request of Seth or put him down. Thus, Seth had the opportunity to learn to handle these situations, and as he learned, he carried his new assertive ability over into his life. He stood up to his girl friend, his sisters, his boss.

During treatment, Seth remarried and subsequently proudly reported, "We had a terrible fight and I felt *very angry.*" Some sessions later he said triumphantly, "This marriage is different. I'm a participant."

In his last session Seth brought in two specific assertion problems, one involving his wife and the other his boss. The group wanted to work on the former, but in a firm voice Seth announced, "I'm more concerned about the job problem. Let's attack that." So natural and firm was his statement that the group readily complied. When I pointed out how Seth had stood up for himself, there was a moment of silence before the group members broke into applause.

In analytic therapy, this kind of detached person usually makes slow progress. Analysis places a lot of emphasis on feeling, and if there are no feelings to work with, progress is slow. With Seth, it would have been easy to formulate his problems in terms of deep-down sexual stimulations of growing up in a household of women, and perhaps in terms of unconscious conflicts concerning his sexual identity. However, I felt the problem was to remedy the behavioral deficit, and to teach him how to feel, not by verbal discussion, but through deliberate training and action. When he did stand up for himself in small situations, he felt himself a stronger person. This made Seth aware that when he didn't stand up for himself, he felt depressed and empty. *The feeling change followed the change in behavior.*

In the course of eight months, Seth's relations with people, his emotional awareness and self-concept changed. Since then, he has gotten raises and a promotion, and has become able to supervise others. His third marriage is working. Seth still has some way to go, but he is learning in a life situation rather than a therapeutic one.

The Neurotic Spiral

Inadequate behavior in one area has repercussions in other areas of your psychological organization, bringing about additional anxieties, tensions, or depressions and influencing your feeling of confidence in other situations. This whirlpool effect I call the *neurotic spiral*. For example, from the fear of losing your job you acquire a whole new set of doubts: "What is wrong with me?" . . . "I am no good" . . . "I never succeed." These thoughts in turn lead to inadequate behaviors, which in turn strengthen the fears and doubts which lead to still more inadequate behavior—and so you can't get out of that spiral.

The neurotic spiral:

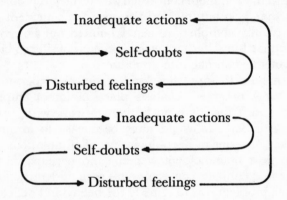

Some of the signs that you may be descending the neurotic spiral in relation to assertiveness are:

You constantly placate others because you fear offending them.

You allow others to maneuver you into situations you don't want.

You cannot express your legitimate wishes.

You feel the rights of others are more important than your own.

You are self-conscious before superior and authority figures.

You are so easily hurt by what others say and do that you constantly inhibit yourself.

You often feel miserable, but you don't know why.

You feel pushed around because you have never learned to stand up for yourself.

You feel lonely because you have no close relationship in your life.

You feel inferior because you are inferior. You limit your experiences, and don't utilize your potential.

By changing your behavior, which will in turn change your thoughts and feelings, you can reverse the spiral. As you do things differently, you feel more adequate. You decrease your resentment, anger, and fears, and you gain good feelings about yourself. This is what happened with Seth Elwyn, the timid soul with two ex-wives. When he became an assertive human being, *he began to like himself.*

Because of its effect on other behaviors, even the change of a seemingly trivial behavior may begin to reverse the spiral and start an upward momentum.

CASE

A successful securities analyst who traveled a great deal in the course of his work frequently lay awake through the night, thinking obsessively about what would happen if after a morning conference in some strange city, he had to go to lunch with fellow businessmen and make conversation. This worry affected his work performance. Therapy showed he barely knew the meaning of the words "small talk," much less the art of telling a story. Through Assertiveness Training, I taught him the art of storytelling. Just as he studied statistics and reports to prepare for a meeting, he learned to make ready a repertoire of anecdotes for lunchtime sessions. With the stories available for use, he became spontaneous instead of anxious, and rarely had to use them. He stopped feeling depressed, and became able to sleep through the night. "My wife says I'm like the man she married twenty years ago," he told me happily.

CASE

Sally Jones lived in a state of chronic upset, feeling she was always the scapegoat. One day she returned to her office after a solitary lunch ("People always pick on me, so it's easier to be by myself"), and the business manager yelled at her. "You left that Xerox room in an awful mess," he accused unfairly, misled by poor information.

Sally started to answer defensively with "I wasn't in the Xerox room today," but just in time remembered her AT. She told her boss, "Now you just apologize."

Startled by her change in manner, the boss shot back, "Apologize for what?"

Said Sally firmly, "For yelling at me for something I didn't do."

She got her apology and realized that having answered one put-down assertively, she could do it on other occasions—and did. As a result, not only did her relations on the job itself change but she began lunching with people and making friends. One simple retort, achieved through six months of AT training, enabled Sally to start feeling good about herself.

Although it may seem so to the uninitiated, Assertiveness Training is neither simple nor simplistic. I reiterate: changing seemingly small behaviors may have a whole impact on relations with others and on your own self-image. AT deals with behaviors of varying complexity.

The *first level* concerns such elementary behaviors as making eye contact, standing straight, speaking in a voice loud enough to be heard by others. Deficits in these areas can have far-reaching consequences. For instance, if you do not look at the other person while you talk to him, you will find you quickly lose contact. Your voice becomes more monotonous, and your communication, rambling and indirect. The other person has trouble following you, gets bored, or annoyed. While patients with this difficulty often have many other assertive problems, the simple act of training yourself to make eye contact can, by itself, bring about major changes.

The *second level* involves the basic skills of assertion: the ability to say no when you want to say no and yes when you want to say yes, to ask favors and make requests, to communicate feelings and thoughts in an open, direct way, handle put-downs, to be in control of such situations as diet and good work habits.

The *third level* pertains to your behavior in more complex interactions with other people: adaptive behavior in job situations, your ability to form and maintain a social network, the achievement of close personal relationships.

Changing these specific behaviors can change the way people react to you, the way you feel about yourself and your very life-style.

Before switching to behavior therapy, I spent twenty years as a practicing traditional psychotherapist. Therefore, I can understand that many people frequently find it difficult to adjust to the empirical approach of BT and its Assertiveness Training programs. They ask pertinent questions which deserve pertinent answers.

Q. What about getting at the roots of the problem that causes the psychological difficulty? Can the patient ever be cured without going thoroughly into his early childhood experiences, traumas, and id versus ego?

A. Does getting "at the roots" really change people? The scientific data show that with the psychoanalytic methods some people get better, some remain the same, and some actually get worse, roughly in equal proportion. From an experimental point of view, little evidence exists (or, at best, doubtful evidence) that getting to the inner psychic conflicts changes people. There is accumulating experimental evidence that directly changing behavior does change people and their lives.

This does not mean psychoanalysis is invalid. Primarily psychoanalysis is a theory about the manner in which neuroses develop. BT scarcely touches this area, feeling that many of the psychoanalytic concepts have little relevance to bringing about the desired behavioral changes.

Q. If you get rid of one symptom, won't another develop?

A. Psychoanalysis says yes. However, the careful experimental data gathered by behavior therapists show that if you get rid of a distressing symptom, the odds are you end up a happier, healthier person. This does not mean you won't have any more problems. Eliminating one problem may produce a series of other difficulties *because you now have the ability to meet more and different challenges.* Take the person who has such a fear of the opposite sex that he can't even ask a girl for a date. Remove this fear to the point where he dates, forms a close relationship with a woman, and marries her. Now he faces a new set of problems he never would have encountered had he remained isolated. I treated one young man whose stutter was so severe he avoided social situations. When forced into them, he backed off into a corner and kept quiet. When I cured his stutter, I learned he had nothing to say, and a course of AT was necessary. Something like this is not a symptom substitution, but a new problem that comes from an expanding life.

Q. How can Assertiveness Training be good when it is so short term?
A. AT is not short term. It is a lifelong process. The only short term part is the formal part, which aims to get you over the initial problem and teach you the skills through which you can keep on training yourself.

The initial results may ensue fairly rapidly, but they serve only as the beginning of the assertive program. As you begin to relate differently to people, they begin to relate differently to you. As you begin to act more openly, people become closer to you. As you learn to stand up for yourself, people have different reactions to you. This leads you into a series of new life experiences, and you change and grow. As a result, you have clearer ideas about what you want and need. These changes don't take place overnight. You never reach a point where you can say "I'm there." There is always room for growth. Obstacles and difficulties will occur and recur, but with assertive skills at your command, you can usually solve them or at least come to grips with them.

Q. Doesn't AT train a person to be manipulative?
A. AT tries to teach you to control yourself, not to let others control you.

Q. If AT does change your life-style, can it cause disruption? Ruin a marriage? Cause you to lose a job? Alienate friends and relatives?
A. The answer is yes. If you have an unsatisfactory life-style and you change it, you disrupt the status quo. For example, a man might have gotten used to living with a destructive wife. A woman might have become accustomed to henpecking her husband. As either of these situations changes, disruption occurs in the relationship with three possible consequences:

(1) Each partner welcomes the change.

(2) The partner who did not undergo AT also changes and grows. Both partners develop better life-styles.

(3) The partner may be unwilling or unable to make the necessary changes. With this last consequence, there is apt to

be trouble. I have seen situations where AT has led to separation and divorce. But the point is: the situation was already unsatisfactory. Your new assertive attitude may win you many pluses, but you may have to pay a price.

Q. Can AT and traditional analysis work together?
A. AT and traditional analysis share similar goals in that both want the patient to be a fulfilled human being. However, the two methods differ sharply on the therapeutic method of achieving the goal.

Whether or not AT and analysis can be carried out simultaneously on the same patient by two different therapists depends on the practitioners involved as well as the individual in treatment. On some occasions, it has proved quite successful. With one patient, I was able to use the insights he had gained in his traditional treatment to establish goals and target behaviors for change. The AT enabled him to communicate feelings more freely, with the result that he was able to gain still further insights in his traditional therapy. At other times, the traditional and AT methods are at cross-purposes. For instance, with obsessive people, I believe they are already too introspective and pay too much attention to what goes on "inside" them, so I try to stop these behaviors. However, these are the very behaviors necessary to carry out traditional psychotherapy, and the other therapist encourages them. This often becomes an impossible situation, and the patient must drop one form of treatment.

Q. Can you become too assertive?
A. To this frequently asked question the answer is no. Part of the definition of assertion is that *the behavior be appropriate.* If it is that, it does not give the impression of being "too assertive." During AT what frequently happens is that the former timid soul goes overboard and becomes inappropriate. However, he soon readjusts his behavior.

AT will not tell you *why* you are the way you are.

It will teach you *how* to live creatively in a complex society by training yourself in the skills needed to be the man or woman who faces and welcomes challenges.

I repeat: just as you have trained yourself to be *neurotic,* you can teach yourself to be *normal.*

Chapter II
Targeting Your Own Assertive Difficulties

What are the various types of assertive difficulties?

How can you recognize the difference between assertion and aggression?

When is it right to stand up for yourself—and when is it wrong?

How can you apply the principles of Assertiveness Training to your own behavior?

Like almost everything else in life, the quality of assertion does not fall into black and white categories. It possesses as many shadings as there are hues in an artist's palette. However, essentially, people with assertive difficulties can be grouped into seven basic types.

ASSERTIVE PROBLEM TYPES

(1) *The timid soul.* You allow yourself to be pushed around, cannot speak up, and remain passive in all situations. If someone steps on your foot, you say "I'm sorry." You may be Caspar Milquetoast, but you are *not* an assertive zero. No matter how great your timidity and irresolution, there is always a point from which you can start to change.

(2) *The person with communication difficulties.* I reiterate that assertion possesses four behavioral characteristics: openness and directness, honesty and appropriateness. You may be deficient in any or all three of these areas, but often you lack assertion in just one:

Indirect communication. You tend to be wordy, a characteristic often accompanied by shallowness of feeling, lack of clear-cut desires, and difficulty with close relationships. Instead of asking your husband, "Would you mind picking up two lamb chops for dinner, since you'll be passing right by the supermarket?" you say, "I know you're getting a haircut today. By any chance will you be on Thirty-eighth Street?" You don't make the direct request; your husband doesn't know what you want, and you don't get what you want. Practice in making simple, direct statements, without qualifications or elaborations, can often change your entire pattern.

Dishonest or pseudoassertive communication. You seem to be open and honest, generally appropriate, often extroverted, but this seeming assertiveness hides a basic lack of honesty. You say, "It's so good to see you—I've been thinking about you for days," when you couldn't care less, and the other person knows it. In this classification fall the stereotyped versions of the hail-fellow-well-met salesman and baby-kissing politicians. Others within this category have problems with closeness and a general lack of satisfaction in life ("nothing turns me on").

Inappropriate communication. Unknowledgeable about the realities of social relations, you say what you think is the right thing at the wrong time. For example, your husband tells you of his "terrible day at the office," and in response, you offer a list of the things he did wrong. You may be open and honest, but the naive and immature way in which you speak up usually leads to numerous interpersonal difficulties, creating a distance from people rather than closeness. At work, your inappropriateness produces dissension and disruption. Because you say the wrong thing at the wrong time, you leave yourself open to exploitation or hurt. This insensitivity to others often leads to self-centered behavior and a disregard for the needs of co-workers, friends, family.

(3) *The split assertive.* People may fail at one area of assertiveness and succeed at another. You can be able to openly express your tender feelings and yet not be able to show your angry feelings—and vice versa.

A man can be the epitome of passivity at the office, and

behave like a tyrant at home. Or he can act assertively at work, in his social relations, and with his children, and yet be unassertive with his wife. For example, in his executive job, Tom Johnson made major decisions all day long. At night, he would fix dinner for his two children, his wife—and her current lover. After supper, he cleaned up, then baby-sat, while Mrs. Johnson and her current Romeo went out on the town. Although Tom rationalized his behavior, he came to me for a few sessions, but found the chance of improvement too threatening. When last heard from, he was still cooking dinner and hoping his wife would solve the problem by running off.

The range for split assertives can be very narrow. You can be assertive at work—except with a superior, a subordinate, or just one specific person. Or you may be assertive in a one-to-one relationship, but not in groups. A woman can be assertive with everyone but the once-a-week cleaning woman. And some people can be assertive with everyone in the world except their mother-in-law.

In general, the narrower the area, the easier it is to change with Assertiveness Training.

(4) *The person with behavioral deficits.* You can't make eye contact or small talk, handle a confrontation, start a conversation. These assertive skills can be learned.

(5) *The person with specific blocks.* You know what you should do, and have the skill to accomplish it, but your fears of rejection, anger, scrutiny, criticism, closeness, tenderness, inhibit you from carrying out the action.

You possess incorrect ideas. You don't comprehend the difference between aggression and assertion. You know the what and how of what has to be done, but question your right to do it.

You have a wrong concept of social reality. You don't understand that different kinds of relationships exist with different people. You think you're supposed to treat a stranger as a friend. It never occurs to you to treat the stranger as a stranger and the friend as a friend. For example, a new patient announced, "I don't trust anybody." Exploration showed she trusted some people with money, others with personal secrets, and still others for business advice. Her misconception: she thought because she couldn't trust everybody with everything that she couldn't trust anybody.

You have an erroneous idea of psychological reality. You worry about worrying, become anxious about being anxious, not realizing that the life situation provides problems where anxiety is the appropriate reaction. One man came to me with an array of problems. His father had just died suddenly, and his wife had undergone surgery for cancer. He had just lost his job, and his son had been arrested for dealing pot. But because he felt depressed by all this, this man had the idea he was neurotic. It is natural to feel anxious when life deals you blows. However, instead of saying "OK, I'm in a stress situation, and I'm uptight about it," you analyze, "I'm worrying so much that I'm a neurotic and I'd better begin worrying about that." Because of your concern about underlying neuroses, you inhibit your spontaneity. In a case like the one I just cited, it is usually far better to reach out to friends and relatives than consult a therapist.

You don't grant independence to other people. You think as long as you're being reasonable, the other person should go along with you. But very often, the other person, because of his own needs, feelings, and hang-ups, just won't.

You feel that as long as you do the right thing, you should win them all. If you don't, there's something wrong with you. Reality doesn't work that way. You can demand a raise and deserve it, but the economic state of your firm may prohibit a salary increase.

(6) *The person with interfering habits.* Because you have learned to do things in the wrong way, you may have trouble doing what you want to do. I call these interfering habits the "peanut butter sandwich syndrome." I tell patients with this syndrome the story of the two workmen eating lunch together. One opened his lunchbox, took out his sandwich, bit into it, and said, "Oh, peanut butter sandwiches again. I hate peanut butter sandwiches."

His friend spoke up, "Why don't you tell your wife to stop making them for lunch?"

The first man answered, "Wife! I make my own lunches."

If you know what the unwanted behavior is, it may be within your power to simply change it. Or you may know what it is, but never think of changing it. *You keep eating peanut butter sandwiches.*

CASE

Rick Shulman, a recent Ph.D., came to me with a career problem. He used to enjoy teaching his college classes, but recently he found the work burdensome and depressing. Our discussion revealed that the change started while he was working on his doctoral thesis. Because he was so busy, he stopped preparing his lectures and depended on off-the-cuff remarks. After completing the thesis, he continued his newly acquired habit of giving the unprepared lectures. Rick realized these lectures were disorganized and superficial; it was this knowledge that brought about his depression and dissatisfaction. The thought never occurred to him to do something about it.

I told Rick the peanut butter sandwich story. He agreed that it was completely within his power to start preparing his classroom lectures again. And it was. In the middle of the next semester, he telephoned to tell me "the fun of teaching is back."

(7) *The person who has assertive difficulties with his own children.* Parents want their children to grow up to be assertive, self-respectful people. Yet they fail to realize the different assertive skills needed to produce both the close relationship and an independent human being, and do not understand how their own assertive difficulties influence their children.

The parent has to be the right kind of model. If the child sees you acting with self-respect, standing up for yourself, communicating honestly, he will learn to do these things. If you are the reincarnation of Caspar Milquetoast, no matter what words you use with your child, and directions you give, he will be unassertive. Remember two points: (1) You may be generally quite assertive, but have difficulty with your children because you want to avoid the same kinds of arguments and disagreeableness that came between you and your parents. (2) If you lead a full life yourself, you are less apt to live vicariously through your children, and will give them elbow room to find their own style.

ASSERTION VS. AGGRESSION

Assertive difficulties lead to inadequate behavior. If you are basically nonassertive, you come on too weak. Because you don't stand up for yourself, you feel hurt, anxious, and self-contemptuous. Your deficient actions and reactions produce feelings of contempt in others.

Conversely, you behave aggressively and come on too strong. Because of various life experiences, you are so filled with hurts and angers that a major core of your psychological organization centers around the goal of hurting others, sometimes out of vindictiveness, at other times out of a perceived need to defend yourself. While this aggressive behavior may accomplish your ends temporarily, in most cases it leads to disrupted communication with friends, calls forth counteraggression from others, and tends to make you even more aggressive. This reverberating circuit keeps you on the neurotic spiral.

By contrast, properly assertive behavior does not always result in the accomplishment of your desired goals, but it does lead to a good feeling about yourself. When things don't work out, you may feel disappointed, but you will not feel irrationally hostile.

Let's take some case examples and see what the appropriate assertive response might be.

CASE A: The teacher calls Mrs. Block to school and in a conference tells her that her six-year-old son does not pay attention in class, and behaves terribly—all because Mrs. Block hasn't brought up Ted in a disciplined way.

CASE B: Jane waits her turn in line at a department store stocking sale. The clerk is just about to finish up with the customer in front of her when a third woman comes by and edges in. Clerk asks, "Who's next?" and this woman says, "I am."

CASE C: Madge and Rose work as secretaries in a two-girl insurance office. Three times a week, Madge leaves early to see her psychiatrist. Rose has to answer the phone and finish the day's work. She doesn't really mind the extra labor; she does have an increasing feeling that the situation is unfair.

CASE D: A year ago John borrowed two hundred dollars from Ken. At the time, John had debts, a sick mother, and no job. Now his mother has regained her health, and John earns a good salary at a government job. Ken wants his money back for a skiing trip, but has done nothing about it. Each day he resents the situation more.

CASE E: Nineteen-year-old Phyllis attends a big midwestern university and will be coming home to Philadelphia for Christmas. Her mother knows that Phyllis has been living with someone at school. In early December, Phyllis implies on the phone that she and her boyfriend will want to sleep together in her bedroom. With two younger siblings in the household, the mother is bitterly opposed.

These examples typify situations that call for an assertive response. Decide how you would handle them.

Here are the answers:

CASE A: Mrs. Block and the complaining teacher.

Unassertive: Mrs. Block says, "Yes, you're right. He does need more discipline at home. Send us a note every time he misbehaves. Meanwhile we'll forbid him to watch TV at night." That night she turns off TV, yells at Ted, brushes aside his attempt to explain, sends him to bed supperless. And she lies awake all night. In this case, Ted has also learned that his needs and feelings don't matter. He feels either that he is "bad" or the world is unfair. In either case, he is being taught to be helpless.

Aggressive: Mrs. Block responds, "You just don't understand my son. From the things I've heard, I think you're a terrible teacher. I'm going to talk to the principal about this and get Ted transferred to Miss Jones's class. She is a *good* teacher." Mrs. Block does talk to the principal, but says nothing to Ted who is transferred. Ted learns that he has no say over what happens to him, that his needs and feelings are irrelevant. He begins to feel he lives in an unreasonable world.

Assertive: Mrs. Block says, "Let me talk to Ted about it. And next week I'll come by with some ideas." That night she has a long discussion with Ted (and her husband) and discovers that a boy in class had bullied him. As a result, he felt upset. She will go back to school, report this to the teacher, and discuss what can be done. Because of her assertive action, Ted learns that what he feels and thinks is important to others, and can influence what happens. He also has the experience of a constructive communication with his parents and the model of the constructive working out of a problem by his mother.

CASE B: Jane in the stocking line.

Unassertive: Jane says nothing, waits her turn, and decides she'll never go back to "that store."

Aggressive: Jane berates both the pushy woman and the clerk.

Assertive: Jane says simply, "Sorry, I was next," and tells the clerk she wants black bikini hose, size small.

CASE C: Rose, who resents Madge's leaving early.

Unassertive: Not wanting to interfere with Madge's psychiatric sessions, Rose keeps quiet. Tension mounts. Rose decides she should look for another job.

Aggressive: Rose fights with Madge and says things like "I'm tired of doing your work" . . . "This office isn't a nice place anymore because you take advantage of me" . . . "Better stop seeing the doctor, or I'll tell the boss about you."

Assertive: Rose brings the subject up for discussion with "We have a problem. What can we do about it?" They discuss possible solutions, such as Madge coming in earlier and doing work ahead, or trying to change her analytic time to an evening hour.

CASE D: Ken, who lent two hundred dollars to John.

Unassertive: Every time Ken sees John, he talks vaguely about things that cost money. He hopes John will take the hint.

Aggressive: He berates John with cracks like "How do you dare wear a new suit when you've owed me two hundred dollars for a year?"

Assertive: Ken says "I'd like you to repay the money you owe me," and they discuss how the money might be paid. Ken suggests, "If you can't do it in one lump, why not give me ten dollars a week?"

CASE E: The college student who wants her boyfriend to share her bed at home.

Unassertive: Mother lets Phyllis and her beau sleep in the same room, but acts hostile to the boy during the entire visit. She ruins Christmas for the whole family.

Aggressive: Mother starts telephoning Phyllis at college and calling her a "slut." She threatens, "Don't you dare bring that boy here."

Assertive: Mother tells Phyllis, "What you do away from home is your own business. However, I have certain rights in my home. If you want to invite him here, he can sleep with your younger brother."

The above situations should give you an idea of the appropriate assertive response. Now, let me offer you two interpersonal "encounters" where *you* provide the response. They were among those used by Michel Herson, Richard M. Eisler, and Peter M. Miller in a behavioral assertiveness test at Veterans Administration Center, Jackson, Mississippi.

(1) You take your car to a service station to have a grease job and the oil changed. The mechanic tells you that the car will be ready in an hour. When you return, you find that in addition to the oil and grease job, they have given your car a major tune-up. The cashier says, "You owe us two hundred and fifteen dollars. Will that be cash or charge?" What do you say?

(2) You are having lunch with a friend, when suddenly she asks you if you would lend her thirty dollars until she gets paid next week. You have the money, but were planning on spending it for something else. Your friend pleads, "Please lend me the money. I'll pay it back next week." What do you say?

As you compare the possible answers to these situations with what you have done in similar life situations, you must realize the cardinal principle: *you cannot be too assertive. Overassertiveness is often aggression and always inappropriate.*

YOUR RIGHTS

As I pointed out in Chapter I, Dr. Arnold Lazarus of Rutgers University feels that some people are so distressfully concerned with an arbitrary range of "rights" and "wrongs" and permit themselves so little freedom of movement that they exist in an emotional prison or confined capsule.

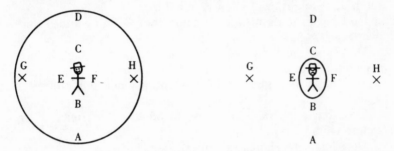

In the figures above the emotionally free individual considers the territory bounded by the poles AD and GH his own psychological terrain, or his own life space. He can move anywhere within these boundaries without feeling he has overstepped his limits or encroached on someone else's emotional property. If somebody enters his territory uninvited, he will unceremoniously stand up for his rights and tell the trespasser to leave.

The encapsulated person is uncomfortable or afraid and very unsure when venturing beyond points B, C, E, or F. He usually feels that he is not entitled to any territory beyond his narrow range inside the capsule.*

You must recognize your rights and stand up for them. If you do not, other people define your role for you, and you stop being yourself. Your life space decreases. You lose freedom of movement. You become the "encapsulated person" and pay the price for this with neurotic behavior.

Many people have this difficulty because they don't have a clear cut idea of what their rights are—or they have an incorrect idea. Others have trouble because they don't know how to stand up for their rights. I think it would be helpful to

---

* From *Behavior Therapy and Beyond*, by Arnold A. Lazarus, Ph.D., 1971. Used with permission of McGraw-Hill Book Company.

both types if I list some of the questions about rights which come up in my practice.

Do I have the right to answer honestly when I am asked if I like something and I don't?

Do I have the right to refuse the car to my son on Saturday night?

Do I have the right to tell my spouse that he/she has gained too much weight, and I am repelled by it?

Do I have the right to tell my boss that I don't want to work overtime?

Do I have the right to go out and work part-time, and leave my children at a day-care center?

Do I have the right to refuse to lend my new golf clubs to a friend?

Do I have the right to refuse to entertain a friend of my spouse whom I don't like?

Do I have the right to pamper myself?

Do I have the right to stand up for my rights?

The following two cases involve the principle of assertive rights.

CASE

Ralph, an amputee patient hospitalized for physical rehabilitation, became extremely agitated, to the point where he couldn't sleep, and required tranquilizing medication. Two weeks previously, he had taken some special diagnostic tests for low back pain, and he had heard nothing of the results. For fourteen days he had been worrying.

In our discussion, Ralph revealed that he thought he didn't have the right to ask any of the doctors about the test results. "They're so busy with so many patients. How would they be concerned about me," he said sadly. Through our talk, Ralph did come around to agreeing that it was his body, and he *did have the right* to know about it. We practiced different ways of approaching the doctor, and then Ralph went and spoke to the doctor in exactly the way we had rehearsed. The doctor assured Ralph it was just a temporary muscular pain and expressed dismay that no one had informed him of the test results earlier. Thus, through standing up for his rights, Ralph secured the information he needed to allay his anxiety.

CASE

Thirty-year-old Margaret Jones, a harried housewife and mother of three young children, came to me with the problem that "my life is falling apart." Because she labored at chores and child care from 6 A.M. to midnight, Margaret felt constantly fatigued and pressured, increasingly depressed, and had developed a series of hypochondriacal fears. All these consequences stemmed from the fact that she did not recognize that she had any rights at all in her own home—to read the paper, play the piano, or rest when she felt tired.

One by one, we took the trivial daily situations: "Do I have the right to sit and read the newspaper for ten minutes in the morning?" . . . "Do I have the right to practice the piano for my own enjoyment?" . . . "Do I have the right to ask my husband to let me know what time he will be home for dinner?" We discussed what she felt her rights were, what she might say and do (a calm, but sure "Mommie is reading now, but I'll be with you in a few minutes"); and we practiced the saying of it in my office. Then I told her to try it at home. In this step-by-step manner, Margaret learned to stand up for her rights. Soon she stopped worrying about dread diseases; her sense of fatigue lessened, and she began to enjoy things more.

Answers to questions about assertive rights must always be based on the personal situation, the persons in the situation, and the possible consequences; but you always have *five basic rights.*

(1) You have the right to do anything as long as it does not hurt someone else.

(2) You have the right to maintain your dignity by being properly assertive—*even if it hurts someone else*—as long as your motive is assertive, not aggressive.

(3) You always have the right to make a request of another person as long as you realize the other person has the right to say no.

(4) You must realize that there are certain borderline cases in interpersonal situations where the rights aren't clear. But you always have the right to discuss the problem with the person involved, and so clarify it.

(5) You have the right to attain your rights!

PINPOINTING YOUR OWN DIFFICULTIES

In determining your own assertive problems, you should evaluate your own specific problems in assertion and the fears that keep you from achieving the assertive state.

Assertiveness Inventory

Purpose: To alert you to your particular problem areas so that this book will become more meaningful to you.

STEP ONE: Buy an Assertiveness Training notebook, which you will use for this exercise and subsequent ones.

STEP TWO: In this (or on a sheet of paper), list the following questions. (Some of these are my own; others have been adapted from the work of Drs. Lazarus; Spencer A. Rathus, psychologist at Samaritan Hospital, Troy, New York; and Joseph Wolpe of Temple University School of Medicine.)

STEP THREE: Answer each question by placing a yes or no alongside it. For a somewhat more precise answer, you can use the terms always, often, sometimes, never.

STEP FOUR: Circle the answers that indicate you have a difficulty in assertion. Now, see if you can write a sentence or a series of sentences after these circled answers explaining your assertive problems in your own words.

For example, if your answer to Question 7 shows you feel dissatisfied with your social life, you might write "I have no social life because I don't like to make overtures and no one makes them to me." Or if your response to Question 22 shows you have assertive difficulties with subordinates, you might state, "I have trouble giving orders to my assistant because I'm afraid he won't like me if I do."

(1) Do you buy things you don't really want because it is difficult to say no to the salesman?

(2) Do you hesitate to return items to a store even when there is a good reason to do so?

(3) If someone talks aloud during a movie, play, or concert, can you ask him to be quiet?

(4) Can you begin a conversation with a stranger?

(5) Do you have trouble maintaining conversations in social situations?

(6) Do people act as if they find you boring?

(7) Are you satisfied with your social life?

(8) When a friend makes an unreasonable request, are you able to refuse?

(9) Are you able to ask favors or make requests of your friends?

(10) Can you criticize a friend?

(11) Can you praise a friend?

(12) When someone compliments you, do you know what to say?

(13) Is there someone with whom you can share your intimate feelings?

(14) Would you rather bottle up your feelings than make a scene?

(15) Are you satisfied with your work habits?

(16) Do people tend to exploit you or push you around?

(17) Can you be open and frank in expressing both tender and angry feelings to men?

(18) Can you be open and frank in expressing both tender and angry feelings to women?

(19) Do you find it difficult to make or accept dates?

(20) Are you spontaneous during sex play and intercourse?

(21) Are you satisfied with your progress in your career?

(22) Do you find it difficult to upbraid a subordinate?

(23) Are you (or would you be) a good model of assertiveness for your own child?

Uptight Inventory

Purpose: To identify the things that make you feel tense and fearful or otherwise disturbed.

STEP ONE: In your AT workbook, list the following stimuli which are either things or experiences:

(1) Loud voices   (5) Failure
(2) Speaking in public   (6) Strangers
(3) People who seem insane   (7) Feeling angry
(4) Being teased   (8) People in authority

(9) Feeling tender
(10) Tough-looking people
(11) Being watched while at work
(12) Receiving a compliment
(13) Being criticized
(14) Angry people
(15) Being ignored
(16) Looking foolish
(17) Being disliked
(18) Making mistakes
(19) A lull in the conversation.

STEP TWO: Add to the list any additional stimuli which produce disturbed feelings in you.

STEP THREE: Indicate the extent to which each of the items sets off uptight feelings in you. Use the scale:

027 Not at all   Much
    A little   Very much

Put your answer next to the item, and, in giving it, show what you feel *at this moment*—not how you reacted at some time in the past, or how you think you should feel.

After you complete this book and, hopefully, apply some of the AT techniques to your life situations, go back and do the Assertiveness Inventory and the Uptight Inventory again.

SETTING YOUR OWN ASSERTIVE GOALS

In addition to using the inventories and applying to your own life situations what you have read so far, these steps will also help you commence your own AT.

(1) Be certain you understand the assertion concept. The test situations presented earlier in the chapter should be useful. I also find that people are helped by reading Andrew Salter's *Conditioned Reflex Therapy* and my own book, *Help Without Psychoanalysis.*

(2) Recognize your rationalizations for not being assertive *as* rationalizations. Generally, they fall into three categories:

(a) People fix on a low probability event as an excuse for nonassertion. For instance, you let someone take your parking place with the rationalization that "If I insist on keeping it, that guy will slash my tires." You can't guarantee this won't happen, but it's unlikely. You should not base your actions on "maybe" events.

(b) People fix on a higher probability event, but give it

added meaning with "it would be terrible if this happened." For example, you feel that if you do stand up for your rights with a friend, he will get angry with you. Then you add the assumption that this will be terrible and devastating.

(c) People, very creatively, make up rationalizations for their lack of assertion that have no validity at all. Champion rationalizers may look back on their lives at seventy and find that all they have are creative reasons for not having had a better life.

(3) Work out the areas where you have assertive problems. Are they in impersonal, social, or personal situations? Do they emerge at work, school, or home? Do they come up more with certain types of people (bullies, superiors, opposite sex) than with others? Do they surface only with a specific person (wife, friend, colleague)?

(4) See what you fear: rejection, anger, or tenderness. Formulate to yourself the very worst that can happen, and then examine this eventuality and its consequences as objectively as possible.

(5) Look for the general behavioral areas where the difficulty comes about, and then try to formulate it in terms of very specific, concrete behaviors. The general area may be that you constantly feel exploited, and the specific behavior may be to say no when you mean no. The general area may be a lack of closeness with others, and the specific behavior may be a more open expression of your feelings.

In formulating these specific behaviors, *start from where you are now*. As your first behavior, learn or practice something you can reasonably expect yourself to master in a relatively short period of time. Then go on to the next step. If you have trouble with your first step, you have selected something too difficult. Look for an easier task in the same or related area. Then move to the more difficult one.

Whatever your problem, there are certain basic principles for the would-be assertive.

Reveal as much of your personal self as is appropriate to the situation and the relationship.

Strive to express all feelings, whether angry or tender.

Act in ways that increase your liking and respect for yourself.

Examine your own behavior and determine areas where you would like to become more assertive. Pay attention to what you can do differently rather than how the world can be different.

Do not confuse aggression with assertion. Aggressiveness is an act against others. Assertion is appropriate standing up for yourself.

Realize you may be unassertive in one area, like business, and assertive in another area, like marriage. Apply the techniques you use successfully in one area to the other.

Practice speaking up with trivia. If you can say "Go to the end of the line" to a woman at the supermarket, you can eventually announce "No, I don't want to do that" to your spouse.

Do not confuse glib, manipulatory behavior with true assertion. The aim of AT is to deepen the experience and expression of your humanness, not turn you into a con artist.

Do. You can always find fifty reasons for not doing things, so that over time you become very skilled at creating an empty life. As your *actions* change, often your feelings will.

Understand assertion is not a permanent state. As you change, life situations change, and you face new challenges and need new skills.

Chapter III
The Assertion Laboratory

The assertive education process can be compared with learning a foreign language. At first you master words, phrases, ground rules. Suddenly you can communicate with a child's vocabulary. You continue to learn until you acquire fluency. With the mastery of your new skill, you feel the freedom to be more creative in what has become your second tongue.

The language of assertion requires knowledge of the subject, practice of the principles, and daily application in your life.

Many people have trouble with assertion, not because of hidden, long-forgotten traumas, but because (1) they have always *avoided* the assertive situation, or (2) they have *never learned* to be assertive.

For these novices, behavior therapists specializing in Assertiveness Training have worked out a program of specific exercises. These include: how to set your own program of goals and sub-goals, behavior assignments (a man who is afraid to ask for a date may be given the task of going to a singles bar and speaking to two people), "feeling talk" dialogue for those with communication difficulties, a guide to how to refuse unreasonable requests, and behavior rehearsal (role-playing of problem situations).

A Goal Program

Through ignorance or fear, many people do not create any action plans for their own lives. As the late Abraham H.

Maslow, chairman of the department of psychology at Brandeis University, wrote, "Let us think of life as a process of choices, one after another. At each point, there is a progression choice and a regression choice. There may be a movement toward defense, toward safety, toward being afraid; but over on the other side, there is the growth choice. To make the growth choice, instead of the fear choice, a dozen times a day is to move a dozen times a day toward self-actualization."

When you don't plan a direction in life, you make a choice—that of *no choice*. This has dull, and sometimes sad, consequences.

To be assertive, you must develop goals.

Goals direct. Without them, you lack a sense of purpose in life.

Goals motivate. When test animals run through a maze, the closer they get to a goal, the faster they hasten toward it. When you take a trip, you become more impatient as you near your destination. If you set a goal, as you approach it, you gain greater motivation to succeed.

Goals reinforce self-esteem. Achievement of goals strengthens your desire to achieve other goals. As a result, you attain a feeling of movement through life and a higher sense of self-worth.

How to Set Goals

(1) *Set your long-term goals.* Ask yourself, "What kind of life do I want to lead?" What would you like your life to be like ten years from now? Consider family and social life, professional aims, avocational interests. Don't ignore your fantasies. Often they can put you in touch with what you really want.

(2) *Set up a series of sub-goals.* If you select a very distant goal without sub-goals, you fail to see progress and become discouraged. With them, not only do you see progress but the achievement of each sub-goal provides a sense of accomplishment.

CASE

Arthur M. had worked as an engineer in middle management for some twenty-five years. His work was considered brilliant

—when he did it, and he was doing less of it these days. Arthur presented his problem as "I'm in a chronic state of depression." This depression was actually due to his difficulty with the setting of sub-goals and the acceptance of their limitations.

With every project Arthur started, he had an unrealistic fantasy goal that would require twenty years work to finish, and for which he would then win the Nobel Prize. Of course, he could not accomplish this in the three to four months allowed him for each project. As a result, he felt so overwhelmed that he couldn't do the work, or if he did, it fell so short of his far distant goal that he was dissatisfied.

Arthur really wanted to come up with a major theoretical formulation within his area of work. I showed him this was a legitimate long-term goal, and that each project he worked on could become a step in that direction. Now he was doing the necessary preliminary work. When he took enough steps toward his goal—perhaps in ten years—then he would be in a position to take a major scientific step.

I knew treatment was over when one day Arthur came in and told me he had just finished a project without any difficulty. In an excited way, he described his findings and exclaimed "That was a two-year goal—and I did it in only four months."

(3) *Conjure up an idealized self-image of yourself.* Ask yourself, "What kind of person would I like to be?" According to Dr. Dorothy J. Susskind, associate professor of educational psychology at Hunter College of the City University of New York, "Goals are the creation of a more positive identity and an enhanced self-esteem."

Close your eyes and imagine your idealized self with all the traits and qualities you would like to possess.

Sit down and write out a description of the kind of person you want to be. Be concrete. Include the way you'd like to dress, things you'd like to talk about, whether you'd prefer to be an introvert or extrovert.

Elaborate on this. Make up a check list of the traits belonging to the kind of person you'd like to be. List them in order of their importance to you so you know where the give has to be. Keep writing down the outstanding characteristics of your idealized self until you have eight to ten qualities.

Work on your idealized self-image. Go through the check list. Do you think you have any of these traits now? Are you "poised," "intellectually curious," "popular"? If there is a big discrepancy between you now and you as you'd like to be, what can you do to develop those desired traits? Some may be impossible to actualize. You may dream of yourself as a famous artist, but have no talent for it at all. However, if in your idealized self-image you see yourself as an informed, aware person, all of us can achieve that.

For example, when Betty Madden, a highly personable woman of thirty-three, came to see me, she said, "I'm miserable. I'm just a high school graduate, and my husband is a professional man. All our friends are college graduates. I can't talk about the things they talk about. I always feel inferior." This intellectual insecurity had turned Betty into an unsure wife and an overprotective mother (she felt "safe" with her three young children, so she sought their company rather than that of adults).

Early in our sessions, I realized that Betty's problems stemmed from the fact that *she did not read*—and even though she had once played the violin well, she now had no cultural interests, or interests that exercised her mind. Working together, we set up a program with these goals: to become an "informed" person by (a) reading, and (b) capitalizing on the artistic interests she possessed, but had never developed.

(a) Betty enrolled in a no-credit English course, where the main emphasis was on vocabulary building, at a nearby college. Her failure to comprehend key words was one of the main reasons she didn't read. As a course corollary, I assigned Betty two daily tasks:

To read two newspaper columnists, look up any words she did not understand, and write down the definitions. She was to read each column twice, and if necessary a third time, until she completely understood the content.

To take her tape recorder and, in her own words, tell the meaning of each column. After that, she should repeat it, starting with the phrase, "I agree," or, "I disagree," and telling why. At the conclusion, she should listen to herself and hear how she sounded.

(b) She started playing the violin again. Betty failed at this. "It's too hard with the house and kids," she told me honestly. So we substituted a record-playing exercise. Each morning, as she vacuumed and dusted, Betty played a classical music record—the same record for five consecutive mornings. Each week she switched to a new record. While she carried out this musical self-improvement campaign, Betty kept her eyes open for announcements of concerts where the music she had studied would be played. Additionally, she attended a thirteen-week art course given by a local high school.

The studying paid off. On her own, she began to read *Time* and *Newsweek*. She reported to me that she had "started to read books." When she came across a book that proved too difficult for her, she said "too hard" and went on to another.

In six months of treatment with the goal of self-education, Betty became a much more contented person, who was beginning to understand many varied subjects. One day she said, "Over the weekend we were discussing politics with some friends who just didn't have the correct facts. So I discreetly showed them where they were wrong, and all four of them, including my own husband, ended up telling me I was right. Imagine me talking up to all those college graduates!"

(4) *Know your limitations.* Make your goal realization of your essential abilities. Do not set goals that are impossible for you to achieve. Many people do this and wind up doing nothing, knowing their aims are out of range. Kurt Goldstein, the late noted neuropsychiatrist, theorized that it is only by recognizing your real limits that you can fulfill yourself. He wrote, "A person . . . is healthy when there is a state of adequacy between the demands and capacities of the individual."

To understand your limitations, you must:

Realize you cannot be everything simultaneously. The day of the Renaissance Man is over. You must have an order of priority and may have to drop some goals completely.

Accept the limitations of goals in terms of talent and age. At fifty, you can learn to play the piano for pleasure, but no matter how great your skill, you have started too late for a concert career. If you have poor coordination obviously you cannot be a tennis champ, but you can learn to play for fun.

Older people must make more compromises and accept more limitations, but they can still set goals. One widow who for thirty-five years had devoted herself to being an attorney's wife came to my office and complained, "I'm a sixty-year-old nothing. My husband is dead. My children are married. I feel my life is over." However, before her marriage, she had acquired an M.A. in psychology and held a series of social welfare jobs. Taking this background into consideration, we worked out a goal for her: to become a marriage counselor. At sixty-one, she entered a two-year training program, and at this point, she is completing her first year. The academic discipline has helped her control her obsessive worrying, and she "loves going back to school."

(5) *As you redefine yourself through action and living, your long-term goal may change.* There is nothing immutable about a long-range goal. Sometimes the change will come about gradually without your being aware of it; on other occasions it becomes a deliberate and anxiety-provoking decision. The danger situation exists (a) when you do not possess a long-term goal and hence have no feeling of movement through life, and (b) when you keep living according to a long-term goal that is no longer desired or appropriate.

CASE

Despite his successful legal career, David Nathanson, a high-living bachelor of twenty-nine, "felt dissatisfied with life." David told me, "I know I have it in me to write a great novel. I just got pressured into law because of my father."

Together we worked out two steps that hopefully would lead to David's goal of writing a novel. To get training, he enrolled in a novel-writing course at New York's New School for Social Research. He also decided to spend two week-night evenings, plus all day Saturday and Sunday, working on the book. At the end of a year and a half, David gave up the whole project without regret, concluding that at best he would be a hack, and that writing was too lonely a life for him. But soul searching on his own, as a supplement to our sessions, made him understand that he did enjoy some things about law: the client contact, the negotiation conferences with fellow lawyers, and the give and take of courtroom trials.

So David switched goals. He spoke up to his firm's partners about getting more of the kind of legal work he wanted. When they couldn't (or wouldn't) make the change, David moved to a different law firm. Now he's happy, because through assertive action, he got to know himself better, learned his limitations, and emerged with a more satisfactory life.

BEHAVIOR ASSIGNMENTS

Recently two men, both in their early thirties, walked into a crowded singles bar on New York's Third Avenue. After ordering drinks, they looked around the room, making a mental survey of the collection of people on the predatory prowl. The bolder of the pair got into a conversation with a pretty stewardess. In turn, she introduced her friend to his friend.

In actuality, the two men had gone to Wyler's Club on orders from their therapist, who at the last group session had instructed: "You both have trouble talking to girls and asking for dates. Your assignment for next week is to go to a singles bar and strike up a conversation with at least one girl. If you feel hesitant about going alone, go with each other."

The "buddy" system represents just one of the techniques used in behavior assignments, an AT method for treating people who have specific problems in assertion. Therapists utilize behavior assignments in different ways, but always with a twofold purpose: (1) to enable the patient to put what he has learned in therapeutic sessions into practice in life. Sometimes the patient must start with very simple behaviors. As he practices these desired behaviors, his fear decreases. (2) The assignments—whether to send back that carbonized steak or to refuse to pay a minor overcharge—serve as a test of treatment; if he can do them, the patient can learn to do other things he once thought impossible.

Here are some of the assignments I have found to be useful to many people. Some involve impersonal situations; some are more personal. To the unknowing they may seem boring and not of major significance, but these inconsequential situations serve as starters in assertion. Eventually you can draw up your own assignments. By practicing them, you may decrease some of your fears and concomitantly feel more elbow room in life—a little or a lot, depending on how assertive you are at the start.

From this list, choose the assignments that will enable you to move in the direction of your own individual goals. Remember two principles always apply:

Pay a lot of attention to the trivial. It is the incidents you tend to dismiss as insignificant that are important in AT. Can you ask for change in a store without buying something? Can you say no easily to the panhandler who accosts you on the street?

Start with what you can reasonably do now, and then progress to more difficult tasks.

Behavior Assignments: Impersonal Situations

(1) In the course of a week go into two stores and ask for change of one dollar. Don't buy anything. The second week ask for change of five dollars, and the third week for change of ten dollars. Visit only stores where you are not known. Remember you do not have to get the change. Just ask. If the proprietor gives it to you, thank him. If he doesn't, say a polite, "Thanks, anyway."

(2) Vary the "demand" technique. Go to a newsstand where you are not known, take out a five-dollar bill, and ask for a fifteen-cent newspaper. Do this twice the first week. The second week try it with ten dollars. Make your request matter-of-fact. Do not apologize. The point: to do the exercise. Remember, you are not forcing the newsstand vendor or storekeeper to do anything, and he or she has the right to say no. I have asked many store proprietors if they resent people coming in to ask for change, and in 90 percent of the cases the answer was, "If they come in, they might buy something."

(3) Go into a luncheonette where you are not known. Do

not pick a time when the countermen are frantic with work. Ask, "May I have a glass of water, please?" If you get it, drink down the water and express your thanks. If you don't get it, say, "Thanks, anyway," and leave.

(4) Go into three stores. In each, try on an article of clothing—jacket, coat, or dress—but buy nothing. This gives you the freedom to say no. If you see something you really want to purchase, go back later.

(5) Stop three people on the street and ask for directions.

(6) In a store, ask for a specific item that is not on display.

(7) Buy something at a store with the deliberate intention of returning it with no apology or explanation. Just say "I would like to return this" to the salesperson. The intent of this task is to be able to return things, not to practice being apologetic.

In carrying out these assignments:

Set a deadline.

Share the assignment with a spouse or friend so you know you will have to report to someone.

If you don't do an assignment for two consecutive weeks, make the assumption that it was too anxiety-provoking and substitute another.

Go back and repeat the assignment again and again. This gives you the feeling of being in control.

In the performance of these behavior assignments, people almost always react in the same way. Before starting the task, they feel increased anxiety. In actually doing the task, they experience little tenseness. If they don't get the change or the glass of water, they usually feel the worst has happened, but "I can do it again." When they successfully complete the assignment, they feel good with themselves and that they have made a start on the assertive road.

Behavior Assignments: Social Interaction

(1) Practice the expression of feeling. Look for opportunities to pay a compliment to a waitress, store clerk, co-worker. Count the number of times you accomplish this in one week, and double the amount in the next week.

(2) In the same way, search out the opportunity to express

displeasure or annoyance to a waitress, store clerk, co-worker. When the occasion comes up, you might say to the waitress, "This soup is cold. Would you mind getting me some hot minestrone?" or, "I asked you for well-done roast beef and this is raw. Please give me what I asked for." To the store clerk you might try, "Sorry, I was next," or "You know you're being rude to me"; to a co-worker, "Do you mind not playing the radio? It's interfering with my work."

As an assertive exercise for more extreme expressions of anger, call up the Department of Sanitation or some other city bureau. Get to as high an official as you can, and in an appropriate way, express your feelings about the fact that your garbage hasn't been picked up for a week, or whatever you're annoyed about. This works best just before Election Day.

(3) If you live in an apartment building, try saying "Good morning" and "Good evening" to fellow residents.

(4) Say "Good morning" to people at work. Don't expect a response. Any response you get is pure plus.

(5) Without expecting a response, make comments to the person sitting next to you at the luncheonette, bus stop, on line at the movie. Your remarks can be simple: "Isn't it a nice day?" . . . "I hear it's a good movie." . . . "Won't that bus ever come?" This task serves to loosen you up socially.

(6) Tell your spouse or a close friend something personal about yourself that you have never told anyone before.

(7) Make it your business to do one task a week that you've wanted to do but have put off. It may be to write your Aunt Fanny, give a dinner party, or just telephone your college roommate to see how she is getting on. Pick a task *that involves another person.*

In following chapters, I will give other behavior assignments. However, these should enable you to start on your own training schedule. Go back to the Assertiveness Inventory in Chapter II, and take specific situations where you scored unassertive and look for specific opportunities to practice your particular behavior problem in assertion.

Some people ask me, "Aren't these assignments unethical and manipulative?" Obviously there's nothing wrong with greeting a neighbor or talking to a stranger in line. However, in some of the exercises, you do make demands of others, such as asking for change. Remember, just as the other person has a perfect right to say no, you have a perfect right to ask. Interestingly enough, the glass of water assignment causes the most comment. It is quite a comment on our society if people question the appropriateness of, or feel uncomfortable about, requesting a glass of water.

I feel the most questionable assignment is the one where you go into a store with no intention of buying or with the plan of returning the item. While we have the "right" to do this, the question remains whether to do it deliberately is ethical. It would be easy to rationalize that many times in the course of such assignments people do spot things they later return and purchase. However, this serves merely as a rationalization. I myself am not certain of the ethics. For this reason, I encourage patients and readers to make their own judgments, analyze their own needs, and base their actions on what *they*, not I, believe to be their rights.

FEELING TALK

Some people voice what they think—not what they feel.
Others cannot say what they feel at the moment they feel it.
Some sad individuals fail to articulate any emotions.
Others aren't even sure of what they do feel.
The inability to express minute-by-minute feelings leads to heartbreaking consequences.

Within yourself you lose contact with your feelings and thus become insensitive to them. Because you have lost control over an important area of your interpersonal relations, you become increasingly resentful and anxious. Your self-esteem declines; your dissatisfactions with yourself and others increases.

With others you limit the amount of closeness you can achieve. You place a tremendous burden on friends and family; they must become mind readers to discover what you feel. Because you never reveal your true self, you can never really be comfortable with others. As e. e. cummings observed:

> *Since feeling is first*
> *who pays any attention*

to the syntax of things
will never wholly kiss you

Assertiveness Training emphasizes the *spontaneous expression and experience of feelings.* It views feelings not as isolated emotions, but as one part of the individual that should be integrated with all his other parts. By teaching specific behaviors, AT aims to merge thought, action, and feeling, so that they become a unity in the person, just as his senses of taste and smell form a unity.

Emphasis on feelings is not unique to AT. Most forms of psychotherapy stress just this and aim to increase the patient's sensitivity to his own feelings. Nor is the stress on overt expression of feelings limited to AT. In the attempt to release unconscious anger or pain, some forms of psychotherapy center around the uninhibited and uncontrolled expression of feelings.

However, unlike many other therapies, AT takes the stand that

by itself experience of feelings is not enough;
by itself expression of feelings is not enough.

You must be able to communicate to another person what you feel at the very moment in a direct, honest and appropriate way. By doing this, you become a more alive person, more sensitive to, and aware of, your own feelings and more open to the feelings of others.

The expression and communication of feeling is not a simple matter of the choice of words; it invokes the whole person and involves tone and expression of voice, facial expression, body stance, and gestures. AT calls these behaviors "feeling talk" (a phrase created by Andrew Salter), and they constitute the very behaviors AT attempts to teach. As an individual gains the concept of experiencing feeling and as he masters the behaviors involved, he becomes more able to express spontaneously what he feels in all situations.

The Behavioral Approach to Expression of Feeling

Some people have only a mild deficiency in expression of feelings. They experience feelings subjectively and manifest them outwardly—but not enough. As a result, their feelings play only a partial, instead of a full, role in their lives.

For people like that, AT changes behavior by *accenting* what *is already there*. It is often possible for the AT therapist to get results by the simple giving of instructions such as: "Put more feeling in your voice" . . . "Be more alive when you speak" . . . "Use more gestures" . . . "Say it more directly" . . . "Let your face show what you feel." At first, people obeying these simple directives feel unreal and unnatural. However, as they find their own unique styles of expression and this new mode of communication becomes more habitual, they often report enriched subjective emotions, increased spontaneity of emotional expressions, and many changes in their attitudes toward themselves and interactions with others.

CASE

Jay Wilkins, a young business executive, originally came to me because he feared speaking in public. But probing showed he had a far deeper difficulty; he lacked emotional closeness. On the surface, he seemed to have good relationships with co-workers, but they rarely developed into close friendships. He had been living with a girl friend for two years, but when I asked how he truly felt about her, he answered, "I'm not sure I really like her."

Jay lacked an involvement in his own feelings. He expressed what he felt, but *not strongly enough*. Through coaching, modeling, and role-playing in our sessions, I was able to get Jay to increase the intensity and aliveness of his expression. Instead of merely telling his secretary, "Nice job," he said, "You did a really fine piece of work here. I'm truly grateful"— and suddenly a new warmth sprang up between them. In discussing a new project with his boss, Jay deliberately accentuated his enthusiasm with gestures and facial expression. And his superior responded with "You *are* excited about this—that makes me feel good." This deliberate stress on his own feelings with his secretary and boss made Jay's own feelings about his girl friend much clearer to him. He realized he had been exploiting her and that he didn't like himself for doing it.

Jay had the first frank talk he had ever had with her, and

admitted, "Look, I'm starting to come alive now, and I see there just isn't that chemistry between us. I like you, but without love, I'm taking advantage of you." Her answer: "I love you, but I've felt something was missing. I'm glad you brought it out in the open." They split. Three months after the discontinuance of treatment, Jay fell in love for the first time in his life.

Sadly, there are many people for whom such an approach is too difficult and advanced. Uncertain of what they feel, they may not even understand the basic concepts of feeling and expression of it. In AT, we approach such emotionally handicapped individuals by stressing the *content* of their communication. By concentrating on content, you

become more aware that you are attempting to express feelings;

consider the feeling you are trying to express, and so you train yourself to be more sensitive in that area;

ensure to some extent that the other person knows what feeling you are trying to express.

As you become more able to say directly what you feel, you often spontaneously develop the other aspects of feeling talk (voice, posture, facial and body expressions).

For a first step in this educational process, I often find it necessary to teach what feeling talk is *not*. Many people believe they express themselves when, in reality, they do no such thing. They may also have an incorrect concept of what feeling expression really is.

You concentrate on saying what you think. On many occasions, it is important to say what you *think*, but don't confuse this with spontaneously saying what you *feel*. Thinking can often get in the way of feeling expression. As soon as you use the phrase "I think," you are not involved with feeling.

Your talk largely concerns facts. Statements about facts reveal nothing of you—neither what you think or feel. Even if the fact happens to be about you, you are talking of yourself as a *thing*, not a *person*.

You say what you think you should feel, or what you believe the other person expects you to feel. Again, your own identity is submerged in this process. You become a mirror of the world around you or what you believe the world is like.

You think you express true inner feelings when you explode with rage or hostility. Such lack of control usually stems from the lack of true feeling expression. However, some people incorrectly believe that feeling talk must be extreme. As nobody really wants to act in this way, this false conception frightens them away from any emotional communication.

You substitute rationalizations for feelings. Because you don't know how to express yourself, you tell yourself, "I'll hurt him," or "He won't like me if I say what I feel," or, simply, "It isn't important." *These aren't feelings. They're excuses.* Recognize them as such.

True feeling talk is the *continuous appropriate communication of your constantly changing state of emotional being.* When you use content to improve your feeling talk, what you say should have certain characteristics:

It is specific, either directed toward a specific person or a specific object or act: "I like your pin" . . . "I want to go to the film at the Rivoli" . . . "I despise Congressman ———— and all he represents" . . . "I admire the way you spoke up to Mrs. Jones."

It stresses the deliberate use of the word "I" followed by a verb of feeling: "I like this" . . . "I feel terrible about what I did to you unintentionally" . . . "I'd love a blind date with him—he sounds so nice" . . . "I want to do that" . . . "Darling, I love you."

It is simple. Too many people begin to qualify statements by adding adjectives, offering so much gratuitous explanation that in the end, the other person doesn't know what they feel—nor do they. For instance, the sentence "I like the way you spoke up at the meeting" is commendatory, clear, concise. Many people are not that clear. They say something like: "When you spoke up at the meeting, I noticed a lot of people were listening intently. Some looked as if they agreed with you. But Joe Blow had a funny look on his face. However, all in all, I think you made your point." With this kind of statement, neither sender nor receiver knows the person liked the way the other spoke up at the meeting. People who use a lot of qualifying words not only fail to communicate feeling but become boring.

It is honest. When you express your emotions dishonestly, you continue to train yourself to hide, to make your emotional mask stronger, to do as T. S. Eliot's J. Alfred Prufrock did when he felt the need to "prepare a face to meet the faces that you meet."

It is appropriate. Many people with difficulties in this area equate expression of emotion with loss of control. They can conceive only of the most extreme expression of emotions. In AT, we concern ourselves with the appropriate expression of emotion by which we mean not just the feeling you want to express, but how you want to express it. A simple criterion: if you saw somebody else expressing the feeling in a similar situation in the way you plan to or did, would you think it peculiar or bizarre?

Feeling talk can be used to express almost any emotion: dislike, liking, love, hate, approval, criticism, complaint, respect. Obviously, in AT the aim is to use feeling-talk exercise until it becomes a natural part of you. Some people find this too general a prescription. For these patients, I have a special exercise.

LABORATORY EXERCISE IN FEELING TALK

Purpose: to increase deliberately expression of feeling by use of feeling-talk phrases.

STEP ONE: Plan to use the following three pairs of phrases as often as you can:

"I like what you said" . . . "I don't like what you said."
"I like what you did" . . . "I don't like what you did."
"I want you to . . ." . . . "I don't want you to . . ."

The verb puts the emphasis on the feeling, and you insure direct communication with a fellow human being. By using "I," you put yourself in the communication. The statement "I like the way you typed that letter" is far more personal than the praise "That's a well-done letter." By limiting the number to three phrases, the task becomes easier for you to do, and you are more likely to carry it out.

STEP TWO: In your AT notebook, make up a chart with a space for each day of the week. At the end of each day, count up the number of times you have used any of the six feeling-talk phrases (or mark them on an index card during the course of the day). At the end of the week, total your count. Do the exercise for three successive weeks. Your chart should look like this.

Use of the Six Feeling-Talk Phrases

Day	Week One	Week Two	Week Three
Mon.			
Tues.			
Wed.			
Thurs.			
Fri.			
Sat.			
Sun.			
Week total			

Often people with difficulty in expressing feelings cannot use the phrases consistently more than once or twice a day, or even week. Some patients are unable to say them even once.

STEP THREE: Monitor your use of the six phrases during the first week, then deliberately increase the number of times you say them during the second week. Set a goal you can reasonably expect to achieve. If you used the phrases only once or twice during the first week, a secondary goal of one a day usually proves realistic. If you used them two or three times a day, you can probably double the number. Keep trying to increase the number of times each day until you reach your goal. Maintain that frequency for the next week. Then set a new goal.

Perhaps these phrases may prove too difficult for you. In that case, substitute another pair. Many patients seem to find

"I agree . . ." . . . "I disagree . . ." somewhat easier. Once you can say your own phrases easily, try mine again.

STEP FOUR: Once you have progressed through the second week of this exercise, analyze your use of the feeling-talk phrases. Study which you had difficulty using, and under what circumstances.

You may find you encounter difficulty with "I want . . ." . . . "I don't want . . ." You feel this makes a demand or puts a pressure on the other person and that this may make him resent you. However, there is a *difference between a demand and a request.* If you utter the phrase "I want . . ." and the other person says no, and you feel disappointment, but not anger or depression, it was a request. You gave the other person the freedom of refusal. However, if you make the statement, receive a negative answer, and then you feel either angry or depressed, you were making a demand and not giving the other person freedom of refusal. As you become aware of this difference and realize the other person's right to his own feelings and needs, you will find it easier to use the "I want" phrases.

Some people have no trouble saying "I don't like . . ." But they can't say "I like . . ."

CASE

Chris Perkins, a thirty-three-year-old accountant, had no difficulty telling his wife everything he didn't like about her. But when he said something as simple as "I like your new dress," his anxiety level zoomed up 30 percent. Somehow, Chris had acquired the peculiar idea that the angry part of him was the only "real part," and when he expressed tender feelings, he was "being a phony."

Chris had never learned to express tender feelings. When he began to practice feeling talk, these feelings quickly became part of him. He had also thought of himself as an "angry man." Now he saw he could be tender, too, and this affected his entire psychological organization. He suddenly found he liked to say "I like . . ."

Once you begin to express your feelings with any consistency, expand into the other aspects of feeling talk.

Get your feeling messages across with face and body talk. Frequently, people lack facial expression and keep their bodies immobile, or they give vent to inappropriate facial or body expression. For example, the man who breathes "I love you darling" and keeps his body rigid does not communicate feeling to the utmost.

Watch for:

Tone of voice: A firm, confident, appropriately loud tone marks assertive behavior.

Eye contact: Look straight at the person to whom you are speaking.

Body expression: Copy the French, who use a lot of gestures as they talk.

Facial expression: Suit your expression to what you feel and say. Don't smile if you are criticizing someone or expressing anger. Conversely, don't look hostile or moody if you express praise or love. Show your inner emotion and put that mask away.

As with behavior assignments, behavior rehearsal, and other exercises presented in this book, you may feel the feeling-talk exercises are artificial and unnatural. They are. That is why they are called exercises!

How then can feeling-talk exercises lead to a more spontaneous and free expression of feeling?

The expression of emotions stimulates and strengthens the excitatory processes in your brain, and so you become a more excitatory person.

The very expression of feelings inhibits the anxiety centers in your brain, and so you feel less anxious. The less anxiety you feel, the more feeling you can experience and express.

By practice of feeling talk, you learn a new skill: expression of feeling. As you gain competence, you will no longer need your chart to make you say, "I like . . ." . . . "I don't like . . ." You will develop your own style.

This can affect the lives of your children. Your use of feeling talk serves as a model for them, so that they can grow into assertive adults, freely expressing their feelings. Because of your model, your children are more apt to share their feelings with you. *This can affect your life-style.*

CASE

Milt Weiner, a thirty-three-year-old married man who worked as a dress salesman, specialized in fact talk and think talk. Because he never felt close to anyone, he needed three simultaneous mistresses. As he started using feeling talk (and he did it very diligently, making use of the phrases with all his customers), he began to see how "dishonest" and "phony" he had made his life. His solution: to give up the mistresses and get out of the selling business, because it encourages "my tendency to phoniness." With his wife's help, he went to graduate school to study to become a psychologist.

This can affect your relationship to yourself and with someone close to you. When Chris Perkins (the Case on page 58) stopped seeing himself as "an angry person," his entire self-concept changed. As his tender side emerged, closeness with his wife increased dramatically. The peak came one night while making love, when, for the first time in his three-year marriage and his life, Chris used the greatest feeling-talk phrase of all—"darling, I love you."

SAYING NO

Judy fears social rejection from the opposite sex. When a man—almost any man—suggests bed, she immediately acquiesces.

At work, Tom passively accepts all the assignments unwanted by others. When the boss says, "Tom, can you take this on?" he does, even though the task has little relation to his particular job area.

Anne resents her husband. Although often she disagrees with what he wants, she feels being a good wife means doing whatever he wants.

Judy, Tom, and Anne differ in age, sex, appearance, economic circumstances, and interests, but they share one quality in common: they never learned to say no.

People in our society always make requests or place

demands on others. You must be able to stand up for yourself by the simple process of saying no. If you can't state this simple two-letter word when you want to say it, you begin to lose control of your life.

This does not mean saying no to everything. You say yes when you *want* to give an affirmative response. If doing a favor for a friend or participating in a community event may inconvenience you, there is still nothing wrong with saying yes if you feel the matter important enough to undergo discommodity for the sake of the friend or activity. Saying yes becomes wrong when you want to say no and it is in your best interest to say no, but instead, you end up with a feeble "OK, I'll do it."

The inability to say no has several consequences.

It leads you into activities you don't respect yourself for doing. From my clinical experience, I can draw the conclusion that with young, single women the greatest cause of unwanted promiscuity stems from their inability to say no. They rationalize by saying, "He won't ask me out again if I refuse," or "This is what I have to do to be popular." Ending up in bed when they don't want to go to bed, they hate themselves.

CASE

Through a mutual referral source, I was treating Alice, a twenty-seven-year-old assistant TV producer, and Fred, a thirty-year-old copywriter. Alice had come to me with the problems of moodiness, depression, low self-esteem, and unwanted promiscuity. Fred felt anxious in relation to women. Along with a fear of impotency, he thought any girl he dated would expect him to take her to bed on the first date, and he feared suggesting this, but thought that otherwise "she'd be contemptuous of me."

While in treatment, Alice and Fred met at the home of the mutual friend who had sent each to me. They dated. At our subsequent sessions, each described this first date in very different terms.

Alice said, "You see, they're all the same. At the end of the evening, he expected me to invite him for a drink. Before I knew it, he pressured me to go to bed. He didn't care about me. He was concerned only with his own satisfaction. I did it—and ever since I've been in one of my moods."

Fred recalled, "They're all the same. I took her out. We had

a pleasant evening. I took her home. She expected me to go up
to her apartment and hit the hay. I didn't really want to
because I felt uptight about whether I'd make it. But she was a
real swinger, and I was sure if I didn't go to bed, she'd spread
the word I was probably homosexual. I forced myself. I made
it. But I didn't enjoy it, and now I'm more reluctant than ever
to ask a girl for a date."

With their permission, I brought Alice and Fred together
for a discussion and showed them how different it would have
been if each could have said no. Subsequently, they dated for a
while, practicing saying no on all kinds of things, including
bed. At some point, they did have intercourse again, this time
by mutual choice. They eventually drifted apart—each with a
greater ability to say no when they wanted to say no.

It distracts you from what you really want to accomplish. You
become so burdened doing the things you don't want to do
that you have neither time nor energy for the things that are
most important.

*Because you allow other people to exploit you continually, the
resentments build up,* and, sometimes, after years of the yes
routine, you lose your temper in an inappropriate outburst. If
you always perform all kinds of errands for others at great
inconvenience to yourself and serve as the family patsy,
eventually someone makes a trivial request and you explode.
This stems not from the most recent incident, but from
hundreds of happenings. What the yes-sayer doesn't realize is
that this behavior often creates lack of respect rather than
liking.

No matter how unreasonable the request, for some thirty
years, my wife always said "yes, I'll do it" to her friend Cathy,
a holdover from elementary school days. One day, over a
ladies' tearoom lunch, Jean made the first demand she had
ever made of Cathy. Cathy's reply, "Sorry, I'm just too busy."
In the middle of the crowded restaurant, Jean lost her temper
and launched into a recounting of what she had done through
the years. Cathy looked at her admiringly. "You've changed
so much," she said. "What a relief to see you this way instead
of being the self-sacrificing martyr." All those years when Jean

had thought Cathy viewed her as the most loving of friends, Cathy really had been contemptuous.

It produces a lack of communication between you and others. As I noted in the feeling-talk section, unless there is honest communication people cannot understand each other. Saying yes when you mean no is not the quality of sweetness and light; it is dishonest. For instance, I treated one patient who had been reared to think that a wife should always give in to her husband's wishes. She complained to me because every Sunday afternoon spouse Alex would ask, "Wouldn't you like to go to the movies?" She couldn't say no, so off they would go to the neighborhood movie. Prompted by my urging, one day she spoke up, "No, I don't like to go to the movies on Sunday afternoon." Much to my patient's surprise, Alex looked at her with relief, and said, "Why didn't you say so? I hate going to the movies on Sunday. I thought I was pleasing you."

This saying-no technique makes so much sense that as soon as you consider it, you say, "Yes, of course." However, therapists did not pay much attention to it as a scientific and important behavior until the work of a brilliant team of researchers at the University of Wisconsin brought it into the light. This group, headed by Richard M. McFall, defined the ability to say no and tested different training methods to determine which proved the most effective.

You, too, can learn to say no. To start your personal training program, do the following exercises, based on those of the Wisconsin team.

LABORATORY EXERCISE IN SAYING NO

Purpose: To make it easier for you to say no when you want to say it, and to help you form your own style of negative responses.

STEP ONE: Take each situation listed below and think of your answer to it. Or better still, write it out so that you don't fool yourself. For each example, assume that you want to say no, that it is appropriate to do so and only one problem exists: are you able to do it?

SITUATION ONE: Co-worker asks to borrow some coins for the office coffee machine. Somehow he always does this and never repays the change. Co-worker says, "I have no silver. Would you lend me twenty cents for the machine?" How do you say no?

SITUATION TWO: A friend had asked you to go with him "sometime soon" to select a new hi-fi set. You had assented. On the Saturday morning when you had been planning to catch up with house chores, he calls and says, "You promised to help me pick out that hi-fi set. Can you come with me this morning?" You really want to sort your bookshelves. How do you say no?

SITUATION THREE: You have been working on the planning committee for a local organization's upcoming fund-raising event. You've already put in more time than anyone else. Now the president makes another demand, asking, "Joan, you're such a terrific worker. Can I count on you to collect tickets at the door?" How do you say no?

STEP TWO: After you have said no to the above situations in your way, read the following instructional models and compare your answers to them. Then try the questions a second time. Remember, the answers you give do not have to be exactly like the models, but you should follow their principles: brevity, clarity, firmness, honesty.

SITUATION ONE: Co-worker and the coffee machine.

Model: "No, sorry, you owe me for too many coffees already."

"No, you never pay back."

Note: Each answer is short and to the point, starts with no so that neither is ambiguous, and does not explain at great length.

SITUATION TWO: The hi-fi set.

Model: "No, I can't make it today. How about next Saturday?"

"I will go with you, but not today. I'm sorry."

Note: The answers recognize the commitment but also the bad timing.

SITUATION THREE: The organization and the hard worker.

Model: "No, you should give that job to someone who hasn't done her share."

"No, I have already done more than my share."

Note: In each case the response is honest, direct, and firm.

STEP THREE: Practice saying no. Think of several unreasonable requests that have been made of you, or that might be made of you. Now imagine each request being made, and then imagine yourself saying no—firmly, succinctly, and without overlong explanation. You can make this assignment even more effective if you put each request on audio tape. Listen to it, stop the machine, and say your answer out loud. Practice each response several times.

Keep in mind some of the model ways to say no:

"No, I can't do it. I have something else scheduled for that time." . . . "No, I don't feel like doing that today. I'd rather do such and such." . . . "No, I don't know you well enough for bed." . . . "No, it's impossible for me to do that. Try someone else."

STEP FOUR: As a final step, look for opportunities to say no in life situations. During your training period, when in doubt, say no.

In my office practice, I use one device to train patients in saying no. Always making clear that this is a test situation, I say to the unassertive patient, "It is important that I get this envelope immediately to another patient. I know it is out of your way, but I wonder if you would mind dropping it off?"

Even though they know I'm simulating, it is very difficult for some patients to say no. Some say yes.

CASE

When Mark Butler, a thirty-five-year-old scriptwriter, answered my unreasonable request to hand deliver my envelope with "No, I just can't do it; but if it's so important, why don't you telephone a messenger service?" it marked a breakthrough in his lifetime pattern of unassertiveness. Even though he possessed great creativity and originality in his work, Mark's passivity had affected both his professional career and his marriage.

One week after he said no to me, a businessman telephoned him and asked him to do a script on speculation. Previously Mark would have said yes. This time he didn't utter a flat no, but offered an alternative, saying, "I can't do a one-hundred-page script on spec; but I'll do one page of outline and two pages of dialogue, and you can make your decision on that."

Not only did Mark win the script assignment, but his new ability to say no also changed his marital relationship. As a result of our Assertiveness Training sessions, he clarified what were his responsibilities to his wife and what were his rights. Mark felt triumphant with his new form of behavior, but his newly acquired assertiveness upset his wife. She had to come to me for several treatment sessions. Her comment: "I always wanted him to be more assertive, but only when I *wanted* him to be assertive!"

BEHAVIOR REHEARSAL

Prior to a press conference, the President of the United States meets with his press secretary and major policy advisors. These assistants ask questions on everything from the national budget to foreign affairs, the same questions they expect the news men and women will pose to the President during the conference. From this dress rehearsal, the President shapes and practices his responses to difficult questions that may be asked, and thus can deliver a better performance at the actual reportorial confrontation.

Reputedly, Presidents Truman, Kennedy, Johnson, Nixon, and Ford have all utilized this strategy at times. These Chiefs of State may not have realized it, but they were employing behavior rehearsal, one of the most successful Assertiveness Training techniques.

Originally referred to as "behavioristic psychodrama," and often termed "role-playing," behavior rehearsal serves as a training process in which patients with deficiencies or inhibitions in their social or interpersonal behaviors receive direct training in more efficient, effective alternate behaviors via such procedures as response rehearsal, modeling, and therapist coaching.

In using behavior rehearsal for Assertiveness Training, we try to correct a "response deficit." Because the patient has never learned to use the assertive response, he acts unassertively. We work in three steps: (1) teach the patient what the response is; (2) have him practice it; (3) apply it to life situation. Naturally the purpose of the first two steps is to speed usage in life situations.

Role-playing has the advantage of simulating reality in a controlled manner, without the risks of reality. It permits experimentation so that the patient can find the assertive response that best suits him and then practice it over and over until he becomes comfortable with it and it becomes part of him. According to experiments, conducted by Dr. Philip H. Friedman of Temple University School of Medicine, even eight to ten minutes of role-playing training may produce a major change in a specific situation—and this change lasts.

How actually does the therapist use behavior rehearsal for Assertiveness Training?

(1) *He defines the behaviors that need training.* These can range from how to ask for a raise or pick up a girl in a singles bar to standing up for yourself in an appropriate manner with a friend, boss, mate, or salesperson and to the acquisition of specific social skills like storytelling. The patient must brief the therapist on all the details of the specific problem so that the latter can play the part of the other person involved. The therapist then sets up a situation in a somewhat simplified form that resembles the patient's life circumstances. Patient and therapist then enact the situation.

(2) *After completion of the scene, the therapist coaches and instructs the patient, pointing out the good and bad points of the performances.* He also tells patient X how he can improve specific actions and express himself more effectively. He may tell him: "be more direct," "use feeling talk," "speak more honestly," "hold your shoulders back so you don't look so listless and without energy." Together patient and therapist work out certain phrases he might say.

For example, at the Institute for Behavior Therapies in New York, Drs. Steven Fishman and Barry Lubetkin treated a shy, passive, twenty-three-year-old medical student. Her problem: she was terrified of examining a patient. Dr. Lubetkin told me, "In session, we role-played everything but actually touching of the hospitalized patient. I enacted various kinds of patients from querulous old women to bad-tempered middle-aged men.

Knowing her insecurity about her lack of experience, I asked questions like 'When will the *real* doctor arrive?' I coached her on making eye contact with patients, voice control (she spoke in a whisper, like Jackie Kennedy), improving her bedside manner. Most important, I showed her how not to come across as a loser—she used to begin our rehearsal sessions with the inadequate sentence 'I'm here as a student.' Slowly, she gained confidence, and was able to apply what she learned in our practice sessions to her work at the hospital."

(3) *After the instruction and coaching, the patient repeats the scene, usually with some improvement.* The therapist reinforces the better performance with such statements as "Good, you spoke up more directly that time." He may then give further instruction.

(4) *To aid the patient in his assertive goal, the therapist may model the desired behaviors.* In this technique patient and therapist switch roles. Now the therapist plays the troubled patient, and the patient enacts the part of the other person. In this way, the therapist demonstrates the actions that have been discussed. Not only does the therapist show what the patient should do but he calls attention to what he himself did. He says, "Did you notice the way I stood?", or "By saying it in that way I was polite, but I stood up for my rights."

Then they switch back to the original roles. The patient again plays himself and tries to follow the therapist's model. The result should be an improved performance which the therapist reinforces with praise. Remember the therapeutic goal: the patient should find his own style and not merely emerge as a carbon copy of the therapist.

(5) *Initial behavior rehearsal may show that the problem posed the patient is too difficult, creating too much anxiety and making demands on the patient that he can't meet yet. Or it may become evident that while the patient can master the situation in the behavior rehearsal lab, he will not be able to carry it over into real life.*

In these instances, we adopt a *hierarchical approach,* starting with situations or behaviors that the patient can easily do and working up to more difficult levels. These may involve either people, tasks, or intensity.

People. Assume the general problem is "telling people off," and that a particularly difficult problem exists with a mother-in-law. The patient might first rehearse his telling-off scene with a good friend whom he does not fear. Then he could enact a scene with a fellow worker that might prove a little harder. In this step-by-step manner we, finally, reach the mother-in-law dilemma. Of course, we tailor each level for the specific patient involved. What one finds hard, another may find easy.

Tasks. Sometimes it is easier to do some things with a given person than to do others. This involves a second type of hierarchy. The patient may find it relatively simple to rebuke his mother-in-law for giving his kids too much candy. He may find it harder to chastize her for upsetting his wife. He can't even try to tell her off for the sly innuendos she makes constantly about him. In a case like this, we role-play each scene in this hierarchical order.

Intensity. We also use hierarchies to approach graded expressions of specific feelings. In this way, we take the patient who has difficulty in expressing anger from a mumbled "I don't like it" to the point where he can role-play a full-bodied, spontaneous anger.

(6) *The patient practices the behavior he wants to perform over and over in the treatment room, thus increasing the likelihood he can do it in the life situation.*

This can be done with many kinds of behavior and with children as well as adults. Dr. Martin Gittelman, chief of Children's Service at the Queens-Nassau Mental Health Service of H.I.P., used the behavior rehearsal technique with Ralph, a thirteen-year-old boy whose temper tantrums had proved so violent that he had been expelled from one school, and was about to be expelled from another. Dr. Gittelman role-played various situations with Ralph, and had him rehearse the behavior of responding with calmness and control rather than with clenched teeth, flare-ups, rude answers, and fistfights. After four sessions using behavior rehearsal, Ralph reported that his behavior at both school and home was much better. He said that while he still *felt* angry, he could *control* what he did. Follow-up nine months later showed that Ralph had had no further outbreaks of aggressive behavior.

(7) *Feedback serves as a final step in behavior rehearsal.* From the patient's reports of successes, partial successes, or failure in life, the therapist learns that new training may be indicated or finds out about new problems. Often, you resolve one problem and move on to other areas. Or treatment may then terminate with the patient maintaining only telephone contact for a period of time.

Reconstruction of a Behavior Rehearsal Training Session

CASE

Dr. Norman Jones, outstanding research pathologist, came to me with two major problems, both stemming from isolation: (1) He had few professional discussions because he lacked contact with other researchers at his level; (2) he failed to get professional recognition, such as invitations to speak or participate in study groups. Logically, he could break the isolation at professional meetings. However, when Norman attended the conferences, he would listen to the papers that interested him, but wouldn't speak with any of the lecturers afterward. When I asked him why not, he stated, "If the person was alone, I didn't want to interrupt his thoughts, and if he was with someone, I didn't want to interrupt the conversation."

I also found out that one of Norman's devices for preserving his aloneness was that when he did get involved in a conversation, he cut it short. Through our discussions, we worked out that his behavioral deficit concerned conversations: starting them, joining them, maintaining them, and decided on behavior rehearsal as his training method. Our goal: better and more social behavior for Norman at the professional meeting he would attend in the near future.

The following patient-therapist dialogue is an almost verbatim reconstruction of my behavior rehearsal session with Norman Jones. It can serve as a model if you decide to use the method.

THERAPIST: "I will be Dr. Smith. We're at the meeting and waiting for an elevator. Your goal is to start a conversation with me and get into shoptalk. Let's see how you do it. We'll make believe the closet door is the door to the elevator, and we'll stand near it. All right. You try to start the conversation."

DR. JONES: *(After a period of silence and fidgeting blurts out)* "Did you ring for the elevator?"

THERAPIST: *(As Dr. Smith)* "Yes, I did. I hope it comes soon."

Period of silence as Dr. Jones continues to fidget.

THERAPIST: *(Out of role)* "Remember, you want to start talking shop with me."

DR. JONES: *(Mumbling)* "Good paper this morning." *(He turns his body half away.)*

THERAPIST: *(As Dr. Smith)* "Why thank you. I'm glad you liked it. Did you think the design was tight enough?" (This query was intended to reinforce the patient for his effort and at the same time to make an answer easy.)

DR. JONES: *(Out of role)* "Look, I'd never be able to talk to Dr. Smith. He's supposed to be sarcastic, and once he wrote a bad review of one of my papers. I'd be too frightened to say a word."

THERAPIST: "I'm glad you told me that" *(reinforcing patient's direct communication)*. "He may be too hard to start off with. Whom do you think we can use first [*forming a hierarchy*]?"

DR. JONES: "They're all too hard." *(Pause)* "How about Brown? I have never talked to him, but he seems to be a good fellow. Besides, once we exchanged letters on a research project. Yes, I think Brown would be the easiest."

THERAPIST: "Fine, I'll be Brown. We're waiting at the elevator, and you start the conversation. Incidentally, last time you were looking down. Try to make eye contact when you talk to me. And talk in a louder voice." *(Coaching)*

DR. JONES: *(Role-playing)* "Dr. Brown, I want to tell you how much I enjoyed your paper this morning."

THERAPIST: *(As Brown)* "Why, thank you. I wonder if you thought my experimental design was tight enough?"

DR. JONES: *(Pause and more fidgets)* "Why yes, it was good. It was fine."

THERAPIST: *(As Brown)* "It was that ion-exchange part. Do you think I handled that all right?"

DR. JONES: *(Mumbling)* "Fine. It was good."

THERAPIST: *(Out of role)* "There must be a better way to do it. Can you think of something?"

(Long pause)

THERAPIST: *(Out of role)* "Let's stop for a minute and think. Your beginning was better. You spoke louder and looked at me. Then you petered out. What happened?"

DR. JONES: "I didn't know what to say. I'd be afraid of saying something wrong and hurting his feelings."

THERAPIST: "The first part is true. You don't know what to say. Once you learn, the fears will disappear. The trouble is the way you began the conversation. You can do better."

DR. JONES: "I told him I liked his paper. People like to hear praise."

THERAPIST: "True, but you were too general. The best way to start would be to say something that would gain his interest and involvement [*instructions*]. Provoke him. Let him know you have something worthwhile to say."

DR. JONES: "I could remind him of our correspondence. He seemed interested enough then."

THERAPIST: "Great. Start out by introducing yourself. Then add something to catch his attention. Let's try it again, and do it that way."

DR. JONES: "I'm not sure I'd have the nerve even in role-playing.

THERAPIST: "I'll tell you what. You be Brown and I'll be you. Watch the way I do it. Incidentally, I won't be perfect either, but maybe I can get the idea across to you." *(Modeling)*

And so I proceeded to train and shape Dr. Norman Jones. Soon Norman was able to walk up to me (as Brown), extend his hand, and say "Dr. Brown, I'm Norman Jones. We corresponded on that tracer project of yours a few years back. Are you still involved in that?" We also shaped and rehearsed his behavior with another colleague and practiced Norman's joining in conversations. We never did have time to get back to the difficult Dr. Smith. Then Norman flew off to the meeting.

During the first day and a half of the conference, Norman continued to act the loner. Then, by chance, he spotted Dr.

Brown alone—not at our practice elevator, but outside of a meeting room. Norman mentally reviewed his speech, mustered up his courage, and walked up to Brown with extended hand. No sooner did he state his name than Brown interrupted him with "I've been looking forward to meeting you. I want to bring you up to date on the tracer project, and I've got some questions about your last paper. Why don't we go up to my room and talk?"

Norman spent the next two days participating in stimulating shoptalk. Only once did he have difficulty. When the formidable Dr. Smith joined a discussion, Norman became briefly tongue-tied, but soon got caught up in the technical discussions.

A year later, his behavior rehearsal training produced unexpected results. Norman was invited to present a paper at an international chemical conference in Switzerland, all expenses paid. The chairman of the meeting turned out to be Dr. Brown!

Through behavior rehearsal, a patient may solve a variety of problems, some simple, some complex; clarify his own attitudes; and change the course of events. Sometimes a complex change in life-style may result from the mastery of a specific, simple act.

CASE

Wanda Midston had a hard-drinking husband who made her life miserable. She knew her solution, and had formulated the entire plan of action: to leave him and take a job in another city where she had family who would care for her two children, while she worked and attempted to rebuild her social life. The job was available, her family willing to babysit, but for two years Wanda made no move to institute the change she wanted so much.

Her explanation for this inertia was quite simple: she was afraid to ask her supervisors for the letters of recommendation she needed to make formal application for the job. We spent part of several AT group sessions shaping and rehearsing the behavior of asking for these references. After this training, Wanda was able to make the request in real life, and was assured she would be given good references. With this problem solved, she began to make final plans for a complete change in life-style.

Even without going for actual behavior rehearsal sessions with a therapist, you can practice the technique.

Find a partner. By playing the other person, the partner can help you shape and evaluate your own behavior, and also serve as model by switching roles with you. Even if the model is not perfect or in your style, you can learn from his or her method of expressing himself. The partner can help by imitating what you do and accentuating your unassertive characteristics. For example, if you talk in too low a voice or make nervous gestures, the partner can ape these. The partner should also pay attention to things you do well in the role-playing. He can comment specifically, "Good, your voice is much firmer this time," or "That was a better way to handle it."

For personal and social problems, a close friend or spouse makes a good partner. With friends you have two choices: (1) to choose as partner a friend with good assertive behavior in the area you will role-play or (2) to elect a friend who has a similar problem. Let's say you're shy with the opposite sex. Should you elect a friend who is confident and outgoing or one who also is shy? As a principle, I suggest you pick the one with whom you would be most comfortable.

Even if the assertive problem involves your spouse, role-playing it directly with him or her can be extremely useful. Role reversal, where the husband and wife change roles, can be particularly beneficial.

In job situations, a co-worker often functions as a good partner. I know one salesman who never calls on an important customer without first role-playing the difficulties that might come up with another salesman who is acquainted with the prospective customer. Similarly, many business executives role-play potentially difficult situations before important conferences.

Define the area of behavior deficit you want to change, role-play it, and rate yourself. Merely playing a situation over and over will usually not lead to the desired changes. You must determine the specific behaviors you want to change (communication of feeling, standing up for self in business, standing up for self with spouse, social small talk) and then evaluate your role-playing to see if you actually achieve these changes.

LABORATORY EXERCISE IN BEHAVIOR REHEARSAL

Purpose: To use role-playing to shape and practice behaviors in problem situations.

To evaluate your role-playing behavior, and thus help you to change, behavior therapists separate this behavior into two parts: a "content" part that concerns *what* you express and a "mode of expression" category concerned with *how* you express it. Often an unassertive mode of expression can nullify good content.

Although you will be trying to change a specific problem, you may have trouble knowing how to rate your performance in behavior rehearsal. Thus, I am providing you with suggested criteria of evaluation plus a rating scale (these are adapted from experiments conducted by Dr. Philip H. Friedman of Temple University School of Medicine and Drs. Michel Herson, Richard M. Eisler, and Peter M. Miller, at the University of Mississippi).

STEP ONE: In your Assertiveness Training workbook, take two pages and at the top of each, put the heading BEHAVIOR REHEARSAL PROBLEM. This should be the problem you select for your behavior rehearsal scene, such as asking for a raise, telling your wife you won't go to a dinner every Friday at her mother's, etc.

STEP TWO: Then draw three vertical lines down each page, making four columns. Label the first column on the first page CONTENT and the next three columns (for rating) in this order: Rehearsal One, Rehearsal Two, and Rehearsal Three.

BEHAVIOR REHEARSAL PROBLEM

CONTENT	Rehearsal One	Rehearsal Two	Rehearsal Three

Follow the same format on page two, but label the first column
MODE OF EXPRESSION.

STEP THREE: Under CONTENT, rate yourself with the
following questions:

A. Did I face the real problem?

B. Does my solution resolve the problem?

C. Did I communicate what I wanted to communicate?

D. Did I avoid being compliant?

E. Did I clearly request a new behavior from the other
person?

STEP FOUR: Under MODE OF EXPRESSION, rate yourself
with the following questions:

A. Was my voice sufficiently loud and firm?

B. Did I talk too long and overexplain, become apologetic,
or confuse things?

Alternate: Was I direct?

C. Did I talk long enough so that the other person could
understand what I said?

D. Did my voice, expression, and gestures communicate
what I felt?

STEP FIVE: Following each behavior rehearsal rate yourself by
the following scale: (1) not at all; (2) a little; (3) some; (4)
much; (5) very much; (6) completely.

Your improvement will be shown by an increase in the
numerical value of the ratings. Try to go up from 1 to 5.

STEP SIX: As you role-play, follow the basic rules:

(a) Keep the scenes specific and simple. Overcomplica-
tion doesn't help.

(b) Use scenes from real life. These may be events that
happened recently (such as somebody putting you down or
interfering with what you wanted to do), or they may be
future events, such as asking a friend for a favor or going for a
job interview.

(c) Give your partner specific instructions on the role you
want him to play and then enact the scene in one minute to
five minutes. During the role-playing, both you and your
partner should strive for realism.

(d) Start with a relatively easy situation and work up to a more difficult one, using the hierarchy approach I described earlier in the chapter. When you feel, and the rating scales indicate, that you have mastered one situation, advance to the next one and keep going until you are ready to tackle the most difficult. Use hierarchies only when you find the troublesome scene is too difficult for you to resolve in initial role-playing or when you believe you would find it too difficult to carry out in life.

(e) Try to become aware of stimuli which cause you difficulty (like a frown, a tone of voice, or a certain context of conversation), and add them to the scene. If you do, you can learn to change your response to them.

STEP SEVEN: If no partner is available, turn a tape recorder into a partner. This technique lacks the interaction and flexibility you can achieve with an actual partner, but you can still practice specific responses to specific situations.

STEP EIGHT: Continue to role-play, evaluate, and discuss until you shape your behavior to your satisfaction. Use the rating scale to make sure you don't slip back. Then try role-playing another situation.

STEP NINE: Most important, now seek out life situations where you can apply what you've learned.

Chapter IV
Achieving a
Social Network

"I'm lonely" . . . "I have no friends" . . . "I don't know how to meet new people" . . . "I meet new people, but I can't ever get close to them."

Every day unhappy and depressed patients make statements like these to me. Often they credit their nonexistent social life to some event, buried deep in their unconscious, that occurred during preschool years. Perhaps it did. However, for these patients, suffering from a cutoff feeling of participation in life, I see the solution not as a remembrance of things past but in giving them the help necessary to achieve a social network in the present.

Complete isolation satisfies only the rare individual. Everyone needs varying kinds of relationships with other people. However, the exact kind of social network best for any one person depends very much on his own requirements and goals. What is best for you may prove wrong for someone else.

THE SATISFACTORY SOCIAL NETWORK

Whatever the different specifics, all satisfactory networks tend to possess certain common characteristics:

Your social network serves as a security base. You feel you belong. The members know you and accept you. You realize what you can and cannot expect from one another. You know who will come when you are sick, who will send flowers, who will telephone, and who will disappear until you are healthy again.

Your social network includes varying kinds of relationships, ranging from the superficial to the intensely close. There is the friend with whom you like to fish but with whom you would never talk shop—and vice versa. There is the friend whom you like to see twice a year and the friend with whom you share your problems and feelings twice-weekly. Hopefully your network includes two to three people with whom you can and want to share what is most personal and close to you.

Your social network suits your own specific needs. If you are by temperament an extrovert, you may require a constantly active network, composed of many people. You would be bored with the few friends and quiet evenings that satisfy the introvert. Be careful not to stereotype though. The greatest extrovert still needs peaceful moments with close friends. The most confirmed introvert may love attending an occasional gala party.

Your network constantly changes—because in the course of living you change; other people change; relationships themselves change. The business acquaintance may turn into a close friend or become a pompous bore to be avoided. You may lose your interest in fishing or bowling and become a bridge buff. You may become richer or poorer, switch professions, marry, become divorced or widowed, have children, move to a different town, or experience other changes so common in life. Each of these may bring about different needs and opportunities, and you must readjust your social network.

THE UNSATISFACTORY SOCIAL NETWORK

People with deficient social networks fall into five categories:

(1) *The loner, the man or woman who lives in isolation.* Perhaps a family exists in the background, but contact with parents, siblings, or cousins is sporadic, superficial, and conflict-ridden. The loner talks with co-workers, shopkeepers, and store clerks, but beyond that there is literally no one. The longer this kind of individual continues this pattern, the more he loses whatever social skills he originally possessed, and the more he avoids any possible social contact.

(2) *The person who has no social network, but does have relationships (usually sporadic) with other people.* As an example of this category, take the bachelor who gets into periodic intense relationships with a woman, or the loner female who embarks on similar relationships with a man. These relationships cannot work out. Each places demands on the other that are impossible to meet. Or you have the loner with a single friend. Again these friendships usually serve merely to perpetuate the isolation each suffers. In these instances, even if the partner has a social network, the other person feels an outsider. He never joins the other's network and when the relationship breaks off, he is back where he started.

(3) *The isolated couple.* This is the husband and wife who exist in isolation from the rest of the world. Each partner is expected to fulfill *all* the needs of the spouse. As this is obviously impossible to do for an extended period of time, tensions and resentments develop and often result in a troubled marriage.

(4) *The barricaded personality who cannot share intimate things.* In his book, *Behavior Therapy and Beyond*, Dr. Arnold Lazarus of Rutgers University offers an excellent visual representation of this level of communication in which the barricaded personality can easily maintain superficial E-D-C relationships, but never lets people into his A zone, thus failing to achieve a close relationship.*

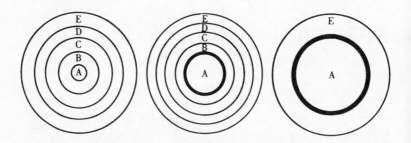

The outermost level E represents the most superficial social

* From *Behavior Therapy and Beyond* by Dr. Arnold Lazarus, Ph.D., 1971. Used with permission of McGraw-Hill Book Co.

situations where you might say "My name is ———" . . . "Chocolate cake is my favorite desert" . . . "I enjoyed that movie on TV last night."

The innermost level, A, denotes the most personal things you can possibly say about yourself, your deep feelings, the ideas that make you vulnerable to others.

The B-D levels symbolize a series of communication levels where it is not so much the content of what you say that matters, but the meaning it has for you. D level for you may represent B to another. However, patients rarely have trouble assigning their own communication to the proper level.

In the left hand concentric circle, the relatively small circle A shows that the personal level is in proportion to the other communication levels.

In the second concentric circle area, A has expanded and is developing a solid wall around it, meaning that the individual has fewer things he can share and is building a wall around his personal communication, so that he can't share thoughts and feelings even in the close relationship.

The third concentric circle presents the culmination of the development of the barricaded personality. The wall has grown thicker and stronger, and now this person has great difficulty communicating anything personal or meaningful to himself. No matter what his façade, he can form only superficial relationships with others, and often lacks awareness of his own desires, thoughts, and feelings.

(5) *The undifferentiated person is the exact opposite,* lacking emotional fences, understanding of relationship layers and varying degrees of privacy needed in varying situations. In contrast to the barricaded person who may have enormous human contact without closeness, the undifferentiated person turns people off, does not give a relationship a chance to develop, feels people push him away when they don't respond to his personal revelations on first meeting, and constantly gets hurt. If you indiscriminately relate your deepest feelings to strangers, some will use them against you.

CASE

Twenty-seven-year-old Susan Armstrong, an English teacher at a public high school, was the daughter of a noted Freudian analyst and had been brought up with talk about penis envy, unconscious drives, and the Oedipus complex. She herself had been in and out of analysis since the age of seven. She had few new friends, dated only spasmodically, could never build up a sustained relationship with a man.

Upset and hurt by a trivial school incident in which she had overheard a fellow teacher say about her, "Oh God, there's Dr. Freud again, with all her prattle," Susan realized people had been avoiding her. She decided to give nonpsychoanalytic treatment a chance and came to me.

In our discussions we found that her concept of conversation was all at the A-B level. She treated every social situation as though it were a chance to probe her innermost feelings and those of others. In this way she never gave a relationship a chance to form, develop, grow.

Explaining to Susan that what was appropriate with close friends was inappropriate with people she had just met, or knew only slightly, I gave her an assignment for a forthcoming blind date: to limit herself to the superficial D and E levels. She tried, but couldn't do it. Before the evening was over, she had relapsed to her rut of analyzing and counteranalyzing. But *this time* she realized what she was doing. My treatment of Susan consisted of getting her to talk at the C-D-E levels. It was hard because discussions of the id and the ego were so ingrained in Susan that she didn't understand the function of small talk.

Finally Susan attended a party, kept away from the A-B levels, but left feeling "I didn't say anything important." She said to me, "Your treatment is putting me in the wrong direction."

But several days later, a C-level friend said to her, "Your new therapy must be working. You were charming at the party. I've never seen you like that."

Once Susan learned the technique, she made rapid progress. As she became accustomed to the outer levels, she began to value her inner feelings more. She got into a long relationship, and when that failed, she accepted the fact that she had broken up with her boyfriend and felt badly. She did not discourse on "the dynamic roots" of her feelings. One day Susan reported that she had a new relationship and that she felt she had really established appropriate communication. At that point, she paid me an accolade. "You know, Doctor," she said, "you're really an A-level person in my life."

Remember that the criterion of an adequate network lies not in the number of people, but rather *the kinds of people* and *variety of relationships*. Many acquaintances, but limited closeness with all, are not good enough. One or two very close relationships, but with no graded series of friends, also prove unsatisfactory.

Your network may be composed of the wrong kinds of people. They are dull, too serious, lack a sense of humor, are too flippant, and you can never discuss anything profound with them. You may find that your network includes no one with whom you can share things that are important to you. Or you may discover that you are becoming just like the people in your network.

Why do you form the wrong kind of social network or have no network at all?

You don't understand the facts of social life. You fail to realize the purpose of various ice-breaking customs and rituals. A number of people come to me with complaints of a limited social life, and then we get down to the point that they don't do the things they have to do when they meet new people. One major problem: they don't understand the social function of small talk, criticizing, "It's superficial" . . . "a waste of time" . . . "too impersonal." With such people, I explain that small talk serves a *feeling out* process. You use it as a ground for an exploration of common interests. I try to give the patient the idea that not everyone he encounters will be interesting to him, but that he can gain an idea exchange even from the dullards.

You have incorrect ideas of active-passive. You think things just happen. They don't. Interesting people don't just appear in your life any more than a knight comes riding on a stark white charger. Entertaining, being a good date, or a good guest requires specific skills that must be learned.

For example, Mort, a spoiled scion of a rich family, had artistic talent, and became a successful dress designer, but always remained a passive personality—especially with women. He could ask a girl for a date, but never planned anything. As a result, his dates were always aimless and dull. Through Assertiveness Training, he started organizing his dates—getting tickets for a ballet, making reservations for supper afterward—and his passivity started to lessen. He lost his anxiety about dating and became more active in planning for many things—like vacations. As he broke his passive pattern, he was able to get closer to women.

You have a whole series of social fears. You fear:

· People will think you're stupid, so you avoid talking.
· Looking foolish. You don't say anything that is different or individual, so your conversation becomes stuffy and conventional. Often you bore yourself.
· Rejection. You tend to stick to people you know and with whom you feel relatively safe. Then you complain you're in a rut.
· Closeness. You keep everything at a small-talk level on a superficial basis. You don't follow up with new people or allow new personal relationships to develop.

As you express them to yourself, your fears appear logical. Yes, there is a chance you will be rejected if you make a social overture. The trick is to bring the irrational element out in the open by adding it to your thought. For example, you think, "If I ask this girl to dance, she may reject me," and then you add the irrational part, "and everyone will be contemptuous of me." By bringing the irrational part out in the open, you make yourself aware of how irrational it is.

Here are some irrational fears that apply to the social network, which I've adapted from those Dr. Albert Ellis lists in a report on "Rational-Emotive Therapy."

It is irrational for you to feel:

· You must be loved or approved by virtually every significant other person in your life.
· That in order to consider yourself worthwhile, you must be thoroughly competent, adequate, and achieving in all possible respects.
· That life is awful and catastrophic when things are not the way you would like them to be.

· You have little or no ability to control your disturbances.

· Your past history must determine your present behavior, and because something once strongly affected your life, it must affect it indefinitely.

THE ASSERTIVE SOCIAL NETWORK

What can be done to vanquish your fears, provide you with a social network if you lack one, better the one you already have? Herewith a guide to developing the assertive social network.

Start where you are. Even if you are extremely socially isolated, usually you possess at least one or two acquaintances in your life situation. Begin to expand your network by increasing contact with them. You can telephone just to ask, "How are you?" Or make a movie date, go shopping, or attend a ball game with them. Increase your use of what already exists.

If you have a truly limited social network, you may rationalize "I wouldn't enjoy calling him—or her." At the beginning stages of the Assertiveness Training program, you don't take enjoyment into consideration. *You do what must be done to increase the number of your friends.* Hopefully, as your confidence increases, so will your enjoyment; but at the starting stage, pleasure is not a major factor. Concentrate on making friends.

Once you have the starting point, you move step by step where you want to go. Keep your eyes out for special events, an office party, lecture, or whatever, where you might begin to meet the people you want to include in your social network. Often patients tell me, "I've gone to hundreds of lectures and nothing ever happens." For some people with assertive difficulties just attending lectures may prove a step forward; for others, it may merely be a repetition of what they've done before. If the latter situation fits you, start to do things differently. If you've attended scads of lectures and never spoken to anyone, now make a point of saying a few words to someone else during or after the talk. Eventually move yourself into a full conversation. Also, if you have frequently attended organizational affairs and spoken to people, but never followed up with a bid for friendship, change your social system. Make a point of contacting one new person you have met *within a week* after the meeting. People like to be liked as much as you do.

Often I use mini-AT groups for the purpose of setting up such systematic assignments. These are groups with three or four members who try to achieve a specific assertiveness goal within four training sessions. One group consisted of three bachelors, ranging in age from thirty-five to forty-one. None had a social network. All had trouble getting dates, often spent solitary weekends, rarely were invited out and never invited people to their homes, had no close friends. The common goal of all the members of this group, undergoing the one-hour weekly, month-long training program: to establish a set of behaviors that would lead to more social contacts, and eventually to becoming part of a group. Let me give you an idea of the scheduling, particularly as it relates to Bruce.

FIRST SESSION: We worked together to prepare a list of assignments for each patient. Bruce's tasks for the next week included: lunch with two people during the week, telephoning two people—one man and one woman—just to chat, and going to the local museum and striking up a conversation with two people.

SECOND SESSION: Bruce reported great success with everything, particularly the phone calls (during the four-week period he made even more than the two weekly phone calls his assignment required, and these calls resulted in two dinner invitations and one party invitation). Next task: again to visit the art museum and speak to two young women. This was to help Bruce meet girls who shared his interests in art and music. Bruce needed some help with this, so we behavior-rehearsed this at the group session.

THIRD SESSION: Bruce reported that he had talked to two women, but barely two sentences worth. Task for next week: to get into a real conversation with a woman at the museum and ask her out for coffee. Again, more behavior rehearsal on this with another group member who had the same assignment.

FOURTH SESSION: Bruce's whole attitude had changed. He had always got to know people superficially, but if they weren't part of his immediate environment, he made no attempt to get in touch with them again. Now he reported to the group: "Through the lunch dates and the calls, I'm making real friends." Furthermore, Bruce had made a date to go to the theater with the young woman he had taken to coffee. Some time later, after termination of the program, Bruce called to tell me that he was marrying her.

In taking this step-by-step approach to expand your network, *go where the action is* and where there are people to meet: parties, singles bars, resorts, classes, etc. (I do want to make a point in reference to singles bars. People with problems in assertion often have difficulty in them because [1] they create a competitive situation, and [2] often they are not satisfying. They lead only to sporadic contacts, and rarely do relationships develop. Singles bars and clubs should be only one minor part of forming a social network.)

The best way of increasing social action is to use your special interests. When you participate in something you like, you are at your social best. Take some interest which is important to you—bird-watching, politics, camping, skiing, tennis—and become actively engaged in this area. *The primary purpose is the area itself.* This proves more satisfying usually than something like a singles bar because you meet kindred souls with whom you can more easily reach out and expand your social network.

Almost every psychological advice book offers the same counsel I have just given: "Get out and do things." . . . "Use your special interests." . . . "Call people." However, in providing these directions for social network expansion, we made the assumption that if you know how to do them, you will do them, and that as your skill increases, your anxiety will lessen. By taking definite action, we assume that you will receive positive reinforcement (perhaps invitations and new friends, or just the feeling of self-satisfaction from trying), and this will eventually mitigate the anxiety.

This is not always true. You may simply avoid the action, and thus the extinction of anxiety cannot take place. Or you may perform the act, but with such anxiety that a noxious feeling becomes associated with the act, making it more difficult to perform the next time.

For such people, Assertiveness Training uses the laboratory exercise covert reinforcement, developed by Dr. Joseph R. Cautela, professor of psychology at Boston College, and a past president of the American Association for the Advancement of Behavior Therapy. This technique utilizes imagery to reduce the fear. The principle of increasing a given behavior is to reward the behavior you want to increase. In covert reinforcement you take the behavior you want to increase; you imagine doing that act; you reinforce your performance of that act *through imagery*. It works like this:

LABORATORY EXERCISE IN COVERT REINFORCEMENT

Purpose: To reduce social anxiety.

STEP ONE. *Take the specific behavior you are afraid to perform.* It may be asking a girl to dance, starting a conversation with a stranger, saying no to an unreasonable request. Concentrate on the act, not the fear.

STEP TWO: *Break down the act into small parts.* For example, you want to ask a girl for a date:

(a) At home, calmly think, "I will call Jill now."

(b) In a relaxed way, walk toward the phone and sit down.

(c) Reach for the phone in a calm, relaxed way.

(d) Dial the number in a calm, relaxed way.

(e) Calmly listen to the number ring.

(f) Hear Jill answer "Hello," and notice that you are still calm and relaxed.

(g) Say hello and ask for the date. Again, you are calm and relaxed.

It is best to write down the parts of the act.

STEP THREE: *Select a reinforcer.* You can use anything that evokes a feeling of pleasure. It does not have to be connected with the act you are trying to reinforce. It can be the image of swimming in Lake Como, eating strawberry ice cream, hearing people praise you, winning the Nobel Prize. One patient used a favorite piece of music, the Brahms Double Concerto. Another enlisted the feeling of skiing. What works for one person doesn't necessarily work for another. As long as your reinforcer gives you a good feeling, it will work.

STEP FOUR: *Read the first item on your list and imagine it.* When your image is clear, say to yourself, "Reinforce," and immediately switch to your reinforcing image. Do this ten times and go on to the next item. Do this exercise every day until you can perform the behavior in actual life with minimal anxiety. If you do this ten times a day, seven days a week, this will give you seventy conditioning trials a week, three hundred a month. It may take hundreds of these trials before the conditioning works. Don't expect magic and get discouraged.

STEP FIVE: *When you have the opportunity, perform the act step by step, just as you did in your imagination.* In the life situation, you can even use your reinforcing image (i.e., you're at a dance and see a girl. You walk toward her in a relaxed way, just as you did in your imagination. As you do this you say to yourself, "Reinforce," and think of your reinforcing image).

STEP SIX: *When you find this technique decreases the anxiety with one behavior, select another and repeat the process.*

Stop brainwashing yourself with the thought that you are a social failure. Some people constantly have put-down thoughts about themselves. Some concern the present: "I'm no good" . . . "I have no ability to relate to people" . . . "I can't do anything." If you fall in this category, you ignore anything good you do. If a person praises you, you feel you've "fooled him," because you find it necessary to maintain your despised image of yourself. I call this the Groucho Marx syndrome because in one picture Groucho said he wouldn't join any club that was willing "to have me as a member."

Other obsessive thoughts concern the future: "If I go to a party, I'll end up being a wallflower" . . . "If I ask her for a date, she'll turn me down" . . . "If I go out with him, it will only be a one-shot because he'll be bored." This kind of thought produces a self-fulfilling prophecy in its victim. If you get caught up in the prophecy—"I will be a failure at the party" . . . "I won't get my work done on time"—you run the risk of starting to act in certain ways that will fulfill the prophecy.

AT offers two steps to stop you from self-put-downs.

(1) *If you suffer from the Groucho Marx syndrome, start setting up the opposite habit—remind yourself of the good things you have done.* Every night list three things you accomplished during the day that made you feel good about yourself. People with the full-blown symptoms sometimes have trouble because they are so insensitive to anything they did well. Again use the principle, "Pay attention to the trivial." When patients say to me, "I didn't do anything good today," I answer, "Think. Were you friendly to someone less fortunate than you? Did you do a kind act?"

(2) *Use thought stoppage.* In this AT technique, we make the basic assumption that you maintain the bad habit by reinforcing it. In most cases we don't know what the reinforcement is. We just assume it is there and aim to withdraw it. If the behavior never gets reinforced, the put-down thoughts disappear. Thought stoppage relates to assertion in that it enables you to express your real feelings, thus freeing you to try new things in life.

LABORATORY EXERCISE IN THOUGHT STOPPAGE

Purpose: To relieve your social obsessions.

STEP ONE: Sit in a comfortable chair. Bring to mind one of the thoughts you want to control. It may be anxiety about a coming event or fear of meeting a new man. If it is a whole series of thoughts, take any one. As soon as the thought forms in your mind, say out loud STOP, then to yourself say "Calm," and deliberately relax your muscles for five to ten seconds. Your aim: at least a momentary break in the thought you're trying to control. If you don't get that break, do the exercise again and say STOP even longer and louder. When you can repeat this twice, getting at least that momentary break, go on to the next step. If you have trouble getting a thought to come to mind, force it. This works as a way of gaining control. Don't be passive. Some people find it helpful to close their eyes while trying to bring the thought to mind.

STEP TWO: Do the exercise the same way, but say the STOP inside yourself instead of out loud. If you experience difficulty in getting a momentary break in the thought, you can also practice fallback positions, such as *yelling* STOP inside yourself, or snapping a rubber band against your wrist as you say it.

In applying the thought-stoppage technique, the two rules are *as soon as* and *every time.* You know the thoughts you want to control. *As soon as* you become aware of having one of those thoughts, go through the STOP routine, say "Calm," and relax your muscles. You want that break in thought. If the thought comes back in two seconds, two minutes, or two hours, *as soon as* you become aware that it's back, repeat the procedure. I say *as soon as* because (1) if you give that thought a chance to build up, it becomes harder to control, and (2) some kind of reinforcement maintains your put-down habit. You must get that momentary break before reinforcement gets into play.

I also say *every time* because (1) you want to set up a counterhabit of not thinking put-down thoughts, followed by relaxation. As with the formation of any new habit, you must try to practice it at every available opportunity and so you must perform this thought-stoppage exercise until STOP-Calm-Relax becomes automatic; (2) without behavior reinforcement the frequency of the behavior lessens and eventually disappears. If sometimes you use the STOP and sometimes you don't, you put yourself on what we call an intermittent random reinforcement schedule. This makes the habit stronger and more difficult to extinguish. You cannot use the thought-stoppage method halfheartedly. *Use it all the time or not at all.*

CASE

Peter, a bright, young assistant history professor, was afraid of women. One strong fear: the simple act of calling up a girl to make a date. For the day prior to making the call, Peter was obsessed with such thoughts as "She'll turn me down" and "Why should such a pretty blonde have anything to do with me?" By the time he actually got on the telephone, he was so filled with anxieties that he handled the call badly, and inevitably got a refusal. I taught Peter thought stoppage. By using it *every time* he had one of those put-down thoughts about the upcoming call, he kept the anxiety from building up, and was able to deliver his invitation with confidence. He started to get a series of acceptances, and his anxiety about asking girls out decreased.

Because put-down thoughts interfere with real feelings, use of the thought-stoppage technique can affect not just your social network but relationships with those even closer to you. As you get these thoughts under control, very often your more human, softer feelings are able to emerge.

CASE

Jane was a very obsessive woman. Constantly thinking put-down thoughts about herself, she turned the most trivial mistakes (like letting boiled eggs get too hard or a misplayed card at bridge) into evidence of "how terrible I am." This led to a constant state of anxiety, depression, and disturbed relationships with other people.

With the thought-stoppage technique, we started to bring Jane's obsessiveness under control; but one night she entered my office with the thoughts fully reestablished, set off by a real catastrophe that had happened to her son.

The fourteen-year-old boy, who wanted to be a professional football player, had just been diagnosed as having softening of the bones and would have to stay out of all sports for four years. Hearing this, Jane started to obsess, "What did I do wrong?" . . . "Will he blame me for this?" She forgot all about thought stoppage.

We zeroed in with thought stoppage to get control of her self-centered, guilt-evoking thoughts. As the technique began to work, Jane's softer feelings of concern emerged, and she became able to experience sadness for her son and to empathize with his feelings of loss. She became a mother rather than a self-centered flagellate.

In using thought stoppage, remember these points:

· If you have constant put-down thoughts, for the first few days you may have to use STOP like a machine gun. One of my patients used STOP 432 times in a single day. By the end of the week, he was down to 20 a day, and in two weeks, down to zero. Grit your teeth and stick with it.

· Initially, the very thoughts you are trying to control may seem to be coming more frequently and with greater intensity. An "operant extinction curve," as this is called, first goes up, but when it comes down, it comes down very fast.

· If in doubt, always use STOP. You can waste so much time deciding whether this is one of the thoughts you want to control that the obsessive thought slips by, and you haven't even tried to stop it.

· The thoughts you may think you have under control can reemerge under three conditions: (1) when you're very tense for whatever reason; (2) when you're fatigued; (3) when you're physically ill. When they reemerge, know that this is the time to press on with the STOP technique to keep them from reestablishing themselves.

Improve your conversation. In Assertiveness Training we devote much time to training socially shy patients in the art of conversation. Some pointers:

(1) *Develop your utilization of small talk,* a skill to be learned like bridge or chess. Small talk may be "superficial," but it serves the purpose of expanding your social network. In making small talk:

(a) Limit your self-revelation. Tell other people things about yourself that are personal, but not too personal. Use the pronoun "I" to talk about the play you saw last week, your most recent job assignment, but don't go into details about your nervous breakdown. At first acquaintance, keep your conversation at the superficial E level, with occasional dips to the D and C levels.

(b) Invite the other person to show something of himself or herself. For example, you tell a story of some travel adventure. Usually the other person will be all primed to tell his own anecdote. All it may take is the simple question, "Have you ever been there?" or even a pause in conversation.

(c) When the other person invites you to show something of yourself, accept his invitation. Reply with your own experience. If you find the conversation bores you or the other person seems restless, change the topic.

(d) Acquire the technique of ending a conversation appropriately and moving on to another group. It's difficult to leave a person alone, so make use of such basic sentences as "Let's go over and join that group," or "I hear them talking about the school board. I'd like to hear what they have to say," or, "I'd better go say a few words to my hostess." In extremity try, "I need more ice for my drink."

(2) *Learn how to start a conversation.* If you can't do this, you may be so anxious about social events that you avoid them. If you go, you may end up speaking to no one. Phrases like "I love your dress. May I ask you where you bought it?" . . . "Are you a member of this club?" serve as ice-breakers. Develop one or two phrases that you become skilled at using.

CASE

When John, a recent college graduate, came to consult me, he was equally afraid of being alone and talking to people. During his entire university stay, he had had only two dates, and these had been arranged by his roommate, who was his only friend. Now, John, a man who even was afraid to stop people in the street and ask for directions, had a more difficult problem. He had accepted a job abroad. "I know no one in the firm. I'll die of loneliness," he told me.

I immediately started training John in the technique of starting conversations. During the treatment period, John was invited to his ex-roommate's wedding, which would be held out-of-town, and where John would know only the bride and groom. With John, I rehearsed how to start a conversation at the wedding.

In my office, I stood up and said, "Make believe you're at the wedding. I'm here. You're there. Come up to me and start a conversation."

John said, "I can't do it."

I told him, "Stand there and say to yourself, 'Should I stand here like a lump on a log or should I try talking to that man.' Say it out loud."

John said the sentence out loud.

I asked him, "How would you answer that?"

John responded, "I want to start talking."

I said, "Fine. Turn toward me. Walk toward me."

John did.

I said, "Say something. Anything."

John remained silent.

I told him, "Look at me. Do you see anything about me or what I'm wearing that you like?"

John looked at me out of the corner of his eye and said "No."

"Do you like my tie?" I asked.

John responded, "No, not really, but I like your tie pin."

I said, "Say to me, 'I like your tie pin.'"

John repeated the sentence.

I showed my pleasure at this step forward. "Good. Make eye contact when you say it." John repeated the sentence again. This time he made eye contact and his voice was louder and more confident.

I responded by telling him a little story about the circumstances under which I had purchased the tie pin, and we easily were off in a give-and-take conversation. We rehearsed this several times. That weekend John flew off to the wedding.

When I saw John on Monday evening, he told me, "It happened just the way we practiced it. I was standing alone, and another man, also alone, was standing near me. I said to myself, 'Would I rather stay here like a lump on a log or would I rather talk to that man? I'll try to talk to him.' I was so nervous that I didn't see whether he wore a tie pin or not, but I said 'I like your tie pin,' and I remembered to make eye contact. Just as you did, he started to tell me a story about the pin. Before I knew it, we were in a conversation, and other people joined in. A group joined us and I met a very pretty girl. She's going to look me up in Rome."

And so John learned to start conversations. Using the same technique, you can too.

(3) *Learn how to join ongoing conversations.* Instead of initiating a conversation on many occasions, you will want to join a group where others already are discussing a definite topic. Your object: to make some kind of statement that calls attention to you and through which the others will view you as part of the group and its ongoing conversation. Accomplish this by elaborating on a remark that has been made, giving some kind of personal experience as you do. Avoid the trap of asking a

question about what the others are talking about. Although this sometimes works, and your query may be extremely pertinent, it is more apt to be regarded as interference, and usually does not make you part of the group. You remain peripheral. Once you manage to become part of the group, you can participate in the ongoing conversation and go wherever it takes you.

For example, Patty, a young social worker, followed through the principles of "meet people through a genuine interest", and "go where the action is" and spent her winter weekends at ski resorts. However, at night she usually sat alone because, as she confessed to me, "I don't know how to join the conversational groups." Since most of the talk concerned different places to ski, I helped Patty recreate several anecdotes from her own experiences. Then we discussed ways of bringing them into the actual conversation. If anyone mentioned Aspen or Zermatt, she could say, "I had an unusual thing happen to me there," and go ahead with her tale. If they talked about another place, she could bridge with "I had a somewhat similar experience at Aspen."

On her very next weekend, Patty, as always, hovering on the periphery of the group, got the chance to test the technique. Someone had just told a story about skiing at Chamonix, and Patty moved in almost automatically with the line, "Something very similar happened to me at Aspen," and told her story.

Patty told me, "As I told my story something very interesting happened. There was a slight physical shift of the group toward me as they moved to make me part of them. When I finished, a man asked me a question about Aspen and from then on I was part of the group."

With this as a beginning, over the next few weekends Patty became even more a part of the group, thus making new friends and expanding her social network.

(4) *Learn to maintain and direct a conversation.* Some tips:

(a) Be careful of the third degree. Don't quiz people with question after question. The principle: show something of yourself and *then* ask the question. For example, instead of asking "Did you like London?," try "I have never been to London. Do you think I would like it?"

(b) Be prepared. Have things ready to say, ideas you want to discuss. Most people have difficulty maintaining conversations because they allow gaps to develop. Because they don't know what to say, they become anxious, and they soon break off the conversation, or the conversation breaks itself off. One useful bridge is the sentence, "I don't know why, but it reminds me of"—and off you go where you want to go.

(c) If the conversation heads in a direction that bores you, or where you can't maintain it, deliberately switch it to an area where you are more comfortable.

(d) Make yourself interesting. That means telling stories in an interesting way. People have the concept that if they have thought through a story ahead of time, it is not spontaneous. It may not be—but it will be a better story. A good story does not require great drama or a fancy punch line. You do want to take an experience with which you have been involved and tell it in an exciting, amusing, or informative way.

For example, I had one patient who worked as an actuary. When I first asked him, "What does an actuary do?" he said something vague and boring about working with figures and insurance rates. When I instructed him to make up a story about a specific project on which he had worked, he became much more interesting. He told me that an official from a southeastern city had referred its civil service pension plan to him, and asked him what it would cost over a period of years if the city raised its pension payments by ten percent. My patient had to figure out the life spans of the various people involved and a number of other intricate points. Together we worked to make this a meaningful story under two minutes in length. Anything can be made into a story if you have something to express. The technique is not enough; you must have something to communicate.

Learn to cope with put-downs. In the course of interrelating with others, you are bound to experience put-downs, whether others do them deliberately or inadvertently. This happens because people have human limits, and, at some point, even a very sensitive person will misunderstand and say something in a wrong way. You must handle put-downs when they happen. If you don't, you become a scapegoat. Friends don't respect you, and you don't respect yourself.

In AT, we mean two things by the word "put-down": (1) an unjustified criticism; (2) justified criticism expressed in a magnified or inappropriate way. The criterion for whether something is a put-down or not is simply: *do you feel it is a put-down?* Don't get caught up in whether it was justified or not. If you feel someone put you down, respond to the remark as a put-down.

A Beginner's Guide to Put-Downs

(1) If you feel someone put you down with a remark, you must answer. Brush aside rationalizations like, "I don't want to create a fuss." Observe the principle: don't be afraid to hurt the innocent. In other words, the other person may not have intended his seeming crack as a put-down, hence he's innocent. He didn't realize what he said. However, if you feel he put you down, always answer him—whether he's innocent or not.

(2) Take time to think. People who say the first sentence that comes to mind are essentially passive. Your answer doesn't have to come out in a micro-second. When you make your response a deliberate one, you take the active approach. Pause momentarily and think of an effective answer.

(3) In most situations, the first sentence of your answer should not contain the words, "I," "me," or "because." Use of any of these makes you sound apologetic or defensive. This can lead to still further put-downs or an inappropriate fight.

Here are some examples of put-down situations with "wrong" and "right" responses. The "right" responses aim to put the other person on the defensive. Instead of your explaining, you make him do it. Remember the criterion for your response is *does it make you feel better about yourself?* The following "right" answers merely illustrate the rules. They may not work for you. You have to try out different things to see what makes you feel better about yourself.

SITUATION ONE: A male friend digs, "That certainly was an ugly girl you were out with last night. Losing your taste?"

Wrong response: "Do you think it made me look bad to be out with her?"

Right response: "Are you still immature enough to judge women by such superficialities?"

SITUATION TWO: A co-worker says, "You did it again. You misfiled the Lesham report."

Wrong response: "I didn't even have that file. I've never looked at it."

Right response: "You're jumping to wrong conclusions again. Why don't you check first?"

(4) Don't fall into the trap of asking another person to elaborate on what's wrong with you. If you ask questions like, "Do you really think that's bad?" or "What's so wrong about that?" you really ask him to kick you in the teeth again.

(5) Learn some stock phrases you can call upon almost automatically—for example, "What are you so angry about?" . . . "Was that a put-down?" . . . "How come you're in such a bad mood today?"

(6) In certain put-down situations in the close relationship, you can use, "I," "me," and "because" in your response. You do this because here your intent is not to counterattack, but to deepen communication.

SITUATION ONE: A seventeen-year-old high school senior brings home a report card with a 95 average. After scanning it, his father asks, "Why isn't this higher? How will you ever make Yale?"

Wrong response: "I tried as hard as I could."

Right response: "I feel hurt, Dad, because you don't give me credit for getting a straight-A average."

SITUATION TWO: A wife works hard on an elegant meal, but her husband says, "Too bad it didn't come out right. When are you going to learn to cook?"

Wrong response: "It took me four hours to make that stew."

Right response: "I feel bad about what you said because I worked so hard trying to prepare an interesting dinner for you."

These are beginners' rules. As you achieve greater creativity in self-expression, you can violate them. As an example, I offer the famous quip of the great British wit John Wilkes. When Lord Sandwich said Wilkes would die either of a pox or on the gallows, Wilkes answered, "That depends, my lord, on whether I embrace your mistress or your principles."

Learn to change a social network when your life changes. Up to this point I have put the emphasis on help for the person who hasn't had an adequate social network. But many people who once possessed an adequate network find major readjustments necessary because of a changed life situation.

If you started going steady at seventeen, married at eighteen and became widowed at thirty-seven, you may find you have no knowledge of how to act on a date.

In other cases the skills may have once been there but have become rusty through disuse. A middle-aged, recently divorced man, who earns over $50,000 a year as a corporation lawyer, told me, "I have forgotten how to act on a date. Am I supposed to do nothing, kiss the woman, or try to get her into bed?"

You may lose a spouse, through death or divorce, and find yourself in what writer Morton Hunt termed "The World of the Formerly Married." Or perhaps you accept a job in a strange city where you have no friends and few connections. Under these circumstances, you may find you possess social deficits and fears you never realized existed.

CASE

A middle-aged couple moved to a new town. They knew no one, and the husband's work kept him on the road three weeks out of four. Tied to the home because of three young children, the wife became excessively lonely and went into a fit of depression. She kept repeating over and over, "We moved here because it's warm, and so I could play tennis, and now I have no one to play with." One Sunday, fed up with her sulks, the husband ordered, "Take a book and let's go to the city tennis courts." Down they went and spent three hours watching other pairs play. During this time, the husband made notes on who played games equivalent to him and his wife. Then he went up to them and said, "Look, you seem to play about the same game we do. Do you think we can play sometimes?" Immediately the couple had two dates for the next weekend, and the wife made three more for herself during the week. The tennis games led to the formation of a social network.

Whatever the situation, if you have to reform your network, you can use all the rules previously outlined: Just remember:

Start from where you are.

Maintain a step-by-step progression toward your goals.

Constantly experiment with your social network and keep on making improvements.

MOVING TOWARD CLOSENESS

"It's fine to make initial contacts through small talk and conversation, but how do you move toward closeness?" one patient asked me. "I don't want to be the kind of person who always tells amusing stories."

To move toward a closer relationship, keep these eight points in mind.

(1) *Follow up.* You can't have a relationship if you see someone only once.

(2) *Realize that merely seeing someone frequently does not automatically lead to closeness.* You must make a deliberate attempt to show how much you can share and how much you want to share with this person.

(3) *Avoid the trap of moving too fast.* In terms of the concentric circles, you don't want to jump from the E to A level without investigating the D-C-B levels. Many people make this mistake, especially singles, those without an adequate network or those with sporadic networks.

Even on a first date, such people tend to evaluate their partner as a potential spouse. They lose sight of the purpose of a first date—to provide pleasure and a preliminary sharing to learn if you want to know each other better. Without really knowing the other person, they are usually disappointed in the date, make a harsh judgment, and don't provide the other with a good evening.

In relationships that move too fast to extreme closeness, you expect more from the other person than the situation warrants, and so you often get hurt. Furthermore, you don't give the relationship a chance to develop.

(4) *As you move from the superficial to the middle range of*

relationships, you can and must choose your people more carefully. At the beginning, you may not have a choice. If you start from the position of isolation, you go with whatever and whomever is available. Once you have formed some kind of network, you can view things as a matter of alternatives. Would you like to become a close friend of Jane's or keep her as a casual acquaintance? Would you like to go out with Man A or Man B on a given night? It is no longer a situation of what you must do to build a social network, but what you would *rather* do to improve it. You are now in the position to choose.

(5) *As your network develops, go by your spontaneous feelings.* You have the reaction "I like him . . . her . . . them." "I'd like to see him . . . her . . . them." "Don't let thoughts get in the way of your feelings. Many people wonder "Am I neurotic to like him?" . . . "Will Mrs. Jones think I'm pushy if I make the first move?" Accept your spontaneous feeling and do something about it. Even the direct statement "I like you. I'd like to see you again," may prove appropriate, provided you recognize the other person has the freedom to say no.

You can train yourself to communicate on a level of increasing closeness. As always, I recommend extensive use of feeling talk, and also increasing your own self-revelation.

LABORATORY EXERCISE IN SELF-REVELATION

Purpose: To help you to tell stories of a very personal nature.

STEP ONE: Take an important emotional experience from each decade of your life and tell it out loud to yourself or into a tape recorder. The stories can be happy, sad, or a little trivial experience that had tremendous emotional significance for you (like running away at the age of six). Work on them one at a time.

STEP TWO: Then tell each story to someone with whom you are striving for a greater closeness—a spouse, close friend, or an acquaintance whom you want to grow into a friend.

STEP THREE: Tell your greatest trauma.

Telling these stories starts you on the track of closeness and you invite others to share their own meaningful experiences.

So the relationship deepens and eventually you become more spontaneous.

(6) *Learn that as closeness develops, the rules for forming a social network become modified.* Because you know the person better, you have greater flexibility of behavior. The question becomes not *if*, but *how* to share your feelings with greater directness and openness. You should learn how to bring misunderstandings into the open, and be willing to fight and argue about personal things. You will share more because you learn more and more what to share. Some rules become more important —for instance, the need to stand up to put-downs, because if you don't, the put-downs become habitual.

(7) *As the relationship gets more personal, your fears of openness may predominate.* You know what you want to do and where you want to go, but you are afraid to head in that direction. Thus you inhibit yourself and prevent closeness from developing.

What can you do about these fears?

Concentrate on actions. Do what you want to do, or say what you want to say, and don't put the stress on the feelings of fear the action generates. Use covert reinforcement or behavior rehearsal. Then go out and do it in your life situation. The anticipatory fear may be much worse than what actually happens.

CASE

I had a patient who was an accountant in his late twenties. During his adolescent years, Pete had been convicted of car theft and sent to a home for delinquents. This had been an unbearable shame to his middle-class family, and Pete lived in terror that someone would discover his past. Whenever talk turned to crime, delinquency, or ethics in social situations, Pete became extremely uncomfortable, and thought, "If these people only knew, they would have nothing to do with me."

In treatment, we figured out how Pete could tell people all about his past: "You know how kids get involved in all kinds of things. I once did something I'm still ashamed of." After that lead-in, Pete would tell what happened. In general people accepted it and remained friends. Pete no longer went through life feeling he had something to hide.

(8) *Realize that as you build your social network, you don't have to like everyone.* Some who exist in peripheral areas of your life you can simply reject. Others imposed into your social life, like in-laws and your husband's old Army buddies, you can accept, but you don't have to give them undue importance.

Sometimes, if you look at the situation from a different point of view and act in a different way, you may even create a close relationship where none existed before. This is what Frank Cousins did with his mother. Once a year Mrs. Cousins would visit Frank and his wife in New York. He hated it, telling me, "She just treats me as if I were still six years old. She criticizes me, the way I bring up my kids, my choice of a wife. She runs her fingers all over the furniture looking for dust. She's got a dust fixation. I hate her."

Frank and I role-played various situations that might come up during Mama's next visit East. He kept insisting that nothing could be done about her critical attitudes. I taught him techniques of responding to her various put-downs (for example, when she complained about the dust, to try: "Yes, there's dust under the piano, but Mom, you're getting red in the face. What did Dr. Jones say about your blood pressure?"). But I didn't stop there. I told him to find out more of the details of his mother's life and to share with her his own feelings of happiness with his wife and children.

His mother made her annual four-day visit. This time Frank first started communication in the area that upset her: her blood pressure. Then he moved on to things she enjoyed (her community work), and then he brought in his own happy experiences. During this time, he allowed for her limitations, but talked about things she could talk about, and for the first time, they communicated.

Frank reported his success to me with "This was the best visit we've ever had. I could really talk with her, and I think we'll be friends. You know, *she never mentioned the word dust.*"

Chapter V
The Close Relationship

At twenty-nine, Susan had a history of never feeling close to anyone. Because her father drank and her mother constantly yelled, as a child she rarely brought friends home ("If they find out what my parents are like, they will be contemptuous of me and reject me, so I have to hide the situation"). Thus Susan trained herself to fear exposure and hide things about herself. As an adolescent, at an age when most peers learned to share feelings, she rarely permitted herself the experience. As a young woman, she fell in love with men where a close relationship would be impossible—for example, a Catholic priest. Eventually Susan married, but even in the intimacy of marriage, she felt the need to disguise her real thoughts and feelings. In desperation, she came to me.

With variations, millions of Susans exist, in male and female versions, the length and breadth of the land. Many husbands and wives fail to achieve closeness in marriage because they hide behind the iron curtain of their public selves, and don't disclose their true selves or feelings. They also, in ways both obvious and subtle, make it difficult for their partners to be open, getting upset when their partners speak freely and combating openness with verbal hits and hurts, or simply withdrawing from it into a closed shell. This sets up a joint spiral of increasing falseness.

Often, like Susan, they don't disclose themselves because they never learned how to do it.

These same people often can work out a more impersonal

social network that provides companionship, stimulation, and shared interests. Yet, the goal of a social network *is* the close relationship.

Many kinds of close relationships exist. You can be close to a child, parents, in-laws and relatives, to friends—but the marital relationship has characteristics that differentiate it from any other. Friendship has been defined as "shared intimacy," while marriage is "intimate sharing." Friendship is intensive; marriage, extensive. It is a relationship between two adults where there is sex, a commitment that is supposed to be permanent, the fact that both are building a life together and that what affects one affects the other. Yet the burgeoning divorce rate proves that fewer and fewer couples achieve or maintain this "intimate sharing."

In the ideal close relationship, you establish a communion with another human being where feeling comes first and you cannot separate giving and taking. In the optimal close relationship, the other person is like part of yourself. In fulfilling the other person's needs as if they were your own, you satisfy your own needs. Yet, you remain yourself as an individual. Thus, both husband and wife are led to deeper, richer experiences, and in the merging, the individuality of each becomes stronger.

Love may produce a desire for closeness or may stem from an experience of closeness. But the wish for closeness, accentuated by love, does not necessarily signify the actualization of the close relationship.

In love situations, in the choice of a husband, wife, lover, in the mode of relating to the partner, individuals often attempt to fulfill magical expectations, satisfy unresolved infantile needs, compulsively repeat conflict situations in the unconscious endeavor to master them.

The new behavior therapy approach maintains that people achieve closeness because *they have learned to achieve closeness.* Assertiveness Training offers a way for patients to learn these necessary skills, with the result that, as they achieve greater approximation to closeness, the feelings of love will emerge.

In the treatment of marital problems, AT puts emphasis on an active approach to achievement of closeness. The therapist:

(1) *Starts by helping each spouse to identify the specific behaviors that need to be changed to better the marriage.*

(2) *Helps the partners to change systematically the behaviors they want to change and acquire the behaviors they want to acquire.*

(3) *Teaches the couple that change in one serves as a precondition for change in the other.* It is important that the couple understand that they are probably maintaining the disruptive behaviors to which they object by continuing reinforcement. By providing or withholding reinforcements for specific behaviors, each partner exercises control over the other. AT teaches that instead of saying "My spouse should be different," you must learn to ask yourself, "What am I doing to reinforce the very behavior I want to stop?"

(4) *Aids each member of the pair to develop channels of verbal and nonverbal communication.* Without good communication, misunderstandings over life-styles, habits, decisions, and feelings develop. The partner must guess what is going on in his spouse's mind.

(5) *Helps the couple to set goals, attainable in a short time.* This provides a feeling of movement and accomplishment. It is simpler to work on "communication of feelings" than the vague task of "improving our marriage." In AT, the couple soon sees that even the most trivial changes begin to change the relationship. The active approach is encouraged both at the treatment session and by the giving of homework assignments that utilize a variety of AT techniques from feeling talk to behavior rehearsal.

As some of my patients do, some readers will question, "Isn't all that contrived? Everything should be spontaneous." But the ancient Greeks realized and performing artists have always known that true spontaneity ensues from self-discipline and mastery of skills. If you have never worked out the problems of two adults in the close relationship of marriage, you have never mastered the skills. Learn the skills and spontaneity will develop.

A BEHAVIORAL PLAN TO MAKE YOUR MARRIAGE WORK BETTER

Both you and your partner should get in the habit of paying a lot of attention to the behaviors you want the other to

increase. Many couples don't understand that a behavior has three possible consequences that will increase or maintain it.

(1) *You do something and the consequence is pleasant or desired.* For example, a husband gives his wife flowers and she thanks him with a kiss. That's called *positive reinforcement.*

(2) *You do something, with the consequence that something bad that has been going on stops.* For example, a wife nags her husband, who then yells at her. As a result, she then stops nagging, and the next time she nags, the husband is more apt to yell. That's *aversion escape.*

(3) *You fear something will happen, and as a consequence of what you do, it does not happen.* For instance, a husband works very late at the office. Fearing his wife's annoyance and even anger, he purchases a bunch of roses for her. As a result, she does not get angry. The next time he works late, he will be apt to buy flowers again. That's *aversion avoidance.*

Both the aversion avoidance and escape methods may lead to certain kinds of apparently desirable behaviors—for example, the saying of something pleasant. However, both have a basic weakness. Through use of either of them, the thrust of the marriage starts to become basically one of keeping bad things from happening rather than one of seeking pleasures from the other and seeking to pleasure the other.

In setting up the replacement behaviors, you should know the things your spouse does that please you, the behaviors that do not, and the behaviors your spouse would like to see changed in you. Concentrating on what you *like* rather than what you *don't like* will change the entire tone of your marriage.

LABORATORY EXERCISE IN MARITAL BEHAVIORS

Purpose: To choose specific target behaviors for change.

STEP ONE: Evaluate the behaviors in your marriage by filling out the following chart, reprinted from the *Marital Pre-Counseling Inventory* by Richard B. and Freida Stuart. Both husband and wife should do this and put the answers down in their Assertiveness Training notebooks.

Please list ten things which your spouse does which please you:

1. _____
2. _____
3. _____
4. _____
5. _____
6. _____
7. _____
8. _____
9. _____
10. _____

Please list three things which you would like your spouse to do *more often*. In answering this question and the next, please be *positive* and *specific*. For example, write "During dinner, ask me how I spent the day" (positive and specific) instead of "Be less preoccupied with himself all the time that we are together" (negative and vague).
How often did he or she do each of these things in the last seven days?
How important are each of these things to you?

1. _____   It was done   Do you consider it:
   _____   ____ times in   ____ very important
                            the last seven days.   ____ important
                                                    ____ not too important

2. _____   It was done   Do you consider it:
   _____   ____ times in   ____ very important
                            the last seven days.   ____ important
                                                    ____ not too important

3. _____   It was done   Do you consider it:
   _____   ____ times in   ____ very important
                            the last seven days   ____ important
                                                    ____ not too important

Please list three things which your spouse would like you to do *more often*, again being positive and specific.
How often have you done each of these in the last seven days?
About how often has your spouse asked you to do each of these things during the last seven days?

1. _____   I did it ____   My spouse asked me
   _____   times in the last   to do this ____ times
                            7 days   in the last 7 days.

2. _____   I did it ____   My spouse asked me
   _____   times in the last   to do this ____ times
                            7 days   in the last 7 days.

3. _____   I did it ____   My spouse asked me
   _____   times in the last   to do this ____ times
                            7 days.   in the last 7 days.

STEP TWO: In telling the things you would like to see your partner do *more often*, make sure you are specific. A wife's list might include, "Tell me what you like about my cooking" (not "Stop telling me what you don't like about my cooking"), "Tell me when I wear a dress you like." A husband's list might include, "Be sweet when I come home exhausted," "Compliment me when I do chores around the house even if I do them badly."

STEP THREE: The wife gives a copy of her list to her husband and explains what she means by each item. Husband gives and explains his list to his wife. The desired items should be something the partner can reasonably be expected to do and is not set against doing. Discuss any disagreements. If at this time your partner feels firmly against doing a specific thing, substitute another more acceptable behavior.

STEP FOUR: Keep a copy of the list you give your partner. Every time he/she performs one of these desired behaviors, put a check mark next to that item on the list. Or use a graph form. Thus you keep count of the times the partner does the desired behavior.

STEP FIVE: At preset times (for instance, every evening before dinner or going to bed), you communicate the count to each other, discussing each episode and how you both feel about it. In this way, you help shape each other's behavior.

Here is a capsule dialogue of a real life husband and wife talking over the wife's account of affectionate touchings—the behavior she wanted her husband to increase:

HUSBAND: "Hey, you didn't count the time you were near the front door and I patted your arm."
WIFE: "No, that seemed too mechanical and none of the affection came through. You seemed in too much of a hurry."
HUSBAND: "What about that time in the pantry? And that time I squeezed your hand helping you out of the car. I really felt extremely affectionate. Didn't it come through?"
WIFE: "You know, you're right. I just didn't pay too much attention. Here is something I say I want, and then when you do it, I ignore you. I'll be more aware in the future!"

By doing this each partner learns not only to please the other but becomes more sensitive to the partner's attempts to please.

BEHAVIORAL MARRIAGE CONTRACTS

Contracts make good intentions workable. You avoid the situation where one partner claims "Here I am doing my share, but my spouse gives me nothing in return. I carry the whole burden. It isn't fair." While it may seem like a cold and businesslike form to use within the close relationship, a contract can actually increase warmth and openness.

The rules for drawing up a marital contract, designed to bring about behavior change, go like this:

The contract involves both people. Each has responsibilities and each receives desired rewards as he fulfills these responsibilities. The responsibilities are directly to the spouse and the rewards stem directly from the spouse. Each partner *gets something he wants* from the other rather than practicing the aversion avoidance or escape type of reinforcement.

The contract must be acceptable to both parties. Each must be willing to accept the specific responsibility in return for the specific rewards.

In negotiating the contract, neither side has any "rights." Anything can be made the subject of negotiation. In this way, you facilitate change instead of staying at an impasse.

The behaviors involved in the contract are specific, positive, observable, and countable. You do not use behaviors like "improve our marriage." You do use such desired behaviors as "number of times he said nice things to me" or "time she spends with me on weekends." While it is not always possible to have countable behaviors, try to get them. You want to avoid unobservable behavior, such as thoughts or feelings. The change in these will follow from the change in observable actions. As one partner increases the number of his feeling communications (observable), both partners will start to feel warmer and closer. Always stress the behaviors you want to increase rather than those you want to decrease.

The contract should be written out in detail so that it makes clear the responsibilities and rewards of each partner. This avoids confusion about the original agreement at a later date. It should be kept in a spot where both partners can refer to it easily. Whenever possible, keep track of the target behaviors with graphs, charts, points, or tokens.

Each partner should rate the behavior of the other.

In advance, set times for deciding on the extension or renegotiation of the contract.

CASE

Mary and Bob had one of those marriages where everything seemed wrong and little right. When they first consulted me, both were so overwhelmed with the "wrongness" of things that it was almost impossible to select specific targets for attempted change. However, in our discussions, one theme constantly recurred. Mary felt their home was not hers. Bob felt their home was not his.

Mary's complaint: "I'm close to my mother and I want to invite her for Sunday dinner. When I do, Bob either leaves the house or acts so terribly that we're all miserable. So I don't invite her. But how can this be my home if I can't even ask my own mother over for dinner?"

Bob's complaint: "Mary is so messy that I live in a continual state of discomfort and inconvenience. I can't shower without removing armfuls of underwear from the overhead rack. Often I can't find a chair to sit in—every one is filled with her books, papers, and packages. How can it be my home when she gives no consideration to my needs and comfort?"

From these complaints, we pinpointed certain desired behaviors. Bob wanted greater neatness from Mary. Mary wanted to have her mother visit, and when she did, to have Bob behave in a "civil" fashion. We made these behaviors the basis for the initial contract.

Mary's responsibilities and rewards. She had to become neater— by Bob's estimate. We broke the desired neatness down into four specific behaviors: (1) bathroom sink free of spilled, or smeared, make-up; (2) she must hang her personal laundry in the pantry rather than the bathroom; (3) books, papers, and packages were to be piled neatly on the living room table or kept on her desk—nowhere else; (4) all articles of clothing were to be kept in closets, drawers, or hamper—out of Bob's sight.

Each day Mary performed these behaviors to Bob's satisfaction, she would earn 1 point for each behavior. Thus, she could acquire 4 points in a day or a maximum of 28 points a week. Mary was not allowed to challenge Bob's rating, but she could ask him to explain the "why" and how she could earn more points. However long it took, when Mary reached 60 points, she could invite her mother for dinner and Bob must behave just as nicely as he would to a guest of his.

Bob's responsibilities and rewards. Of course, his reward was Mary's increasing neatness. His responsibility: to act civilly when Mary's mother actually visited. If he did not (in Mary's judgment), Mary received an additional 10 points and so hastened mother's next invitation. We found it difficult to pinpoint the specific behavior called "civil," and this led to an ongoing discussion between Bob and Mary of how he could please her during mother's visit.

During the first two weeks of the contract, Mary earned only 15 points. This made her realize how inconsiderate she was of Bob's comfort. For the first time in years, she began paying attention to Bob's needs around the house and started doing other things not covered in the contract (like wearing a pretty negligee to breakfast instead of a torn smock).

As Mary accumulated points and the mother's visit neared, Bob became increasingly concerned about his own "civil" behavior. He started discussions about "offensive" things he had done in the past (both with her family and friends), and about various social actions he might perform to please Mary. These discussions spontaneously broadened into talks of how each felt about his own parents and eventually how they felt about each other. Soon an openness and warmth started to return to their marital relationship.

Mary and Bob kept this contract going through three Sunday dinners and then went on to other contracts. However, by that time this mechanical and impersonal "clean-up contract" had led to an improved communication, an increased feeling in each that "this is my home," and the optimistic feeling that they had reached a turning point in their marriage.

Marriage contracts don't always have to concern something as comparatively simple as Sunday dinners with a mother-in-law. Richard B. Stuart, formerly professor of social work at the University of Michigan and now professor, department of psychiatry, University of British Columbia, used the contract system with tokens as rewards with four couples making a last desperate attempt to save their marriages. In each instance, the wife listed as her first wish that the husband converse with her more. Each husband wanted more physical affection.

Dr. Stuart set up an exchange of conversation for sex. Every time the husband conversed in a manner the wife found satisfactory, he would receive a token. He could exchange his tokens for physical affection or sex—"paying" 3 for kissing and "lightly petting," 5 for heavy petting, and 15 for intercourse. Mechanical, yes. But the rates of conversation and sex increased sharply after the start of treatment and continued through twenty-four- and forty-eight-week follow-up periods. Divorce was avoided in all cases.

Learn to communicate. Wearing a "public face" proves effective in certain job or uncomplicated social situations (like cocktail parties); it cannot work in the close relationship. If you adopt a mask, you will be unable to communicate intimately.

Good communication exists as the core of a successful marriage. If you don't express your feelings openly, the intimacy of sharing decreases. Misunderstandings develop. When things don't work out, good communication provides a corrective factor. Without this, small irritating situations grow into giant problems. Your dissatisfactions continue without abatement, and may come out in the most destructive ways. Eventually, the lack of openness makes strangers of two people who once promised at the altar to "love, honor, and cherish" each other until death. The relationship ceases to grow. The couple then has a choice: dead marriage or divorce.

Here are some communication caveats that may prevent you from having to make that choice.

Speak up about trivia, because most marital problems concern trivial matters

In this way, you (1) keep habits from building up that in the long run can become major problem areas, (2) begin to set a general pattern of openness in marriage, (3) resolve the difficulty to the satisfaction—or dissatisfaction—of both. For example:

WIFE ONE: Ruth disliked her husband's sister. She particularly resented the fact that she and her husband went out with "that girl" and her husband every Friday night, and "I pretend I enjoy it." Finally, Ruth spoke out with, "I'm sick of this Friday night foursome. I don't like your sister. I never have." Mark retaliated with an accusation, "When we go to your house, you talk to your sister and ignore me." They fought, but the air was cleared. Now Ruth talks to Mark when they visit her family, and the Friday night quartet has been cut to once a month. Says Ruth, "I was trying to please him, so I squelched my own ideas and felt miserable. Since I gave it to him straight about his sister, our marriage is much better."

WIFE TWO: Like many wives of professionals and executives, Louise was lonely and upset because her husband's new job kept him working from 9 A.M. to 11 P.M. When she came down with an ulcer, she decided to confront Mike with her unhappiness—and arrived at a compromise. Mike answered her tale of woe with "Look, this is my job. If I have a nine to five job, I get a nine to five pay check." He asked tenderly, "What can I do to help the situation?" The couple worked out a solution. Mike would try to get home by 9 P.M., would call her an hour before he planned to leave his office so she wouldn't ruin the roast, would never work late Friday night. For Mondays through Thursdays, Louise would find some evening activities of her own.

In both cases, speaking up prevented an upsetting situation from turning into *Sturm und Drang*.

In learning to communicate, follow this guideline: *It is never should you speak up, but how and when.* It is not aggressive to speak up. It is assertive. You have to figure out a way to tell your partner something in a way that increases communication rather than in a way that hurts. For example, your husband worships his mother, but she has done something that has got you very uptight. One technique: You say "We have a problem. Your mother did such and such. I feel hurt." That way you have not attacked his mother; you have presented the situation as a mutual problem, hopefully when your mate feels calm and relaxed, not exhausted.

LABORATORY EXERCISE IN COMMUNICATION

Purpose: To bring about closeness, not distance, through appropriate communication.

STEP ONE: Write out what you want to say. Go over it and improve the "how." Make sure you are talking about what you want to talk about.

STEP TWO: Read it into a tape machine and listen to the playback. Make any "script" changes you think necessary. Check your emotional communication and your voice loudness. Do it over and over until it feels right to you.

STEP THREE: Set in advance a specific time to deliver your speech. Choose the hour wisely. If you're a wife, don't pick half time of the Jets game. If you're a husband, don't start talking before dinner when she's busy at the stove. Of course, something unexpected may come up that would make it wise to defer the talk, but this occurs rarely. If you find that unexpected things keep coming up and you continually put off the confrontation, figure that you are just too anxious. Keep practicing, or try Step Four below.

STEP FOUR: Your paralyzing anxiety may be due to anticipation of your partner's responses. In this case:

· Make a list of several possible responses.

· Read each response into an audio tape, leaving a two-minute gap between each.

· Listen to the partner's first possible response. Stop the machine and imagine what you might say. Then say it into the tape and go on to the next until all are done.

· Start the tape from the beginning, listen to your reaction to your mate's first response, and stop the machine. Think how you can make it better. Does it say what you want to say? How can you put it in a better way? Does the tone of your voice communicate the appropriate emotions?

· Imagine doing this new way as vividly as you can. Then

rewind the tape and listen to your partner's possible response again. This time say your new response into the tape.

· If you still feel dissatisfied with any of the responses, do them over a third time.

· Now reset a new time to make your speech and do it!

STEP FIVE: If you still cannot tell your partner what you want to say, you may have to resort to other methods. You may state: "Look, there's something important about what I feel that I want to tell you, but I'm too anxious to do it directly. So I wrote it out [or put it on tape]. I want you to read it [or listen to it], and then I'd appreciate talking about it."

This way sounds very mechanical. It is, but it also is a scientifically proven way to commence communicating.

Make sure you are getting your message across. Sometimes you think you are sending one message—and your partner is receiving another.

CASE

Thirty-four-year-old Tom and thirty-year-old Wendy, married for six years and parents of a four-year-old son, came to me because of sexual difficulties. In reality their problem was communication.

Their sexual troubles had a pattern. In his rather impersonal style, Tom would begin sexual advances. Feeling the lack of warmth and love, Wendy became resentful, and withdrew emotionally from the situation even though she continued sexual behavior. Tom responded to this withdrawal by feeling dissatisfied and frustrated. Often he expressed his anger during coitus. This made Wendy even more resentful and she withdrew even more. In the period just before they came to see me, Tom, enraged by the deteriorating sexual relations in the marriage, had started an affair with his secretary. For six weeks he moved into her apartment before he decided to go "back home and give my marriage another try."

After a proper evaluation, I presented them with a plan which stressed working on communication and assertion. When I asked them to bring in specific problems, Wendy brought in an incident that had happened several weeks prior to the six-week separation.

Wendy's version: "For several nights in a row, Tom ate his dinner very quickly and said he had to go back to work. Even during dinner he acted uninterested in my conversation and completely ignored my objections to his working late every night. I grew increasingly resentful. One night Tom returned home after midnight, woke me, and, with no exchange of words, began to make love. I felt extremely hostile. When we finished, he had a temper outburst at me."

Tom's version: "I had been involved in a very important project which might mean life or death for my firm. The deadline was approaching and I had to work very hard. I felt under great pressure. I needed comfort and support from Wendy. What she gave me was remoteness. On the night in question I came home exhausted and dispirited. My sexual advances this time weren't for sexual reasons—I wanted a tender contact. Instead, Wendy was more distant than ever, just when I needed her most. It made me furious and I lost my temper."

When I asked Tom why he had not told Wendy any of this, he answered, "She should have known." When I asked Wendy why she hadn't inquired if anything were wrong, she stated, "It never occurred to me."

With these revelations, the failure of communication became obvious to them. Among the methods we used to improve their communication were the feeling talk exercises (described in Chapter III) which proved particularly helpful in relation to sex. Tom and Wendy's discussions of what each liked and didn't like in their lovemaking brought increased sexual pleasure. We also used role-reversal, which they called "playing switch." When either felt some message was not getting through, he or she would call out "switch." At that point, Wendy would role-play Tom, and Tom, Wendy. Each would try to express the message he thought the other was sending. Then they would correct each other. In that way, they aborted misunderstandings and trained themselves to be more sensitive to the other.

Over time, they felt less need for the exercises but used them whenever they had a particular difficulty. Formal AT treatment took four months, and at the end of a one-year follow-up, Tom and Wendy reported, "Closeness is growing and sex is better than it ever was!"

Remember, communication need not be verbal.

Create specific projects that say things without words, like intimate dinners, sweet notes, thoughtful little gifts. This is nonverbal speaking up. The best communication combines actions and words. Hug her but also tell her that you love her. Kiss him but also tell him that you love him. People like to hear things as well as experience them.

Learn to fight—but fight fair.

In the book *The Intimate Enemy*, authors George R. Bach, founder and director of the Institute of Group Psychotherapy, Beverly Hills, California, and Peter Wyden write, "Verbal conflict between intimates is not only acceptable, especially between husbands and wives; it is constructive and highly desirable. Couples who fight together are couples who stay together—provided they know how to fight properly." In a close relationship, the expression of anger is as important as the expression of tenderness. A marriage without at least occasional fighting becomes a union lacking in closeness.

In learning to fight, you want to accomplish three things: to understand and achieve your fighting goals, to express emotions through fights, and to control destructive fighting.

UNDERSTAND AND ACHIEVE THE GOALS OF FIGHTING. You may experience confusion about the goal of fighting. You think of your partner as an enemy, and, with enemies, you are out to win or destroy them. This attitude may be right in the superficial relationship, where some people are antagonists out to demolish you, but not in the close relationship. You don't fight to win, but clear the air, find a solution, share feelings, gain greater understanding of each other—and thus both of you win. To accomplish this, you must do certain things:

Set ground rules. To bring up certain sensitive areas leads only to hurt. Make these clear with "Don't bring up my sexual difficulties in a fight," or "Don't compare me to my father— say anything you want about my faults but treat me as a person on my own." When your partner exceeds the limits you have set, you have the right to cry "foul," and the partner must stop. If he thinks the limit is wrong, discuss it or even fight about it. But in your fighting, you should be able to fight freely without fearing emotional destruction.

The core of the fight should be what you think your partner has done—not the kind of person you think he is. The kind of fighting where you hurl diatribes, like "You are a latent homosexual" . . . "You have a father fixation," cannot work. Even if you are correct, what can she/he do about it? Can your partner resolve her Oedipal complex then and there or even in the next month? This fighting error leads only to frustration, disruption, and growing distance. This does not mean a husband can never call his wife a "bitch," or that a wife can't call her husband a "mama's boy." It is OK to call her a bitch when it is an expression of your feelings, and you mean, "I am goddamn mad at you." It is not OK when you issue it as an ultimatum meaning "we won't make it unless you change the very essence of you as a person."

Equalize your fighting. Some people fight better than others. They verbalize more easily, yell louder, or think more quickly on their feet. As the point is not to win but grow closer, the difference between the partners has to be minimized. One way: to establish the rule that the weaker person can start a fight at any time, but the stronger one must give advance notice or can only commence a fight when the weaker one feels strong.

Don't drive your partner into a corner. That kind of victory produces desperation and vindictiveness in your partner rather than closeness.

Talk about your fights afterward the way you may talk about your sex life. Did you gain your point in a fair way? Did it increase trust? Was the fight open and direct? Tell what you liked, what you didn't like.

LEARN TO EXPRESS YOUR EMOTIONS THROUGH FIGHTS. Some people have just never learned to express anger. For such people I suggest deliberate use of the negative feeling-talk phrases. These people are very adept at the "I like what you said" sweet talk when they really think, "I'd like to tell you to drop dead for what you've just said; but if I do, we'll get into a fight, and I really don't want that." This way constipates your emotions. Start saying, "I don't like what you did," and see what happens. Another technique for those afraid to fight is the staging of mock fights. Take a relatively trivial thing and role-play as if you were truly fighting about it. At first, you may feel artificial about this, but as you loosen up, you will act more spontaneously, and you may start to engage in honest fights.

LEARN TO BRING YOUR UNCONTROLLED FIGHTING UNDER CONTROL. Many types of uncontrolled fights exist: the pointless *recurring* fight that happens over and over again and never gets anywhere . . . the *eruption* in which one partner just blows off steam, and which rarely concerns an issue between husband and wife . . . *fighting about the wrong thing* in which you start fights about everything else, but never confront the real problem . . . the *no limit fight* where because you bring in every hurt and grievance, you can't communicate about anything.

If you have learned the bad and essentially passive habit of uncontrolled fighting, you can take a much more active approach.

Prepare for a fight. Think through beforehand what you expect to gain from the fight. Do you want to make your partner understand how you feel? To simply get it off your chest? If you choose a goal like "humiliate him the way he humiliates me," better stop, evaluate, and see if that's what you really want. It helps to ask yourself key questions:

> Should I really fight about this or not?
> Can I tolerate the tension this fight will produce?
> Am I prepared to be honest?

Stop fighting at random. Make an appointment with your partner for the fight. Tell him/her what the fight will be about. Try something in the vein of "I'm furious about the way you acted at the party last night and I have to get it off my chest. How about after dinner tonight?" Don't pick a time just before an important conference or when you've both drunk too many highballs but don't let your anger simmer more than twenty-four hours. The time limit keeps your feelings from being diluted, and when you know you will have it out soon, you feel less frustration.

Keep to the topic of the fight. If you want to fight about extravagance and your partner drags in "your terrible Uncle Otto" or how you "snore too loudly," you have the right to stop him. The challenged partner must prove the topic he has introduced bears relevance to the fight core—or drop it.

Remember a fight does not have to have an end or ultimate resolution. It is part of a continuing exchange of feeling and understanding in a relationship that grows ever closer. Just as you exchange tenderness, you exchange anger and, in this way, better the relationship.

Communicate to improve the way you feel about, and make decisions in, your home

Sometimes you think your partner does not do his share. Because you believe you make too many of the decisions, they have come to represent a burden, not a shared bond. Or you may resent that your partner makes all the decisions. Many husbands feel their wives make all the decisions about schools, social life, which church to attend, leaving them only decisions about moneymaking—never money-spending.

Communication can help you to understand the percentage of family decisions you now make and the percentage you would like to make. It can also help you to know if your perception is accurate, what changes can be made, and which areas are most important.

LABORATORY EXERCISE IN DECISION-MAKING

Purpose: To improve decision-making via communication.

STEP ONE: Draw two vertical lines on a page in your AT workbook. Head the three columns with: DECISION-MAKING AREA, PERCENT CONTRIBUTES TO DECISION NOW, and PERCENT WOULD LIKE TO CONTRIBUTE.

Under DECISION-MAKING AREA, list the following:

> household responsibilities
> vocational activities
> communication
> personal independence
> financial management
> interaction with in-laws
> religious activities

Add any others with which you experience difficulty.

STEP TWO: Each partner fills out the form separately.

STEP THREE: Compare ratings. Expect differences of opinion in what now exists and what you want. These discrepancies serve as good starting points for discussion.

STEP FOUR: Select one area where you and your partner have general agreement about what is and what each wants. Discuss what you can each do to move in the desired area. Be sure to choose the area first where you have the greatest chance of success. As you start making progress in that area, move on to the next most likely area.

DANGER SIGNALS

In working to achieve the close relationship, there are four things to guard against:

(1) *Don't finger point* with the "he-should-she-should" or the "it's her-fault-his-fault" attitude. Many of the people who consult me about marital problems have become experts at analyzing their partners. However, when I ask the patient, "What could you have done differently?" all I get is a blank look. What such people don't understand is that very often they are setting up circumstances that maintain the very behavior about which they complain. Your partner cannot change until you change.

CASE

Marge, a saleswoman for a large computer company, and her lawyer-husband, Frank, loved each other, but couldn't live together. Married for seven years, they had maintained separate apartments for the last four. One reason: their continuing disagreements. When they disagreed, each tried to establish his case by proving the other wrong. They glorified this behavior by saying they "were searching for the truth." In actuality, they forgot all about the feeling interaction they wanted to go on between the two of them.

One day, Marge and Frank were shopping together at the supermarket. He saw a can of olives and put it in the cart. On the checkout line, he asked her how much his can cost. Marge replied, "Fifty-nine cents." Frank gave her the money and she put it in her purse. This ate away at Frank. "I'm always giving her things. She never gives me anything," he thought to himself. He burst out, "You never should have taken that money!"

Marge felt, "It was so trivial. I did it without thinking. It never occurred to me he might pay. I just took the money absently."

In discussing this situation in my office, each became the lawyer, picking on every detail over and over just to prove his version the correct one.

When I suggested, "Look, by expressing tender feelings, you could have changed the whole thing," neither knew of anything that would have made a difference.

I made a feeling-talk suggestion. Starting at the point where Marge put the money in her purse, Frank could have turned and said, "I am hurt and angry that you took the fifty-nine cents. It's not that the money means so much to me, but it expresses your attitude."

Frank agreed that that was what he really felt. Marge concurred that this statement would have gotten through to her.

Then I asked Marge what she could have done that would have made Frank feel better about the incident. She turned lawyer again with "Nothing. He shouldn't have spoken to me that way."

Then I asked Marge, "Look, Frank just told you that you hurt him. Think again—what could you have said or done in the situation?"

This time she answered, "Put my arm around him and kissed him on the cheek—right in the checkout line."

Frank's face lit up. He said, "That would have made everything all right."

Thus, when this couple cut through the litigant attitude and the need to prove themselves right, and managed to communicate direct expression of feeling, things improved, and they took a step toward closeness.

(2) *Giving up your own identity*—and sometimes not knowing you have done so. Beware of the couple who constantly use the

pronoun "we" and never "I." They are smothering each other to death. If you live in a close relationship with someone, there is extensive sharing of all the details of living. This constant sharing and close physical proximity dictate the need for some degree of emotional privacy. Each partner is entitled to be a "self."

(3) *The partner may move in and take over in the other person's territory and not allow him freedom.* Here the partner does not allow the spouse "territory," but often moves in with the mistaken idea that "it is good to share *everything*." One partner becomes interested in bird-watching and the other rushes out to buy binoculars and a field guide. One becomes fascinated by the Italian Renaissance and the other starts reading Berenson from cover to cover. I had one case where a middle-aged widow, married to a widower with two grown children, nearly brought about divorce because she decided she "was the children's mother." It took quite a few sessions to get her to understand that her husband's relationship to his children was his territory.

In marriage, sharing is good—but not 100 percent sharing. Each partner needs a territory of his own. Constant together-ness becomes bondage.

(4) *The area of independence may become threatening or create a distance between the partners.* This places a limit on point three. In the close relationship there cannot be complete freedom in the choice of territory. Anything either partner does may influence the relationship, make the partner anxious or insecure, threaten their common fate. The outside territory chosen must take these effects into consideration.

CASE

John and Roger, a homosexual couple, had lived together for twelve years. They considered themselves "married" and the relationship permanent. Through the years, each had had a great deal of sexual experience on the outside with both men and women. John was about ten years older than Roger, approaching his mid-forties and starting to feel extremely insecure. He said to me, "If I lose Roger, I'm afraid I'll end up a lonely old auntie."

Basically, John feared Roger would become seriously involved with another younger man. He began to become very upset about Roger's extramarital affairs and this created tension and disruption in the relationship. They started to fight. John's solution: they should both give up having sex outside their own relationship. Roger refused to accept this idea. He said, "Why, we've both been doing this for as long as we've known each other. Why should we change now?"

We finally reached a compromise. *Roger would have sex only with women.* John knew Roger wouldn't leave him for a female, and so he no longer felt threatened. The solution did not completely satisfy Roger, but for the sake of his relationship with John, he accepted it.

True closeness with another human being at a depth level is an experience that those who have not experienced it find hard to understand. It becomes a process of growth that may take years. Achieve it and you will know what Mark Twain meant when he wrote, "Love seems the swiftest but it is the slowest of all growths. No man or woman knows what perfect love is until they have been married a quarter of a century."

Chapter VI
The Active Approach to Sex

In the ideal sexual union, a man and a woman share tenderness, excitement, love, with the goal of complete release of inhibitions and complete immersion in feelings. Their bodies merge so that two individuals become a single unit. As Erich Fromm wrote, "Erotic love begins with separateness and ends in oneness."

True intimacy does not represent an "I-excite-her-and-then-she-excites-me-in-return" exchange of favors between mates. To get the essence of your partner's warmth, you give of yourself primarily for his or her pleasure. Rather than acting like an uninvolved spectator, you share your partner's feelings and sensations as if they were yours.

Even though *almost all human beings are born with the capacity for normal sexual response,* many things block this ultimate fulfill-ment in the close relationship. Some people feel sex is "bad" . . . "dirty" . . . "perverted," because parents, teachers, church, society instilled these thoughts in them during the formative years. Others have learned to connect fears, anx-ieties, and I-can't-make-it thoughts with the sexual act. Still others behave passively about bettering sex; they *don't know* they can achieve an improved performance in the marital bed.

But all the reasons come down to this. We do not learn *how* to have orgasms. We learn how *not* to have them. What we have learned in this area we can usually unlearn. This principle serves as the major basis for the new sex therapies.

Sexual failure stems not only from dysfunctions but also

from more common causes such as lack of sexual frequency, variety, and freedom. Experts estimate that sexual problems of one kind or another affect more than half of all married couples in the United States today. But bad sex represents more than a failure of the biological mechanism; it reverberates through the entire relationship, inhibiting closeness and producing tension and rifts. The simple relief of a sexual problem can have a profound effect upon a marriage, making the entire relationship more mature, trusting, and close.

THE BASIS FOR CHANGE

Passive acceptance of an unsatisfactory sex situation is the mark of an unassertive person. You cheat yourself if you don't look into and try techniques that have worked for others, and can make sex better for you. Why suffer unnecessarily? With this tenet, Assertiveness Training in the sexual area has a threefold goal:

(1) *To provide information about sex.* To have an orgasm you have to let go of reality and experience abandonment. Unfortunately, lack of knowledge or incorrect or outdated information often leads to inhibited actions and prevents spontaneity and expression of feelings.

(2) *To develop an active orientation toward sex through setting and achieving sex goals.* Although it is easy to say that the ultimate goal of sex in a close relationship is the deepest exchange of feelings, this concept can seem rather abstract. You are in pursuit of this happiness. For most people, other goals are also present, temporarily or permanently. Since sex serves as a way of having fun, playfulness and enjoyment can be a primary goal. During times of stress, sex may serve as a source of comfort. At other times, the emphasis may be on conception. But unfortunate goals also may develop or exist. For example, sex may become a duty or ritualistic habit, and thus lose its spontaneity.

You can change this.

Taking the active attitude means you examine and evaluate your sexual relationship. Then you examine areas where you can do something to produce improvement and go about

doing this in a systematic fashion, always working coopera-
tively with your partner. By taking action, you develop a
feeling of movement and command in your search for the
ultimate intimacy.

(3) *To help you learn to communicate.* Many people who show
their feelings openly in superficial relationships pull back from
the final step of complete openness in a sexual situation within
a close relationship. Since sex involves such an intense sharing
of much that is personal, they fear they are making themselves
vulnerable. However, through AT, they *can* learn to communicate on this intimate level and, in the process of learning, can
achieve a new closeness.

Sexual Knowledge

Just as you have to have a correct conception of the role of
small talk in forming a social network and the importance of
fair fighting in the close relationship, so you must know about
sex to achieve fulfillment. There are two common difficulties:

(1) *Some people lack sexual knowledge.* In some instances, men
and women have rigid ideas about what is allowable and
normal in sex. Some highly educated people who know all
about the various possibilities for intercourse are naive and
inexperienced about techniques for sex play. Often they don't
recognize how little they know.

(2) *Others don't realize how the emergence of scientific and clinical
data has completely changed our sexual knowledge.* The work of
Kinsey and, later, Masters and Johnson threw open the doors
of scientific research in this sensitive area.

With the disclosure of new data, many concepts about the
mechanics and physiology of sex have been revised. We used
to distinguish between a clitoral and vaginal orgasm. Now
Masters and Johnson have shown that there are not two kinds
of orgasm; in women, *all* climaxes stem from the clitoris. Lack
of vaginal orgasm is not due to the unconscious conflicts
assigned by Freud (like penis envy), but may be brought about
by the simple fear of not having orgasm during intercourse or
may be a mechanical problem—such as when the woman has
not had sufficient time to warm up prior to intercourse. What

makes the vaginal and clitoral orgasms seem different are the emotional factors involved and the meaning they possess for the woman.

Ideas about masturbation have also changed. Not too many years ago, masturbation was thought to be both "neurotic" and the cause of diseases, ranging from cancer to mental illness. Next, masturbation was regarded as acceptable, but, because people misunderstood its nature, they felt guilty and depressed when they practiced it. Today, we recognize masturbation as a good thing, and in the newer sex therapies teaching a person to masturbate often proves the first step to better sex. Many couples find it enjoyable and exciting to masturbate in each other's presence.

Here are some of the most commonly posed questions about sex, which I will answer with current conceptions in this rapidly changing field and hopefully, with these answers, provide new knowledge that will remove inhibitions.

QUESTION ONE: *"What is normal sex? What are the limits of sexual activities permitted in a close relationship?"*

The specific activities in question might run the gamut from oral or anal sex to having sex on the living-room floor to exchange-of-dirty-word tenderness. How can you truly let go when you are frightened of doing something "abnormal," or you become upset when your partner does something you consider "wrong"? Your concern is understandable. Even today, many highly reputable theorists and practitioners in the area of human behavior still believe that the only "normal" sex is that which culminates in "heterosexual genital union" (that is conventional intercourse between members of the opposite sex). For them, any other form of sex indicates immaturity or conflict or something gone awry in the psyche. Many are even leery of sexual foreplay, which they regard, at least in part, as a regression to infantile sexuality where there is no specific outlet for sexual activities.

It is hard to isolate the scientific data on which this narrow viewpoint is based. Studies of other mammals and human societies show a wide variety of acceptable sexual behaviors. *Just about anything that is anatomically possible probably has been accepted somewhere, sometime, and someplace as normal.*

Contemporary theorists in the sexual area take the general position that *just about anything is normal between consenting adults as long as it is acceptable to both. The more you can let go in actions, the more you can let go in feelings.*

This does not mean that no such thing exists as abnormal sexual behavior with consenting adults. It does mean that the label "abnormal" is not imposed because of the content of the act—in other words, because of what it is you want to do or actually do. Oral sex, anal sex, fetishes are neither normal nor abnormal because of what they are. The degree of normalcy relates to *the freedom of choice you have.* When the act goes out of control, becomes compulsive, and you lack freedom of choice, it then becomes abnormal.

It is "normal" sex if:

> *you do it because you want to do it, either for your own satisfaction or to pleasure your partner;*
> *you feel free to do something else if you want to.*

If you follow these basics, you can stop worrying about being "abnormal." Just go ahead, let go, and be you.

QUESTION TWO: *"Just what do you mean by consenting partners? How do I know if there is consent?"*

Consenting partners are people who know enough about their own desires to make a decision about whether they want to say yes or no without coercion or restrictions.

You know if there is consent by communicating, by asking, discussing, and bringing sexual matters out into the open. When one partner mind-reads the other and comes up with the wrong answer, inhibitions result.

Asking is a request. You have the right to say no. For instance, your husband desires oral sex, but you do not. If you really dislike it, refuse. It is far better to say no than force yourself to do something you do not want to perform. But disliking it does not mean you should never do it. At times, you may be willing to perform an act you dislike to pleasure your partner and show your love. But you do it from choice, not because you feel forced. Also make sure your dislike is the true emotion you feel, not merely your own anxiety or that Mother taught you "that is wrong."

QUESTION THREE: *"You encourage freedom in actual sexual behavior, but in my fantasies I am way out. I'm afraid that if I really let go, my fantasies will take over, and I'll really be a pervert. Is there much chance of that?"*

If sex is always the same, this indicates a problem—either one of a passive attitude toward sex or the presence of an inhibiting anxiety. Sexual feelings gain in spontaneity and depth through freedom of action, and fantasies are one way to achieve this. Fantasies may point out potential sources of satisfaction that you haven't tried, but should. Sharing them with your partner may result in increased physical stimulation and closeness.

These truths about sexual fantasies may prove helpful:

Sexual fantasies do not necessarily reflect the play of deep unconscious forces. Many are merely habits, ways you have learned to turn yourself on. Some evidence shows that you can acquire the content of sexual fantasies quite accidentally, just as you accumulate learning accidentally in other life areas.

A difference exists between fantasy and action. Just because you have a sexual fantasy about being with someone other than your partner does not mean that in actuality you would like to have sex with that person. Because you have a homosexual fantasy does not imply you are a homosexual or that you crave homosexual activity. Usually, it signifies only that you had the fantasy, and it excited you. Period.

Fantasies can cause difficulties if they control you and become the only way you can experience sexual satisfaction, or if the fantasy comes between you and your partner, creating a distance both of you experience. If this happens deliberately focus your attention on your partner as you reach the stage where climax is inevitable. In this way you begin to associate the sexual excitement with your partner rather than with the fantasy, and eventually the partner may replace the fantasy as an excitement source. Once you can do that fairly consistently, start the fantasy interruption process earlier in your lovemaking. At first you may be able to hold this attention for only a few seconds before you feel the need to return to your fantasy, but stick with it and try to get that time to be longer and longer.

QUESTION FOUR: *"What about the 'real' sexual problems? What about when the man cannot achieve an erection or comes too fast? What about when the woman cannot achieve orgasm or when her vagina tightens up so that either the man cannot enter it or it is painful when he does?"*

These represent the most common of the sexual dysfunctions. There are variations of these, plus many others. Current thinking on the causes of sexual dysfunctions goes like this:

(1) The sexual response is a natural reaction to sexual stimulation. It comes about spontaneously and cannot be forced.

(2) If you feel anxious, this anxiety interferes with the sexual stimuli and keeps them from getting through. Hence, the natural sexual reaction cannot take place.

(3) The most common anxiety is the fear of dysfunction. The woman worries whether she will have a climax; the man worries whether he will have an erection. These anxieties become self-fulfilling prophecies. *The very thing they worry about is more apt to take place.* So, the next time they worry more, making the dysfunction more probable. And so goes the neurotic sexual spiral.

(4) The anxieties of the "uninvolved" partner begin to contribute to this spiral and also serve to insure the continuation of the problem. As an example, take the possible reactions of a woman whose husband has a problem with impotency.

(a) Her frustrations cause anger—even rage—with him. She becomes contemptuous of him.

(b) She begins to doubt herself as a woman. This may lead to an extramarital affair, which is both a search for sexual satisfaction and a seeking for reassurance about her womanliness.

(c) She may avoid all sexual contact, even any expression of affection. This generates continual tension between the partners and also guarantees that they will not resolve the sexual difficulty.

(d) Because of her tension, she may develop a sexual dysfunction of her own.

The person who suffers from the dysfunction suffers enormous feelings of guilt and inadequacy. But the "uninvolved" partner also contributes anxieties and conflicts that disrupt the relationship.

(5) The major premise of the newly developed sex therapies (which stem from Masters and Johnson) is *to decrease anxiety and increase receptivity to sexual stimuli.* To accomplish this, sex therapists have devised some rather complex techniques, and those who desire information should read *Human Sexual Inadequacy,* by William H. Masters and Virginia E. Johnson, and *The New Sex Therapy,* by Helen S. Kaplan.

(6) Because many of the new therapeutic approaches are based on rather technical exercises, they appear to be rather mechanistic and impersonal. The very opposite is true. Even though the exercises themselves may be mechanistic, treatment always stresses communication and exchange of feelings between partners. Handled with mutual respect and love, communication and negotiation about sexual problems can solve a great many difficulties. A few simple basics re dysfunctions:

(a) *Always have a medical examination* before you come to any conclusion. People are all too quick to ascribe psychological causes to sex problems. A number of medical conditions can bring about sexual dysfunctions.

(b) *Talk about the problem. Make sure you know what it really is.* Many couples think the sexual problem between them is one thing, when in reality, it is another. For example, a newly married student came to me with the problem of premature ejaculation, even though he could remain erect inside his wife's vagina for periods up to one half hour without ejaculation. Further investigation showed his wife was mildly frigid, and because he couldn't hold up long enough for her to have a climax, they both blamed him, when actually he was performing very adequately. I ended up treating *the wife's* frigidity, and the problem was resolved.

(c) *Remember the general principle in trying to change a dysfunction:* to decrease anxiety and increase stimulation. De-emphasize the aspect of sex that gives you trouble. Build up the pleasure of other sexual aspects.

For example, if the problem is the man's potency, he fears

he will not be sufficiently erect to penetrate the woman. For a period of several weeks, they might try to make sex play as exciting, pleasurable, and tender as possible, but make *no attempt at intercourse*. When the woman does not have a climax, use the same method, with the understanding there will be no attempt to bring her to climax. The worry "Will I have an orgasm?" underlies her anxiety. In this way, you remove the anxiety and increase sexual stimulation in other areas.

(d) *Pay a lot of attention to the conditions (time, place, lights on or off)* under which you achieve sexual success and utilize them.

CASE

A forty-year-old man came to my office with the problem of lack of sexual potency. During love play, he could get no erection at all. However, when he and his wife caressed each other and both were fully clothed, he could achieve full erection. Martin attributed this to two things: the pressure of his clothing on the genital area and that he knew he was *not* expected to perform sexually. His wife realized that Martin could have an erection during these conditions, but neither she nor he had any idea of how they could use this to help his sexual problem.

I gave them the task, "Figure out how you can use this." At the next session, they came back with a plan—and it worked. Martin wore all his clothing from shoes to navy-blue suit. His wife had wanted to be nude, but he felt that would prove a pressure; so they compromised. She wore a dress with nothing underneath. They would sit and caress each other. When Martin had a full erection and she was ready, she opened his fly, allowing the erect penis to emerge, and sat on his lap facing him. In this way, they took the first step to resolving his dysfunction.

For some ideas about making sex play more exciting, I recommend *Sexual Stimulation*, by S. G. Tuffill.

(e) *Examine your satisfactions and dissatisfactions in other areas of your relationship.* Sex does not exist in a vacuum, and often you may aggravate your sexual problems by unexpressed resentments about other things.

(f) *You may make a mutual decision to seek professional help.* You don't have to suffer or anticipate long, endless treatment of doubtful outcome. The new therapeutic methods for sexual dysfunctions are relatively brief and often quite effective. If you don't know about available treatment, ask your family physician.

QUESTION FIVE: *"How does the changing concept of the woman's role influence the sexual relationship?"*

The woman's role in sex certainly has changed. Gone is the idea that she is the passive vessel of a man's search for his own satisfactions, or that it is "wrong" for her to initiate and participate actively in sex. She has the rights and responsibility that come with equality, and thus she has acquired the responsibility for her own satisfaction.

However, many a woman still passively places the burden for satisfying her needs on her partner. To achieve good sex she must teach her partner how best to satisfy her. This means saying, "I liked that," or "Be more gentle," or whatever she wants to communicate, exchanging feelings and ideas, taking the partner's hand and demonstrating what, where, and how she wants something done. Assumption of responsibility also signifies she acts to increase her own pleasure, such as moving her pelvis in such a way that she maximizes stimulation.

She must also take responsibility for satisfying her partner. She allows herself to be taught how best to fulfill him, asking when she doesn't know something and listening when he explains. By developing a sensitivity to him and his feelings, she achieves greater fulfillment; both achieve greater closeness.

This attainment of sexual equality by women has produced problems. Growing evidence shows that the recognition that women have the right to sexual fulfillment has been experienced by many men as a demand and a pressure. This brings anxiety into the sexual act, which may lead to a dysfunction. Reports indicate an increasing rate of impotence among men. Now women must help to remove this anxiety through understanding and communication.

THE ACTIVE ORIENTATION

Unlike the techniques that search for the deep, unconscious fears that affect the libido, the Assertiveness Training method utilizes graphs, tests, assignments, and graded approaches to better lovemaking. As a result, when patients come to me because of sexual difficulties and learn what treatment will be, they rebel initially against "mechanics." They say, "I want to have sex when I feel turned on to it. The entire system you propose is artificial and depersonalized. It will rob sex of spontaneity."

They miss the point. Of course, the aim is spontaneous and free sex. However, if you have sexual difficulties, you *already* have learned unsatisfying habits. Assertiveness Training merely attempts to establish new habits more to your liking. Once these are set, you can discard the record-keeping and the exercises, and spontaneity will return or commence in a new way.

Would you like to have sex more often?

Do you feel your partner possesses physical skill, but always remains aloof and uninvolved while making love?

Would you like your partner to be more active in sex play?

In taking an active approach to improving your sex life, you must determine where you are now and where you want to go. Then take steps to achieve this goal. Basically this process involves the following three parts:

(1) *Pinpoint the sexual behavior you want to change.* This pinpointing of behavior differs from others I discuss in this book because here two people are involved. It is important that both see the problem in the same way and formulate a mutually acceptable goal. The very act of negotiating the goal may bring greater closeness and understanding. For example, if you talk about frequency of sex, the tête-à-tête may bring out many feelings you have about sex, your partner, and your own desires. The warmth between you increases.

(2) *Organize a systematic plan of behavioral change.* Define the behaviors concerned very specifically and preferably in such a way that you can count or measure them. To illustrate this method in the sexual area, I am going to offer laboratory exercise programs in the areas of sexual decision-making, sexual satisfaction, and frequency of sex. Remember you want a series of successes and movement toward a long-range goal, so the goals you set for each step should be reasonably attainable.

(3) *Put the plan in operation.* Monitoring serves as an effective way of observing changes taking place. As with any new habit, initially these new behaviors may seem artificial and forced, but eventually they will become part of you. You will modify them to fit your personal style and go on to the next step. If you can't achieve or maintain the desired success, assume something is wrong with your program. Either the step was too difficult or you and your partner were not really in agreement regarding the goal or the procedure. Discuss it and reformulate.

Adjusting the Sexual Decision-Making Process

Recently Tom and Beth Jones came to consult me because of a sexual problem. What had started out as a happy marriage had in five years turned into a mess. Basic problem: each felt the other made all the decisions about everything from where and when to have sex to termination of coitus. Both felt coerced, but they had never discussed their feelings. Beth told me "I can't talk about sex." Tom echoed Beth.

I had them fill out a quiz on sexual marital responsibility, modeled after the one devised by Richard and Freida Stuart in the *Marital Pre-Counseling Inventory.* When I confronted Beth and Tom with their respective answers, their first reaction was disbelief. Beth said to Tom, "You can't think *I* decide when to have sex. *You* always make the decision." Tom said, "You can't feel I decide when we have sex. *You* always make the decision." They made similar "*You* can't think this—this is the way *I* feel" comments about their answers to all the questions on the quiz. Next they turned into litigants, with each trying to prove his case. I stopped that. Suddenly, they saw a humorous side to their answers, started to laugh, and they went home resolved to change their feelings by first changing their actions. In this case, the major problem was that of communication. Once they defined the problem, they were easily able to take corrective action.

LABORATORY SEXUAL EXERCISE I

Purpose: To determine satisfaction with present sexual decision-making in your marriage.

STEP ONE: Take your AT notebook or a sheet of paper and set up this chart:

Decisions Made About	Who Makes It	Whom You Would Like To Make It	The Difference
A. When to have sex			
B. Takes initiative to start			
C. Where to have sex			
D. Surroundings of sex			
E. Starts coitus			
F. Determines how to have sex play			
G. Determines position for intercourse			
H. Terminates coitus			

STEP TWO: Under the column Who Makes It, indicate who does make the decision (as you see it) about each part of the sex act. Indicate this by using the following scale.

1. Man every single time
2. Almost always man
3. More man than woman
4. Just about equal
5. More woman than man
6. Almost always woman
7. Woman every single time

STEP THREE: In the next column, using the same scale, show whom you would like to make the decision.

STEP FOUR: If the numbers differ, subtract the smallest from the largest and enter in column three. This will give you an indication of the desire of your own satisfaction with your sexual decision-making process. For example, if item A on "When to have sex" shows a 5 ("more woman than man") both in the second and third column, you are satisfied with this state. However, item B, "Takes initiative to start," may show number 7 ("woman every single time") in the second column and number 4 ("just about equal") as whom you would like to make it. Thus if you're female, you see yourself as always taking the initiative and feel dissatisfied because you would like this decision to be equally shared.

The important thing is not who makes the decision, but how satisfied you are with it.

STEP FIVE: Just as you have filled out this chart, your partner should fill out a similar one independently. Do not look at one another's rating until both of you have finished.

STEP SIX: Compare the charts. Discuss any discrepancy of two points or more. If there is a difference in the ratings, don't try to prove your rating is the better one; assume your partner has a reasonable basis for the way he scores it, and try to understand what it is.

If the charts reveal only mild discrepancies, you can start taking necessary action.

A SIMPLE CASE

Rita and Leonard, a young unmarried couple who shared a Soho loft, weren't getting along too well sexually. The decision-making quiz showed they both felt Leonard made the decisions almost always (#2), that he wanted #3 (more man than woman), that Rita wanted #4 (equality). Both agreed she should initiate more sexual activity. Their intercourse, or love-play, pattern averaged three times a week. My assignment: for the next month Rita was to initiate any sex play they had, whether she felt like doing it or not, and strive to do this three times a week. This was hard for Rita. She had her mother's attitude—"It's wrong for a woman to take an active sex role"—and because of this, she had never learned what to do. With Leonard as the coach, she practiced being the initiator and learned to talk sexy, started playful sex play, and just put her arms around him and said, "Now." Within four weeks, Rita had learned these skills well enough so that she could stop treatment. At that time, she was able to initiate sex often enough to satisfy both herself and Leonard.

If you find a marked difference exists between you and your partner concerning one or more of the sexual decisions, you may first have to work on areas with smaller discrepancies, and lead up to the larger one.

Improving the Quality of Your Sexual Relationship

In the following laboratory exercise, you are going to determine the area of sex where improvement is needed and learn how certain techniques of open discussion can help bring about better sex.

Purpose: An assessment of your sexual dissatisfactions and satisfactions.

This is a simple way for you to analyze your own sexual reactions.

STEP ONE: Take your Assertiveness Training workbook or a piece of paper and identify the different aspects and stages of sex as follows:

A. Preliminaries to sex play
B. Sex play
C. Coitus
D. Postcoitus
E. Partner's expression of feeling.

F. Own expression of feelings
G. Frequency of sex play
H. Duration of sex play
I. Frequency of intercourse
J. Duration of intercourse

STEP TWO: Show how satisfying each act is by placing the appropriate number next to each letter. These numbers represent the usual degree of satisfaction you have experienced in the recent past.

0 . . . Terrible
1 . . . Bad
2 . . . Poor

3 . . . OK
4 . . . Great
5 . . . Ecstasy

As you score yourself, in this test adapted from a similar one by Richard B. Stuart, beware of the "halo effect," a common result in ratings of this type. There are two kinds of "halo effects": You have a general overall impression of your sexual satisfaction, and you apply this to every item. Or you let the feelings from one item overflow into the others. For instance, you feel coitus is "terrible" (0), and you let this influence your judgment of sex play—whereas in actuality you may find sex play OK (3). Try to consider each act separately.

STEP THREE: In your AT workbook or on a piece of paper, list three things you can do to make your partner more sexually content. Then list three things your partner can do to make you more sexually content. These should be:

Specific. Do not say, "Should be more loving." State the behaviors that indicate lovingness. Perhaps, "Should say more tender things," or "should kiss me more."

Positive. Do not say, "Should not get out of bed so soon after intercourse." Do say what should be done: "should be closer to me longer after intercourse."

STEP FOUR: Both you and your partner should complete these assignments independently and then compare forms. Sometimes the very recognition of a specific problem will result in a spontaneous discussion, which then leads to changes. In this manner, the situation improves, satisfaction and closeness increase.

STEP FIVE: You may need to structure your discussion. Although it is easy to say "talk about your sexual problems," people have difficulty following the advice because sex is a highly charged, emotional subject. Some of us can't discuss it in a constructive manner, and some of us can't discuss it at all.

Set up a series of three 20-minute scheduled discussions. In these you must obey two ground rules. *Do not bring up the past*—whether something that happened last night or that occurred ten years ago—unless the experience illustrates a *desired* behavior. Do not make *any mention of what you want your partner to stop doing.* Put the emphasis on the specific behaviors you want to increase. Wrong way: "Don't bite me so hard!" Right way: "Bite me more tenderly."

In your discussions utilize the questionnaire as a base. (I am making the assumption that you have difficulty talking about sex and require a step-by-step program.) Each discussion should last no longer than twenty minutes, and you should decide in advance who will talk first. Each partner gets ten minutes. Use a timer. You *must* stop when the bell rings even if it is in the middle of an important sentence. The purpose of this is to prevent the discussion from getting out of hand during the early stage of sex-talk training. The discussion can even last less than the twenty assigned minutes.

First discussion: Partner one describes a minimum of three actions (maximum of six) that partner two can do to improve partner one's sexual experience. During this initial talk partner two's part is simply to comprehend what is wanted. He/she may ask questions and make statements but only for the purpose of clarification. When the first partner finishes or the timer rings, partner two gets his turn and describes the actions he wants.

Second discussion: Partner one reveals his feelings and thoughts about the wants of partner two. A simple OK won't work. He/she must say what he really thinks about each desired behavior change.

If appropriate, he/she can open up about fantasies. At this point, partner two does not argue or challenge. His goal: to understand how partner one feels. Then partner two reveals his thoughts about the desires of partner one. He might say, "It's obvious you want more oral sex during sex play; but I feel uptight about it, and I'm not even sure I like doing it. I'm not sure that in this area I can give you what you want. But you also say you'd like to have intercourse more often with you on top. I'd love to do that."

Third discussion. At this point, both partners should have established some communication and gained knowledge and understanding about the needs and wishes of the other. In this discussion, they plan a course of action. There may be complete agreement. If not, they negotiate or even draw up a sexual contract.

OTHER ACTIVE COMMUNICATION STEPS

Encourage the next step in a positive direction. Nothing is zero. Even if a couple gains satisfaction only from lying quietly and holding each other, that is a starting point. What is the next step that can be taken that leads in the right direction? Think

"What can we do?" rather than "How terrible everything is." Also, stick with the specific.

Limit your discussions about sex to behavior rather than the core of the person. Many people fall into the trap of blaming the person rather than the act. The stabs "You're not woman enough" or "You're not a man" leave the partner helpless, hurt, or increasingly indifferent. But the statement "You seem to worry too much about sex" can lead to the constructive question "What can each of us do to get you to worry less?"

Tell what you like. The simple "I like what you're doing" during sex play can be a very helpful communication. Tell your partner the specific things that he/she can do to excite you—things that actually have been done or that you would like to try. If you have disagreements, discuss them.

Bring the things that bother you out into the open. The occasional phrase "We have a problem," or "I'm sorry about last night," does not accomplish this. Again, discuss the specifics.

A real communications block occurs when one partner simulates climax and the other believes the simulation. Very often a woman will act as if she came to climax and fool her lover. This leads the man to think he's doing the right thing, and as a result, sex doesn't improve. Men also fake climax. They may actually have physical ejaculation, but without experiencing any actual orgiastic feeling along with it. In a close relationship, dishonesty will always keep a couple from resolving their sexual difficulties.

If you've had a lengthy history of sexual difficulty, share it with your mate. At the very least, your revelation may relieve your partner's doubts about his/her sexuality and so take some of the tension out of the situation. It will also help determine the next step.

Pay attention to what you can do *differently.* Ask yourself "What can I do to make my mate less anxious? What can I do to make sex more exciting for my partner? . . . For me?" Don't fall into the trap of, "He should be different," or "She should resolve her hang-up." These accusations cannot lead to constructive actions.

Practice nonverbal teaching. Showing how may be worth thousands of words. For example, most men do not know how to stimulate the clitoris. They tend to play with the top, whereas the majority of women prefer stroking along the sides of it. Guide your partner's hand. Move it in a way that pleases you, showing him where to go, how much pressure to apply, the rhythm you like. Then add verbal cues, "gentler," "stronger," "faster," "slower," as he repeats the motion.

Increasing the Frequency of Sex

Many people want change in many sexual behaviors—particularly in the frequency of sexual contact. It helps when both partners agree to attempt a change even though they differ on the ultimate goal.

How often do you have sex?

How often would you like to have sex?

To determine this *you must define what you mean by sex,* distinguishing between sexual intercourse and sex play without intercourse.

The distinction is major. Many people believe that all sex play must lead to intercourse or at least to climax. Thus, if for any reason at some time they are incapable of intercourse or achieving a climax, they avoid all sex play. In that way they deprive both themselves and their partners of a potentially satisfying and enjoyable experience. This insistence on intercourse may actually interfere with increasing the frequency of it.

To increase frequency of intercourse, you must first *find out how often you actually have it.* In such a sensitive area as sex, it is easy to distort what actually happens. You must check reality.

LABORATORY SEXUAL EXERCISE III

Purpose: Record-keeping so that you will know at a glance when you had different kinds of sexual activities, what they were, and how frequently they occurred each week.

STEP ONE: Buy a good-sized calendar, preferably one where each day is printed in its own box; the boxes make for clarity as you annotate. It should provide plenty of space for record-keeping and have fairly wide margins. You will be using the right-hand margin to record weekly totals.

STEP TWO: Use the following code to note the sexual behaviors that actually take place.

P . . . means sex play took place.

C . . . means sex play took place where one or both partners reached climax

I . . . means intercourse took place that day. It assumes the intercourse was preceded by sex play.

STEP THREE: On days when sex behavior occurs, put the appropriate symbol in the upper right hand corner for that day. If more than one sexual contact takes place, place a second symbol beneath the first.

STEP FOUR: At the week's conclusion, mark the totals for each act on the margin of the calendar. To get a good sample of this behavior, keep this record for four weeks.

For example, during the first week, Mark and Mary had sexual intercourse twice and sex play without climax once, for a total of three sexual experiences. During week two there were also three sexual experiences—one of each kind. Within week three there were four sexual contacts: sex play without climax twice, sex play with climax once, intercourse once. In this week Mark and Mary had two sexual experiences on a Saturday.

I asked them, "How do you account for the Saturday sexual experiences?" This led to a specific explanation, one they both knew but had never verbalized. On Saturday mornings their twelve-year-old boy and ten-year-old girl left the house early for club activities. They had no "must" duties, so after the children's departure, they frequently made love. They had never fully realized how frequently this occurred or the implications: Mary felt more comfortable having sex with the children out of the house, and Mark had more sexual desire on a weekend morning, when he was more relaxed and rested.

The very recognition of these feelings led to change. Mark and Mary started to go out of town occasionally for weekends—minus the children. The fact that both knew sex was the main reason for the mini-vacation added excitement. "It makes me feel delightfully wicked," Mary said.

By making up and keeping a chart, you can begin to get a clearer picture of things you want to change.

In deciding about frequency of sex, you may find yourself hindered by some psychological obstacles. As my patients do, you may ask these questions:

"What is normal frequency?" We have been brought up to entertain such doubts about our sexual adequacy, such fears of deviant behavior, that to be either above or below "normal" frequency emerges as a threat. Normal frequency depends on your physical health and condition, age, your feeling for your partner and the kind of relationship you have, your immediate surroundings and general life-style, and a host of other variables. You cannot determine what is normal, so forget about normalcy and *do what you want.*

"How do I know how often I want sex? In my fantasies there is constant intercourse, and I know I'm not capable of that." This is where record-keeping ties you to reality. Last week you had intercourse four times. Would you like to stay at that level or increase it? Try it out and see what really satisfies you. You won't really know until you determine it in action.

"What is the point of deciding what I want? My partner won't go along with me." As with many other entities in the close relationship, the needs and desires of each partner may differ. You may not get what you want, but remember that active discussion is better than passive acceptance of the unsatisfactory.

"How do you get from too little to more sex?" One AT technique: to use the method of successive approximations, which involves both setting dates for sex and keeping records.

CASE

Thirty-five-year-old Roy and thirty-year-old Peggy, married for six years and with no children (nor any desired at this point), wanted to increase the frequency of intercourse. Their marital difficulties came to a head when Peggy discovered that Roy had had several brief affairs with other women. He claimed this was because he continually felt frustrated. "Peggy and I rarely have sexual relations," he told me. Peggy complained that Roy hounded her constantly about sex.

At the time we were working on other problems in

treatment, but we did determine their sexual frequency by using the calendar method for four weeks. The record showed that during the first two weeks Roy and Peggy had intercourse once, and during the second two weeks, they had intercourse twice and sex play with climax once (she brought him to climax manually). They could not agree on a frequency goal. He wanted sex three to four times a week and once was more than enough for her.

We used the method of successive approximation in the form of sex dates. Each week they were to have at least one "date" for sex and more if both wanted it. Each date had to be set twenty-four hours in advance and the time chosen with discretion. For example, they were not to set a date when he knew he had to work overtime and would come home late. The aim of the date was not intercourse, but sex play: touching, caressing, talking intimately about sex with each other. They drew up a special contract about intercourse, made necessary by Peggy's feelings of being sexually exploited and Roy's actual exploitation of her. The aim: for Roy to arouse Peggy so she would want intercourse. Contract provisions:

· There was to be no attempt at intercourse unless Peggy said aloud, "I want you." If she did not wish intercourse, she was to offer no reasons or apologies. However, at breakfast the following morning, she was to tell Roy two specific things he might have done—or done more of—that might have made her want intercourse. She was not to utter one word about what he did wrong.

· If there were no intercourse, but sex play occurred, every other time (if Roy wanted it) she was to bring him to climax either manually or orally (the choice was hers). The purpose of this every-other-time rule was to begin changing their notion that *all* sex play must lead to climax. There was one exception to this rule: on an unscheduled time, if she strongly wanted to bring him to climax, this was permitted.

Because of the exercise two things happened. Roy became more sensitive to Peggy's sexual needs. He ceased to exploit her. As he changed, Peggy began to feel less exploited, stood up for her sexual rights, instead of withdrawing from sex, and began to derive enormous pleasure from exciting Roy. Both became more respectful of each other and closeness grew.

At the end of two months, while they still had many problems to resolve, Roy had relinquished his one-night stands, and sex was occurring spontaneously with such frequency that they no longer felt the need for preset dates.

If you use the successive approximation method to increase sexual frequency, keep your aim in mind: a series of successes.

· Set the dates in advance at a frequency level just slightly higher than your current sexual action.

· Increase the number of dates in small steps. Don't set too many and find you can't keep them. It can be as small an increase as one date every three weeks.

· The aim of the date is sexual contact, not necessarily intercourse.

· Use the previously described calendar method to keep records.

· When you achieve the desired frequency, continue the scheduling and record-keeping for several additional weeks.

· If at some point you start to backslide, start scheduling dates again.

SEXUAL TALK

In intimate communication words can have an effect beyond pure instruction or praise. By proving exciting in themselves, they can increase the sharing of feeling.

You can use specific words to improve your sexual life in three ways:

(1) *Utilize words to share your tender feelings* such as the very basic, "I love you."

(2) *Use words with the purpose of arousing each other.* These range from simple words, like "great" and "wonderful," to calling attention to body reactions, with "I'm trembling" . . . "Look how hard you made me," or telling your feelings, "I'm exploding" . . . "You drive me mad."

Some words or phrases can be exciting in themselves. Words like "prick" or "cunt," or sentences containing them, may intensify the sexual experience. Using these words to ask for something or to describe what you're doing can excite. For example, "Suck on my prick," or "Your cock feels so big in my cunt," can add an extra dimension to your sex life.

If you object to these words and phrases, substitute what appeals to you. Some people are turned on by the assignment of names to different parts of the anatomy, and by treating the parts as individuals and friends. "Hi there, Johnny" says the wife to the husband's penis. "I'm glad to see you again. Let me kiss you hello." Some people develop a language all their own.

Such a use of sex language does more than increase your excitement. Expressed between husband and wife, this sort of conversation shuts out the rest of the world and brings the two of you closer.

(3) *Practice after-sharing.* Talk and reminisce about your sexual experiences, just as you do about other shared activities. Also talk about ways you might experiment. The simple statement "I hear a lot of talk about vibrators . . . I'd like to try one sometime" may lead to a new area of sexual activity.

Share your fantasies with your partner. This can lead to greater intimacy and new sources of enjoyment.

· If you don't have sexual fantasies, train yourself to develop them. Make up one a day. Then try to make them longer and more exciting (popular fantasy situations: sex in a Paris bordello, working as a prostitute, having a harem, wearing sensuous clothing, being overpowered). At first your fantasies may be wooden, but there is the chance that eventually they will become imaginative and spontaneous.

· If you experience anxiety about revealing your fantasies or your partner seems tense about hearing them, tell them in easy stages. First, give the general outline, and gradually disclose more of the details. As you become comfortable, you should be able to share the complete fantasy.

CASE

A woman came to me with a case of partial frigidity. She could not achieve climax during intercourse. She told me of her favorite masturbation fantasy in which she became a young Polynesian girl who services an entire shipload of sailors. The patient thought that if she used the fantasy during intercourse, she would be able to have an orgasm. But she felt doing this would mean "disloyalty to my husband."

At my urging, she told him her South Sea Island fantasy. To her surprise, he encouraged her to use it during intercourse, and it did bring on a climax. Furthermore, he added improvements—for example, during sex he started talking like one of the crew members. Engrossed in the play-acting, he continued it long after she no longer needed the fantasy to achieve climax.

By changing a sexual behavior, you can change your life and, thus, make your total life and personality happier. Like this woman, you, too, can take an active approach to sex. If you can't experiment with all the AT ideas I've advanced here, try one—and then a second one. It may change your life. But as you work toward the goal of deepest intimacy in the close relationship, remember one thing: the greatest aphrodisiac of all is love.

Chapter VII
Assertiveness Through Self-Control

In *The Odyssey*, Homer tells how after winning the battle of Troy, Ulysses and his crew set sail for home. Their route to Ithaca would take them past the Isle of the Sirens, home of those heartless creatures, half-woman, half-bird, who enticed sailors ashore with enchanting music for the purpose of devouring them. Warned by the sexy Circe of his prospective fate, Ulysses decided to circumvent almost certain death. He put wax in the ears of all the crew members, leaving his own unplugged so only he would hear the sirens' song as the ship neared the island. He did take the precaution of having the sailors lash him firmly to the mast. Thus, Ulysses managed to lead the ship past the lethal sirens and save the lives of himself and all his men.

Ulysses accomplished this mythological feat via two actions that in modern psychological parlance are known as *stimulus removal* and *response prevention*. When a dieter keeps food out of sight, he practices stimulus removal. When he padlocks the refrigerator door so he can't get at the food, he exercises response prevention.

You can modify, control, and change your own behavior. By using a series of behavioral techniques you can arrange the contingencies (chances of things happening), activities, rewards, even punishments so that your behavior becomes what you want it to be. Even if a bad habit has become a lifetime personal trademark, you can get rid of it. You can exchange undesired behaviors for desired behaviors.

In changing your own behavior you become truly assertive.

For mastery over self, which is often termed self-control or willpower, is an important part of assertion.

When you perform an act which wins you your own self-respect, your own self-esteem increases. In equation form this means:

Desired behavior → Satisfaction → Increased self-esteem

Conversely, when you procrastinate, overeat, or perform any act which causes you to lose self-respect, your self-esteem dips. In Chapter I, I discussed the formula, Assertion = Self-Esteem. Self-regulatory behaviors must be considered part of assertion, for to be truly assertive you must be in command of yourself.

It is difficult to know how to take action about such vague phrases as "in command of yourself," "to possess willpower." However, if you analyze these terms, you will discover that all they really imply is a series of specific habits that may concern anything from the amount of food you eat to the unsatisfactory way you work. Almost any habit can be changed, eliminated, or learned. Very often the trick is to identify the specific habit you want to change. Once you know what it is, you may be able to change it just by telling yourself to do so. Effecting change in other bad habits may prove far more difficult and require a complex training program. Realize that altering even a trivial bad habit (like putting away your clothes before you go to bed instead of throwing them on a chair) gives you the good feeling of being in control of yourself.

B. F. Skinner, who is Edgar Pierce Professor of Psychology Emeritus at Harvard University, and perhaps the most influential of living psychologists, writes "It is of little help to tell a man to use his 'willpower' or his 'self-control.' He does not know what to do. By considering the specific components that make up the thing we call 'self-control,' we do have the practical advantage of knowing what measures to take in the attempt to change them."

WHY YOU FAIL WITH SELF-CONTROL

Changing your relationship to yourself is just as important as changing yourself to improve your relations with others. Other people don't care about many of your behaviors. They don't have real concern about the state of your bureau drawers, whether you weigh fifteen pounds too much, or waste your leisure time. But your control of your own habits matters very much to *you*. Bad habits can create such anxiety that they influence your moods, your feelings about yourself, your life-style.

Why can't you simply change bad habits into good ones by making the decision to do it?

You fail because you have never learned the skills of self-change. You cannot do what you don't know how to do—and this lack of knowledge may keep you from trying. People often rationalize their inability to change by believing the unwanted behavior satisfies some unconscious need.

You fail because you are passive. You don't like the behavior, but you do not try to change it. This lack of action increases your feeling of helplessness.

You fail because you have not learned the concept of willpower. The term "use willpower" signifies that you possess some control over your actions if only you would exercise it. But there's a disadvantage to the term: it doesn't tell you what it is you have to do. Willpower can serve as the focal point of self-change only if you make *action* a corollary.

CASE

Frank Edwards, a forty-year-old business executive at the middle-management level, came to me with the problem of "procrastination." He did brilliant work, but never handed it in until months after the due date. As a result, he had continually been passed over for promotion and always felt tense and depressed.

For over twenty years, Frank had tried varying kinds of treatment to overcome this problem. Six months of behavior therapy helped no more than analysis or hypnosis.

In the middle of one session when Frank was talking about the tension he felt because a report was overdue, I turned to him and said, "Look, you know you're quite capable of finishing that report. Make yourself do it. Use willpower."

I went on to explain to Frank that he had the wrong concept about life. He had the idea that without any *new* behavior on his part, the right behavior would suddenly emerge. He thought he could maintain his essentially passive attitude, and still somehow get the work done on time. "Willpower," I defined, "means that it is *up to you,* not some outer circumstance or inner force. You have to *make things happen*—in this case finish the report that's due in three weeks."

Frank was startled, and said, "In over twenty years of therapy, nobody has ever told me to use willpower. I may as well try it." The term "willpower" oriented Frank to take control of his own life—in this case to hand in the report on time. He didn't find it easy to complete the report, but *he did it.* Frank's new understanding of the word "willpower" and the action he took because of it proved the turning point in his treatment.

THE THEORY OF BEHAVIOR CHANGE

To understand how to add the "how" to "willpower," you must comprehend the work of B. F. Skinner.

Whereas Pavlov was interested in processes that went on *inside* the person (such as changes in the nervous system), Skinner stresses that the crucial relationship occurs between the person and his surroundings. A person *emits* a behavior. This behavior *operates* on the environment (the world around you). In other words, the behavior has consequences, and according to Skinner, behavior "is shaped and maintained by its consequences." It is these consequences, which Skinner calls "reinforcement," that determine the probability that a human being will repeat his behavior. The consequences—events that occur *immediately* after you perform a certain act—will affect behavior in one of three ways:

(1) *Reinforcement. The consequences make the behavior stronger and more apt to be performed again.* This happens under two conditions:

(a) *The consequence can be that something is added to the situation.* This is called *positive reinforcement.* Usually reward is thought of as a synonym for positive reinforcement. It can take the form of material things like money, gifts, food. The reward can be a social reinforcer like praise, attention, affection, love. Or it can be your own inner feelings of joy or satisfaction.

Many people misinterpret the term positive reinforcement

and think it has to be something good. All positive reinforcers are not rewards. The consequence of your behavior may be that your spouse yells at you or you yourself feel anxiety. If these consequences fortify and strengthen the behavior that immediately preceded them, they must be considered positive reinforcers. They have been *added* to the situation.

In changing your self-control behavior, this becomes an important point. If you want to change a specific habit, seek out the positive reinforcers that maintain your unwanted behavior and remove them. In looking for these reinforcers, do not limit yourself to those that are pleasant or rewarding. Any consequence following the behavior may provide the reinforcement. If you remove it, you weaken the behavior.

Any response a mother makes to her child's behavior—whether it takes the form of sympathetic attention or yelling—can provide positive reinforcement. Sometimes the reinforcers can be extremely subtle. One patient had the compulsive habit of overspending in restaurants. We had difficulty in determining the reinforcers that maintained this extravagance until he recalled, "Every time I do it, my wife gets a momentary look of annoyance." Consciously, Herb did not want to annoy her, and when she deliberately controlled this reaction (on my instruction), his overspending behavior decreased. Hence the principle for recognizing the reinforcers of unwanted behaviors: if target behavior eventually decreases when you stop adding a particular consequence to a situation, then that consequence was the reinforcer.

(b) *The consequence can be that something is subtracted* from the situation. *This is called negative reinforcement.* People mistakenly think of negative as something bad happening, confusing it with punishment. In Skinner's terms, negative means minus—something has been removed from the situation, and thus increases or maintains your behavior. For example, you fall behind in your work at the office, and your supervisor criticizes you. When you catch up with your work, he stops criticizing. The consequence of your catching up with assignments is the subtraction of the boss's saying, "What's the matter with you?" Thus negative reinforcement maintains or increases your better work behavior. The unpleasant consequence has been removed.

Negative reinforcement maintains much self-control behavior. But, as with any reinforcement, it can work in two ways—good and bad. Let's take the instance of two men who hate to pay bills. Both feel extremely pressured by the huge pile and find this feeling most unpleasant.

One man may go to his desk, sit down, and write out checks to Internal Revenue, Consolidated Edison, and Jason Realty, and send them off. This act takes away the feeling of pressure. In the future, he is more apt to pay his bills. The bad feeling has been subtracted. He will gain a good feeling about his bill-paying action, which will further strengthen the habit and his own self-esteem.

Another man may start to watch TV to get away from the bill-paying situation. This, too, takes away the feeling of pressure, but it maintains the bad habit of procrastination. If he actually enjoys the TV show, he makes this behavior of procrastination even stronger, equating it with a feeling of satisfaction. But he will feel unhappy with himself for procrastination, and his self-esteem will go down.

(2) *Extinction—when a behavior has no consequence, that behavior weakens and eventually disappears from the behavioral repertory.* If you tell a joke and nobody laughs or responds in any way, you are less likely to tell that joke in the future.

To have no reinforcement is the only way to extinguish a given behavior. If you have a bad habit and can identify and remove the reinforcers, your behavior will stop. If you use this extinction technique, technically known as *withdrawal of reinforcement*, keep four things in mind:

(a) The first result may be an actual increase in the very behavior you want to extinguish. This is often followed by a sharp decrease in the behavior. Just remember that extinction takes time.

(b) If you use extinction, your bad habit behavior must *never* be reinforced. Allow even a rare reinforcement and you make the behavior more difficult to extinguish. Even a single reinforcement can have a strong effect.

(c) Once you have extinguished the behavior, it may return *if the reinforcement contingencies change.* If you have gotten rid of a bad habit and it begins to come back, look for changed consequences to that habit. You will probably find that you have reestablished old reinforcers or developed new reinforcers.

(d) Sometimes you extinguish *desired* habits through the inadvertent removal of reinforcers. By restoring the original reinforcers, you can restore the desired habit.

CASE

"I used to be very good about saving money, but suddenly I'm not," Marty Wilden said to me, in one of our treatment sessions. I investigated what the reinforcements were that had previously maintained Marty's saving behavior. He told me that for many years he would go every Friday at lunchtime to the savings bank near his office and make a deposit. The tellers were generally pretty, young women who would smile, say a warm "thank you," and sometimes even flirt a little with him. Then Marty accepted a new job three miles away from this particular savings bank. He began to mail in his deposits. Suddenly he stopped saving. To reestablish the reinforcers, and to restore the desired, now-extinguished behavior of saving money on a weekly basis, I had Marty transfer his account to a bank near his new office. Here again the tellers were pretty, polite, and flirtatious. Marty now makes his Friday noontime trip and saves his money.

(3) *Punishment*—the suppression of behavior. This occurs under conditions that are directly the opposite of reinforcement. Either a positive reinforcement is taken away from the situation or an unpleasant consequence is added to it *immediately following the behavior. In other words, something good stops happening or something bad starts to happen.*

Punishment does not extinguish the unwanted behavior (only removal of reinforcement can do that), but merely suppresses it. Remove the punishment and the behavior tends to recur. Hence, punishment proves a rather ineffective way of changing habits. Use it, and as the unwanted behavior starts to reemerge, you will have to use punishment to suppress it again. You will have to give yourself a constant series of booster shots.

Under one circumstance, punishment may prove extremely

effective: the suppression of the habit allows for the development of an alternate behavior. You punish the unwanted behavior, substitute the alternate behavior, and strengthen it.

CASE

A psychiatric resident I was training felt upset because he was putting on too much weight. Chuck analyzed his own behavior and narrowed the problem to compulsive dessert eating. Unfortunately, Chuck could never reinforce the non-dessert-eating behavior, because he never performed it. He decided to use punishment to suppress his passion for high-calorie sweets.

Chuck made up a list of organizations he really hated (like the Ku Klux Klan), wrote out a series of checks for twenty-five dollars, and also wrote covering letters, explaining his contribution was to "help keep up the good work." He gave the collection of letters and checks to another resident with the instructions, "I'll call every morning to report that I didn't eat dessert the night before. If I don't call, assume I've slipped and mail off the first letter—and just keep on with the procedure."

Because he hated these organizations, Chuck controlled his behavior for two weeks. Then he ate two pieces of apple pie for dinner, did not make his morning phone call, and his friend promptly sent off Chuck's first letter with its contribution to the Ku Klux Klan.

It worked. Chuck told me, "Through that letter to the Ku Klux Klan, I got on the mailing list of a whole series of 'hate' organizations. Now, every time I see a dessert, I also think of this terrible 'hate' mail."

Remember, the only way to increase a behavior is to reinforce it. The only way to get rid of a behavior is to extinguish it. Punishment has only certain limited uses.

Lack of Reinforcement Control

One special behavioral situation exists in which you have *no control over your reinforcements.* For instance, the child with an irrational mother never knows whether his behavior will be reinforced, ignored, or punished. There is no relationship between what he does and the consequences that follow. Another example might be the employee with the erratic boss. A superb piece of work wins him praise one day, no attention the next. In this and similar situations, victims learn to feel helpless about what happens to them. They are not in control of their reinforcers. Some theorists maintain that this "learned helplessness" serves as the greatest inducer of depression.

Interestingly enough, this fits in with one of the psychoanalytic theories of depression, advanced by Dr. Edward Bibring. Dr. Bibring places as a central core of depression the awareness of the ego that it is helpless and powerless, and he traces this back to early childhood trauma. Whether due to childhood trauma or not, the unassertive person does tend to feel helpless and powerless, and depression follows. As he becomes more assertive, he gains a "learned competency" and thus relieves the depression.

Discriminative Stimuli

Let's say, you have a pigeon in a box. If a red light flashes, the pigeon presses a bar and receives food. The pigeon soon learns to press the bar when the red light goes on. If a white light flashes and the pigeon presses a bar, he gets no food. With the white light on, he gets food only if he makes a circle. So the pigeon learns to discriminate between the two situations. He learns that when the red light goes on and he presses the bar, he will be reinforced with food. He learns that when the white light flashes, he will get his food only if he turns in a circle. The different response to lights is called *discrimination*. The lights themselves are *discriminative stimuli. They signal which behavior will be reinforced.*

Adult human beings spend much of their lives under the influence of discriminative stimuli. They signal which of your behaviors will have consequences—be reinforced or punished. In this way, you learn to behave differently in different situations. You learn a series of discriminative stimuli that signal you that if you shout at a ball game, you will receive reinforcement in some way, like feeling part of the crowd or having the person in the seat next to you start a friendly conversation. In this same manner, you have absorbed a series of discriminative stimuli that signal you that if you shout in church you will be punished by glares, disapproving looks, and instructions to "be quiet." So you shout at the ball game and remain quiet in church.

You get into trouble if you have learned the wrong S^Ds (Skinner's symbol for discriminative stimuli) for behavior. If you equate the very *sight* of food—a cake in a pastry shop window, a bowl of potato chips on the table—as an S^D to eat, you probably are overweight, have trouble dieting, and tell yourself you lack willpower.

Inappropriate S^Ds can dominate your life. A work or study situation can contain S^Ds that signal talking on the phone with friends will make you feel good. So you talk with friends—a behavior that is incompatible with working or studying. Soon, you berate yourself for being lazy, procrastinating, and possessing other poor work habits. The difference is not in your behavior or the reinforcements, but in the cues to which you respond. To establish self-control you may have to change the S^Ds.

You'll notice that I have not referred to the unconscious, emotional conflicts, or instinctual drives. Skinner is not concerned with these. He maintains that understanding of the interaction between the individual and the environment is enough to change behavior. He points out that science did not advance as long as pre-Galilean scientists were trying to figure out what went on *inside* falling stones as they responded to gravity. Science didn't advance until Galileo considered only *outside* forces acting on stone and thus determined that all falling bodies, whatever their weights, fell at the same rate.

Starting in the 1930s, Skinner formulated a science of behavior based on the relationship between the frequency of behavior and its consequences. Eventually he found that by controlling reinforcement, he could even teach pigeons such a complicated act as playing Ping-Pong.

Skinner is concerned with behavior that "operates upon the environment to produce effects," and he calls this behavior "operant behavior." When the pigeons' operant behavior fulfilled Skinner's demands, he (positively) reinforced them with food. He controlled their behavior by setting up "contingencies of reinforcement"—circumstances under which a particular bit of desired behavior is reinforced or rewarded to make sure it will be repeated. It is interesting to note that not only is it more humane to train animals, children, or people through rewarding desired behavior rather than through punishing undesired behavior but it is also more effective.

Skinner thus proved that behavior could be modified in a predictable way, purely by controlling the external consequences of that behavior and without any reference to what goes on inside the animal. He and others have shown that human behavior can be shaped in the same predictable way. The proponents of Skinner maintain that all behaviors are subject to those consequences.

His opponents say "people aren't pigeons." They believe Skinner's approach is limited, and ignores the behaviors that are unique to human beings—especially the areas involving thinking (so influenced by man's ability to use language) and conation (a psychological term which concerns impulse, desire, volition, and purposive striving).

Whether Skinner is right or wrong about all behaviors, you can certainly apply his techniques of reinforcement, extinction, and punishment to improve your self-control habits. If you do not like the way you behave, do not blame yourself for lacking willpower, self-discipline, or drive. Consider these to be habits. Decide what changes you want to effect, and deliberately embark on a program to carry these out.

Chapter VIII
A Guide to Changing Habits

How can you create new improved habits and break old bad habits?

Is it possible to start showing up on time for appointments when all your life you have arrived for everything one half hour late?

Can you learn to diet successfully when your record shows continual failure with food resistance?

Can you make the switch from being extravagant to saving money?

Many kinds of habits exist in human beings. Some are personal, such as lack of neatness, uncontrolled nail-biting, or the unwanted habit of extreme tenseness. Some concern work, such as procrastination, chronic lateness, and the inability to concentrate. Others are social. These include sarcasm, clowning, or even the inability to remember names.

Whatever the habit, to ensure change you must follow these six steps.

I: Identify the habit you want to change.

This essential procedure also includes the identification of the conditions under which the behavior (lack of studying, sloppiness, for example) occurs. Through changing these conditions, you can gain control and thus change the behavior in the desired direction.

(1) *Pinpoint the behaviors involved in your undesired habit.* Unless you know the exact behaviors you want to change, you will

experience difficulty changing them. Rule: *Express the behaviors in such a way that you can count or measure them.*

For example, twenty-nine-year-old David Martin came to me with the bad habit of sloppiness. His untidiness had reached the point that he never invited friends to visit his apartment and loathed going there himself. David wanted to "become neat," but "being neat" consists of many behaviors. I had David keep notes for a week, and here are some of the specific behaviors that he noted:

> Didn't make his bed before leaving the house
> Left the dirty dishes from the night before on the dining table
> Scattered his underwear, socks, shirts, papers, haphazardly in drawers, so that he could never locate anything with ease
> Littered his bathroom sink with shaving cream and toothpaste

Once David knew the precise behaviors involved, he was able to set up a course of action to establish the habit of neatness. Useful technique: follow yourself around with a notebook for a week. Every time you come across something in the habit category you want to change, write it down. Remember it is easier to learn to make your bed before you leave the house than it is to "become neat."

(2) *Measure the pinpointed behavior to see how often it occurs before you plan your program.* This "before" phase will tell you where you started so that you can check your progress later. There are a number of ways to count: the frequency with which the behavior occurs, the rate at which it occurs in a given time, the duration of the behavior.

(3) *Study your chain of behavior.* You may not be able to control the final act, but this doesn't just happen out of the blue. It is usually preceded by a series of acts. It may be possible to change a habit at the beginning or midpoint of the chain before it begins to gather momentum.

CASE

When I first saw Stan Block, he revealed that he was a compulsive gambler who had tried everything from therapy to

Gamblers Anonymous in an effort to get control of his horseplaying addiction.

Stan had a pattern. Every morning as he dressed, he promised himself, "Today I won't bet." Over breakfast, he repeated the vow to his wife. On the way to his office, or over coffee on weekends, he went through the newspaper, eventually reaching the sports section. There he read about the horseracing and began to think about the different horses that might win, place, or draw. The sense of urgency built up until, just before track time, it got out of control, and Stan, using every cent he could lay his hands on, would place a bet.

I wondered if it would be easier to intervene earlier in the chain than the final act of the actual gambling, so I asked Stan if he could stop reading the morning newspaper. He stopped. The gambling stopped, too, and the loan sharks disappeared from his life. Dissatisfied, Mrs. Block telephoned me regularly. "But, Doctor," she said, "Stan still doesn't understand why he gambled. He has no insights." She felt without insights the problem would return. I did a three-year follow-up. Stan hadn't placed a single bet. For his daily newspaper he uses the *Wall Street Journal*, which lacks a sports section.

II: Make a contract of intention that you want to change your behavior. Do this either with yourself or someone else.

(1) *This statement of intention must be extremely specific.* To vow "I will study harder" is too vague. How can you count or really measure this? To say "I will study two hours a day" is better. You can count the number of days when you do study those two hours. Even "I will get to work on time" may be too vague. Is getting there just two minutes late being on time? How about ten minutes late? What if you arrive late and your supervisor doesn't notice? It is far better to state something specific, such as "I will arrive at the office each morning no later than nine o'clock." Even that "will arrive" may be unclear. Does that mean the time you arrived at the lobby of the building . . . punched in . . . sat down at your desk?

This underscores the necessity of pinpointing the various behaviors involved in "not procrastinating," "being more orderly," "dressing better," "making better use of my time."

Without a specific statement of intention, it becomes easy to
fool yourself into believing you have carried out this vow. Dr.
Allen Marlatt, of the University of Washington, and Dr. Burt
E. Kaplan, of the University of South Florida, found this to be
true when they studied the carrying out of New Year's
resolutions. The vaguer the resolution, the more apt it was to
be reported as fulfilled. It is easier to believe you "are more in
tune with the world" than to believe you have lost ten pounds
when the scale shows you have gained three pounds. *Write
down the intention so you cannot change it inadvertently.*

(2) *Tell your intention to another person or, preferably, show it in
written form to this person, who ideally should be in a position to monitor
the change.* If you want to change office behavior, reveal what
you want to do to a fellow worker, not to a friend who bowls
with you on Tuesday nights. If it concerns bowling, tell it to
someone who bowls with you, and not to that nice man in the
mimeograph room. Be specific. He can't know if you've
"stopped thinking evil thoughts"; he can note if you finish an
assignment on time.

Caution: The friend should not reinforce the intention with
praise. Nor should you praise yourself for having the intention.
However, don't go to the opposite extreme and express your
intention to someone who would disapprove, thus making it
harder for you to develop future intentions.

(3) *Set as your intention something you can accomplish in the near
future.* The promise, made on Christmas Day, that "I will never
again get drunk at an office Christmas party" does not prove a
good working contract because the opportunity to carry it out
is too far off.

(4) *Aim for a series of successes.* Select a behavior where you
have a strong chance of success and work on that. Your success
will make it easier for you to take action on other behaviors
and simpler for you to formulate new intentions as a basis for
self-change projects. For instance, you procrastinate about
household chores. It's unrealistic to tell yourself "I must spend
all day Saturday working around the house." Set up a series of
goals: (a) to work around the house for one hour on Saturday
morning; (b) when that habit is set, your goal becomes to work
around the house for two hours on Saturday morning; (c) then

two hours in the morning and two hours in the afternoon. Continue this pattern until you accomplish your objective.

III: Examine the situation to see if you can make the unwanted act harder to perform and the desired act easier to perform.

(1) *Control the stimuli that set off the undesired behavior.* This is what Ulysses did when he put wax in the ears of his crew so that they could not hear the enchanting song; he made the stimulus ineffective.

Often the physical arrangements of the area where you function send out the wrong message.

(a) If you do not have sufficient closet and drawer space, the physical situation may send out the cue that keeping clothes and accessories neat is a problem, and neatness behavior will not be reinforced. Hence, you are less likely to rearrange your closet and straighten your drawers.

(b) If a student tries to study physics, while his kid brother watches TV in the same room, he may get the discriminative stimulus that tells him that he, too, would get pleasure from seeing the program (positive reinforcement) or that watching the program would take away the pressure of learning about Boyle's Law (negative reinforcement). So he stops studying physics and settles down to TV.

Rearrange your environment so that you eliminate cues for unwanted behavior and strengthen cues for the wanted behavior. For instance, adding additional closet and drawer space may start sending out S^Ds that neatness behavior will be easier to perform. Doing homework alone in a room without a TV set removes the undesirable stimulus of the TV set. The S^Ds for study become dominant.

(2) *Prevent the unwanted response.* Often you cannot control the stimulus, but by rearranging the environment, you can keep the unwanted response from occurring. For instance, a writer had the habit of telephoning friends instead of working. His solution: every morning he locked the dial of the phone and presented his wife with the key. She would unlock it at 2 PM, the time he usually finished his day's stint. Eventually, he no longer required the lock and key and felt proud of his "improved self-control."

(3) *Suppress the unwanted behavior by using self-punishment.* I reiterate that punishment is not usually an effective technique for changing behavior. Far better to effect it through reinforcement or withdrawal of reinforcement. However, sometimes the desired behavior never shows, or you cannot reinforce it because the bad habit is so strong, or you cannot uncover the reinforcers that maintain your bad habit, and thus cannot extinguish it. In these circumstances, punishment may help.

It may also prove useful if you need an *immediate* change in behavior. Perhaps your unwanted habit may lead to losing your job unless you bring it into line right away. In this case, punishment may serve as the only possible technique. Remember it must be strong, and administered right after you perform the unwanted behavior.

CASE

Because of Alan Wood's lack of politeness with customers, he had lost three jobs, and felt he was about to get fired from his new one as a salesman in a department store. With a mortgage payment due, he had to get his bad habit under control right away.

So I devised a punishment technique. I told Alan to go to a novelty store and buy a little gadget that resembled a cigarette lighter, but, in actuality, when pressed, delivered a rather strong electric shock. Its primary use was playing practical jokes on people, but I had another purpose in mind. Alan kept this gadget in one of his jacket pockets. Every time he became aware that he said anything that a customer might consider rude, he reached into his pocket, squeezed the gadget, and administered the electric shock to himself. The shock was fairly strong. Within a few days Alan noticed a change in his behavior. In a few more days he started to receive reinforcement for this change from his supervisor and fellow workers, and this strengthened his polite behavior. His customers also helped reinforce him. After about a week, Alan rarely had to use the shocker, but he kept it in his pocket for a while. "Just knowing it's there keeps me from being rude," he told me.

(4) *Shape the desired behavior.* If you have trouble coming up immediately with the desired behavior you want, start where

you are and gradually change to where you want to go. Sometimes the "warm-up" technique accomplishes this. For example, a copywriter had the problem of starting work. For her warm-up exercise, she chose to file all her copy from the day before. She got so involved with reading over what she had written and thinking of how she could improve her next draft that she could easily begin that day's work.

A student may find it easier to start studying math rather than history, or vice versa. An executive may find it easier to commence the day's work with a conference or dictation because of the social stimuli these situations provide, rather than organizing a year-end report.

Warning: Stay with each step only until you can go on to the next one. If you remain with an early step too long, you may get stuck there.

IV: Discover what consequences of your unwanted behavior serve to reinforce it. You must search out the immediate consequences of the act (but they do not have to be "pleasant" ones). Whatever they are, assume they are the reinforcers.

Always consider the immediate consequence. The dieter complains about the negative consequences of overeating. She doesn't want to wear a half size instead of size 10. Knowing this, why don't the unpleasant consequences repress her huge caloric intake? They don't because she gets such a momentary feeling of enjoyment or relief from tension when she devours that platter of meatballs and spaghetti that she forgets the end result—fat.

In theory we know:

· *A behavior followed by reinforcement (whether negative or positive) leads to an increase in that behavior.*

· *A behavior followed by a punishment leads to a decrease in that behavior.*

What happens when a behavior is first followed by a reinforcing consequence, and then, by a punishment? *The behavior will be maintained or even increase.* Only the consequence that *immediately* follows the act matters. Others don't count. For instance, a compulsive drinker belts down a series of Scotches.

He feels less tense, good, high. Later, he becomes terribly sick.
That second consequence doesn't matter. He will continue to
drink because the first consequence made him feel good.

(1) *You may have to change the behavior of the people around you to
avoid the consequences that maintain or increase the desired habit.* For
instance, Teodora Ayllon and Jack Michael, two leading
experimenters in the operant field, tell the story of Lucille, a
hospitalized, mentally defective patient whose visits to the
nurses' station constantly interrupted and interfered with their
work. For two years, Lucille had carried on her harassment.
The nurses continually expressed their annoyance to her.
When this didn't work, the nurses developed the attitude that
"She's too dumb to understand."

When behavior therapists entered the case, they decided
that the nurses' behavior needed changing. They instructed
the nurses to give Lucille no attention when she came visiting,
but to ignore her completely. They did. For the previous two
years Lucille had averaged sixteen visits a day to the nurses'
station. After the nurses stopped reinforcing her behavior with
attention, her visits dropped to two a day.

In everyday life, there is an example familiar to every
person who has tried to stick with a diet. When the dieter
succumbs to some high calorie food, everyone around remarks,
"You shouldn't eat that," or "Hey, what happened to your
diet?" By paying attention to the diet-breaking habit, they
reinforce it. However, when the person stays with the diet,
others tend to ignore it, thus withdrawing reinforcement from
the diet-keeping behavior and so tending to decrease the
frequency of that behavior. Their reinforcements are the exact
opposite of those needed to keep the dieter on the diet.

(2) *Remove the reinforcers that are maintaining the undesired
behavior.* You must identify the consequences that *immediately*
follow the unwanted act and either take them out of the
situation or render them ineffective. Without this reinforcement the behavior will decrease and disappear.

(a) *Remove the reinforcer entirely so that it can't function at all.* In
this way, you change the situation so that the current
unwanted consequences do not occur.

CASE

A twenty-one-year-old college student came to me with the

problem of hairpulling (a very common unwanted habit among both men and women). As Dina studied, she would yank out hairs from her pretty blonde head. Dina's pattern: she would take two to three strands of hair and wind them tightly around her index finger at the point of the nail so that the pressure would be on the sides of the nail. She reported that she "loved that feeling of pressure." So we decided to remove the feeling of pressure that was providing the reinforcement. I directed Dina to put a bandage around her index finger so that she couldn't experience the pleasurable pressure. After a number of weeks going around with a bandaged finger, Dina had the habit under control.

(b) *If you can't remove the reinforcer, you may be able to override it by adding a different consequence*—one that is more important or stronger so that the previous consequence loses its hold.

CASE
A man who worked as a nightclub pianist came to me with the problem of nail-biting. The nail-biting concerned him because his ugly hands were always on display. I suggested that he check his druggist for what he could put on his fingernails that might make nail-biting less of a pleasant experience for him. Preparations exist that produce a sharp, definitely unsatisfactory taste when you paint them on your nails. He did, and that was all there was to it. Several weeks later he telephoned to say, "My nails have started to grow" and six months later reported, "I no longer need the preparation and everything is under control."

(c) *Use imagery to control the reinforcements.* In the technique covert sensitization, developed by Joseph R. Cautela, professor of psychology at Boston College and past president of the Association for the Advancement of Behavior Therapy, you devise an extremely unpleasant scene (such as feeling sick, being bitten by a mad dog, rats crawling all over you). Then, when you begin to perform the unwanted behavior, you begin to *imagine the scene.* You make the scene as vivid as possible and just keep on imagining it until you *stop doing what you don't want to do.* As soon as you stop, switch immediately to an imagined pleasant scene—something that is the very opposite of the aversive scene. In the therapist's office the patient carries out both the unwanted act and the offensive scene in imagery and then goes on to practice the method in real life situations. While the scenes may be distasteful to both patient and therapist, they prove extremely helpful in bringing about change.

V: Establish the desired habit. For this, you need a pinpointed knowledge of exactly what you want your behavior to become and a system of reinforcers that will work for you. Even if it is logical for something to be a reinforcer and all your friends might think of it as a marvelous reward, it may not serve that function for you. The person who detests freezing weather and any form of sports won't find a promised weekend at Aspen a reward. Choose reinforcers that suit you.

(1) In choosing positive reinforcers, consider three kinds.

(a) *Social reinforcers.* As I've noted, your friends can encourage your progress with smiles, attention, interest, praise.

(b) *Things that give you pleasure.* This can be something you want badly such as a new dress, a night on the town, a fishing trip. Or it can take the form of something you enjoy like a lunchtime martini or an orgy of whodunit reading.

(c) *Something you tend to do a lot of*—brushing your hair, fluffing pillows, putting on make-up, looking in store windows. If you can't think of a reinforcer, see what you do a lot of and use this as a reward. This law of behavior is called "Premack's Principle" (after Dr. David Premack who formulated it). Dr. Premack has demonstrated that the thing you do most often in a free situation can be used as a reinforcer. To increase a seldomly performed behavior, do it, and immediately follow it with a more frequently performed behavior. For instance, you have trouble getting started on your morning program of exercises. You *always* listen to the morning news on the radio. As soon as you start doing your exercises, turn on the news.

(2) *Using your positive reinforcers.*

(a) *Reinforcement cannot come before you perform the desired behavior.* Think of it as earning a reward. No desired behavior, no reward. For instance, if you have the bad habit of consistent lateness for work, you cannot drink your morning coffee unless you are completely dressed and ready to leave for the office by 8 A.M.

My wife, Jean, claims that with this technique, even with a full-time job, she managed to write four books. If she gets up at 6 A.M. every morning to work on a book, she presents herself with a Bloody Mary and steak tartare for Saturday lunch. If she manages the 6 A.M. getting up on Saturday too, she goes out to lunch. All this is contingent on the 6 A.M. getting up—no 6 A.M., no Bloody Mary, no steak tartare, no lunch out.

Long before Skinner, Benjamin Franklin put this reinforcement contingency principle to good use. When Franklin was president of the American Philosophical Society, he advised the society's chaplain, "a zealous Presbyterian minister, Mr. Beatty," about how to get more members to the meetings in time for prayers. As each member was given a daily ration of "one gill of rum" (four ounces), Franklin suggested to chaplain Beatty "that if you were to deal it out and only just after prayers, you would have them all about you." Beatty obeyed Franklin's injunction and "never were prayers more generally and punctually attended." Franklin's comment: "I thought this method preferable to the punishment inflicted by some military laws for nonattendance on divine service."

(b) *Remember it is the behavior immediately preceding reinforcement that tends to increase.* If you wait too long before reinforcing your good behavior, irrelevant behaviors will intrude, and it is these irrelevant behaviors that will be strengthened—not the one you want. Of course, you don't have to receive the concrete reward at the very moment you perform the desired action. A token, a score, or just the knowledge that you've earned the reinforcer proves just as effective. Jean knows she will give herself that Bloody Mary on Saturday if she gets up at 6 A.M. all week.

(c) *Monitor yourself. The keeping of records can serve as a reinforcement.* Do this with tables, graphs, or any kind of record-keeping that works for you. Count the number of times you perform the act each day. For example, if it is an act you perform only once a day, like getting to work at 9 A.M., you can keep a very simple chart.

The very act of self-monitoring may change your behavior. A golf counter serves as a simple way of doing this. For instance, if you have a habit of daydreaming at work, every time you catch yourself looking out of the window or getting lost in fantasy when your attention should be on work, click the counter. Keep a record of your clicks, and at the end of the day, transfer the total to a graph or chart posted where you must see it. A graph is usually better because you can see immediately what is happening. Don't be surprised if changes start occurring immediately once you begin the self-monitoring.

I have found self-monitoring proves a very effective device for salesmen, stockbrokers, and other businessmen and women who have to make a lot of telephone calls to develop business. Often they don't get down to the task of making these calls. Then they feel depressed, disgusted with themselves, and worried about falling commissions and possible job loss. Usually they know the number of calls they should make each day. When a patient with this problem consults me, I have him buy a notebook. Every time he makes a phone call to a prospective customer, he notes it in the book, using a separate page for each working day and adding up the total at the end of the day. This simple, self-monitoring device often enables the patient to perform to his own satisfaction.

(d) *You can reward yourself mentally for performing a certain behavior.* This is the covert reinforcement technique, developed by Joseph R. Cautela, which I applied to social situations on page 88 in Chapter IV. You take the behavior you want to increase, imagine doing it, and reinforce your performance of it through imagery. You can also apply this method with habits. To recall it to you:

· Think of the behavior you want to perform.
· Imagine yourself doing it.
· Then tell yourself "Reinforce" and switch to a rewarding image.
· Do this over and over in sets of ten reinforcements. That way you give positive reinforcement to the actual act you want to establish, all done in imagery. Remember you may have to do this hundreds of times.

One college junior who had developed a creative block about writing his term paper on the Irish theater had great success with this technique. His imagined scene: the various steps involved in completion of the paper. His imagined reinforcement scene: kissing his girl friend!

(e) *Make the rewards more difficult to earn.* Set your standards higher and higher. For example, initially, you give yourself your reward every time you arrive at work punctually. Then, to earn the reward, you must get to the office on time for three successive days . . . then for a week . . . then for two weeks. As soon as you've earned three successive rewards, make them harder to earn. One way: *establish a point system.* Each act in your desired behavior earns you points, but you must amass a series of points before you present yourself with your reward. Another way: *use intermittent random reinforcement.* Sometimes you earn the reward; sometimes you don't. Decide by tossing a coin. Third way: *use the shaping system.* You reinforce closer and closer approximations of the desired behavior. First reward yourself for being only twenty-five minutes late, then fifteen minutes, then five. Again, the important thing is not to stay at a preliminary step in the desired behavior for too long.

(f) *Know that the feeling that you are doing something for your own good can serve as a very powerful reinforcer.*

I treated one very successful young lawyer. His problem: he couldn't save money. We set up a rather complex training program to increase his saving behavior, using such reinforcers as his secretary's approval, a self-monitoring program, and the accruing bank account. Eventually, Ken felt he had conquered his extravagance and developed the desired savings habit. At this point he told me, "You know the best reinforcer wasn't any of those things we set up. The best reinforcer was the fact that every time I go to the bank I feel proud of myself. I know I am in command of my own life."

Chapter IX
Lack of
Reinforcers
=Depression

Because they have no positive reinforcers in their lives, some people suffer from a chronic state of depression.

Usually this situation stems from one of the following three conditions:

(1) *You may have formed a general life-style that permits few opportunities for reinforcement.* Your depression may be a very natural reaction to a bleak way of life. I have known many people who work at jobs they hate, have few friends or social contacts, possess no interests or hobbies. Alone and friendless, night after night, weekend after weekend, they sit at home, watching TV shows that bore them and hating themselves. Some haven't taken a vacation for years. They rationalize their inactivity with statements like "there's nowhere I want to go," or "there's nothing I want to do." It is natural to see no end to your gloomy existence when you don't like your job, social life, home, friends, way of life, and even yourself, but *do nothing to change any of this.* Because of your dull, meaningless existence, you have created a situation where something good cannot happen.

(2) *You may have possessed positive reinforcers in your life—and lost them.* A number of life situations remove positive reinforcers or potential sources of positive reinforcement. A husband dies, leaving a grieving wife. At fifty-five, an aging executive loses the job to which he gave "his all for thirty-three years." An older person retires, without preparation, and faces an un-

structured existence. An only child marries and moves three thousand miles away. Mother, busy for years with her offspring, has time on her hands—often she occupies her empty hours with depressive thoughts. The loss can be a part of the body, like a limb or breast. Or the loss can be more ephemeral, such as youth.

Many theorists maintain that it is the *meaning* of the reinforcers you lose that produces depression—in the empty-nest syndrome, it means to the mother that she is no longer needed . . . to the man who got fired, the loss of his job signifies his professional inadequacy . . . personal disfigurement means "no man (or woman) will want me" . . . the death of someone close signifies loss of affection and possibly loneliness.

While "meaning" is the obvious interpretation, it is not always necessary to produce depression. Loss of opportunities of reinforcement may produce a depressed reaction where no "meaning" is involved. For instance, take my own feelings the day I acquired my Ph.D.

After long years of courses, study, and examinations, I met with the faculty committee for the last step in the lengthy process: the defense of my dissertation. After two hours of questioning, the chairman looked at me, smiled, and said, "Congratulations, *Doctor!*" My reaction to finally winning my doctorate was a full-bodied depression which lasted several days. The reason: the almost lifelong source of reinforcement —grades, teacher approval, acceptance of term papers—was no longer present. A similar reaction often occurs with men and women after their discharge from the Armed Services. They return home and feel depressed without the familiar reinforcement potentials of barracks life, set duties, and authority figures.

(3) *You center your life around negative reinforcements.* I have explained that negative reinforcement is when something, usually unpleasant, is subtracted from the situation or *is kept from happening.* If this type of reinforcement becomes dominant, you set a goal: to keep the situation from getting worse, to minimize your losses rather than effect gains. Your reinforcement comes not from having good things happen to you, but from *keeping the bad things from getting worse.* Unfortunately this

no-win situation exists as the unhappy base of many marriages. At best, you don't lose, and you set things up so pleasant things can't happen. In this no-win situation, you believe one way to keep from losing is to do less and less. You begin to feel apathetic and unmotivated.

Whether your lack of positive reinforcers stems from your life-style, a change in your life situation, or the predominance of negative reinforcements, to get positive reinforcement you must *deliberately* seek new sources of pleasure, things which will provide you with a positive—rather than a negative—view of the world around you, yourself, the future. You must do things that serve as sources of satisfaction. You must pay great attention to whatever feelings of pleasure develop. The old saw about the woman who felt depressed and went out and bought a new hat possesses much theoretical merit.

With depressed people, it is easy to issue this injunction, hard for them to accomplish it. One of the characteristics of depression is the inability to take action. Over and over patients say to me: "I can't think of anything satisfying to do. Even if I did, what's the use? I wouldn't enjoy it. I would still feel depressed."

However, as with most Assertiveness Training programs, it is possible to find some starting point. Even if you are unable to take any outward action in search of reinforcements, you may be able to do so in fantasy.

LABORATORY EXERCISE FOR DEPRESSION I

Purpose: To provide positive reinforcement through fantasy, as the first step in relieving depression.

STEP ONE: Make a list of things that will give you a feeling of satisfaction *if you imagine them.* Systematically check out the following areas: food, drink, hobbies, entertainment, sports, sex, work, social interactions, travel, or any other categories that come to your mind. You are looking for specific acts that will produce even a minimal feeling of pleasure. The act can be something as simple as licking a chocolate ice cream cone, listening to classical music, or reading a mystery book. Or it can be much more complex, such as having people seek out your company or being in a love relationship with another person. In selecting your act, don't limit yourself to reality. Try anything that might give you a good feeling—like the idea of winning the Nobel Prize. No matter how down and ugly you feel, almost everyone can find one thing that will produce at least a twinge of pleasure.

STEP TWO: Select one (or several) of the acts you've chosen that has a relatively high point of pleasure (you may have to choose between tiny and tiny, tiny pleasure). *Imagine* doing this act, and try to capture whatever good feelings you gain from the fantasy. Practice this fantasy several times. Each time try to make the image more clear and detailed, and capture whatever good feelings that may emerge. Repeat the procedure with each imagined act.

STEP THREE: Do this exercise every day. *You are trying to provide yourself with the positive reinforcement that you cannot get through actual activity.* Your AT goal: to relieve your depression sufficiently so that you can take *some action in life instead of in your imagination.*

You may be able to start your depression cure with a more active approach than fantasy reinforcement. In this case, your goal is to set up the *habit of doing more things that may bring about some enjoyment.* Follow the rules for establishing new habits.

LABORATORY EXERCISE FOR DEPRESSION II

Purpose: To provide a plan for increasing activity so that eventually you will find new sources for positive reinforcement.

STEP ONE: Make a list of specific activities that hold some potential for reinforcement. These can run the gamut from going to a museum and shopping in a department store to telephoning a friend, dining in a favorite restaurant, or going fishing. The action should be something you can accomplish and that you have not performed for the past six months. If you are extremely depressed, it might be something as simple as taking a half-hour walk in the park.

STEP TWO: Write down the day and time you are going to perform the action. When the time comes, *you must perform your chosen act.* I make a special point of this. No exceptions.

STEP THREE: Start by doing at least one action a week. As time goes on, perform more acts. Monitor your behavior by keeping a chart on which you place a check mark *every time* you perform the action.

STEP FOUR: Remember you are doing this exercise to increase activity. *Enjoyment is not the purpose of the task.* Initially, you may feel no pleasure. However, to attain the eventual goal of positive reinforcement, you must pay attention to any pleasurable reaction—even if very slight and fleeting. Therefore, after completing each task, jot down the highest amount of good feeling you had while doing it. For this purpose, use a numerical scale where 0 represents no good feeling whatever and 100 means complete ecstacy. This serves to reawaken your awareness of pleasant feelings, which you have learned to ignore. It also introduces active orientation. You learn to take responsibility for your pleasures rather than demanding they pop out of the woodwork.

I do not pretend that these plans are easy to follow. I know they will increase in difficulty with the severity of the depression. *They are for mild depressions.* However, in my practice, I have seen practice of these simple exercises help all kinds of depressed people regain a thrust in life.

One more point: sometimes you may have many reinforcers in your life, but somehow you have become insensitive to them, and feel depressed. For example, a single girl may concentrate so much on the fact that she has no husband that she doesn't see what she does have—good looks, good job, a collection of male and female friends. Or take the man who has lost his wife of thirty-five years and goes through a period of grief and mourning. Long after her death, he still centers his life around this loss and ignores the friendliness and concern of others and the good things that remain. The loss is real. Just as real is the fact that many nice things exist in his life. If he shuts out these entities, depression (not sadness) builds up.

If you don't realize that pleasures do actually exist in your life, the reinforcer that may get through to you is the knowledge that you are starting to *control your depression.*

CASE

At forty, Jack Phelan, a distinguished Australian biologist, had a loving wife, three adjusted kids, and his research was considered brilliant. He moved from his homeland to the Caribbean, London, and finally New York, each time getting a better research opportunity. All these good things had no effect, however, on what Jack called his "growing deadness."

When Jack came to me, his work had been affected by his continual down feeling; he couldn't muster the final bit of energy he needed to reach the brilliant point that had characterized his past research. He had stopped enjoying sex, and he was beginning to avoid people. More and more he ate lunch by himself.

At first, I tried the fantasy approach with him. In my office, he was able to experience the good feelings in imagery, but they didn't affect his depressed state in real life. After this failure, I set up programs for him to do things he had enjoyed in the past and new things he had never tried. But the deadness increased.

Finally, I started him on self-monitoring; he was to keep a graph of how depressed he was each day. This appealed to Jack's scientific mind. After a number of weeks, he found he could deliberately start lowering the level of his depression at a slow, but steady, pace. He said, "When I became aware of feeling the deadness, I would somehow summon up some kind of energy and make myself feel alive for a brief period of time."

What had happened, I think, is that Jack had fallen into the bad habit of depression and had become increasingly passive about letting it take over. Instead of doing something about it, he sought refuge in medications, reading psychoanalytic literature, and visiting an endless procession of therapists. As he traveled from country to country, he often found a therapist before he found a house. The self-monitoring technique, which is a very effective method for changing habits, enabled him to take a more active role and to set up the counter habit of feeling alive and involved.

By the end of ten weeks, Jack's problem was gone, and he stopped treatment. About a year and a half later, he telephoned to say that occasionally he does get the feeling of deadness, but manages to bring it under control with monitoring.

Chapter X
How to Get Thin — and Stay Thin

While millions of unfortunate human beings throughout the world suffer from problems of undernutrition and starvation, the major nutritional affliction in this country is obesity. Dieting has become the nation's most popular indoor sport.

However, the sad statistics show that of the millions of Americans who diet every year, *fewer than 10 percent actually keep the weight off.* Whatever plan they follow may make them temporarily thin, but *they don't stay thin.*

The average dieter has a pattern. His clothes become tight. A friend or spouse criticizes, "You're too fat." He *feels* fat and unattractive. Upset, he embarks on a crash diet that will probably last from sixty to ninety days. He loses weight. And six months later he has gained it all back! This happens because he does not change his basic eating habits. To get permanent change, you must alter your eating habits and exercise patterns for the rest of your life, not just for a short time.

People maintain poor weight-control behaviors for three main reasons.

(1) Overweight people are very much under the control of outside stimuli (the sight and smell of food). If food is around, they eat it; the availability, rather than hunger, triggers the eating. The sight of a mouth-watering ad in a magazine sends them on a refrigerator raid. Many indirect stimuli also become signals for eating. Because they associate food with viewing

TV or reading, they nibble peanuts as they watch the nightly news or read.

(2) At some point in life, they learned poor eating behavior. The habit of overeating has become a life-style, maintained because they enjoy it, feel insecure without it, or because it gives temporary relief to feelings like anxiety, anger, or depression. Some eat to avoid stress. By being overweight, they can avoid certain tension-producing circumstances—like closeness with the opposite sex.

(3) Some people weigh too much because of poor exercise habits. They may not eat too much, but they don't burn up what they do eat. Sometimes their restricted activity leads to increased food intake.

The Assertiveness Training approach to weight control helps you to gain command of these three areas. You do *not* go on a crash diet. A crash diet aims to change your weight, not your behavior. It takes time to establish a permanent new habit, and extreme and rapid weight loss can rarely be maintained long enough for this purpose. *Hence, you aim at an average weight loss of one to two pounds a week and a long-term change in your eating habits.*

To do this, you apply the principles of self-control. You search for the stimuli that set off your unwanted eating and eliminate them. You pinpoint the specific eating or exercise behavior you want to change. You eliminate the reinforcers that currently maintain your unwanted overeating, and you substitute or strengthen reinforcers that will increase your desired eating behavior.

Controlled experiments, particularly at the University of Michigan, Columbia University, and the University of Pennsylvania Medical College, have proved the success of this approach. According to obesity expert Dr. Albert J. Stunkard, formerly chief of psychiatry at the University of Pennsylvania and now chairman of the department of psychiatry, Stanford University School of Medicine, application of behavior therapy to weight gain "represents the first significant advance in years. . . . Earlier weight-reduction programs asked only that one suffer and endure; this one provides an opportunity to work hard and succeed."

CHANGING YOUR EATING HABITS:
A FIVE-POINT PROGRAM

POINT ONE: *Learn your own eating habits.* You can't change them until you know what they are. Prepare a diet diary. Keep it for a week and cover the who, what, when, why, and where of your food intake. Set it up in the following way: in your Assertiveness Training workbook, take a separate page for each day of the week. And on each, set up columns with the following headings:

Time you ate	Where you ate
What food you consumed	With whom you ate
How much you ate	or if alone
What you were doing when you ate	How you felt when you ate

Keeping this record will make you much more aware of what you really eat and the environmental and psychological stimuli associated with your food intake. One thirty-year-old housewife reported that after two weeks of self-monitoring, for the first time, she realized that anger stimulated her eating. Once she knew that, whenever she felt angry, she left the kitchen and wrote down how she felt, thereby decreasing her anger and aborting her eating. Another woman had an unhappy, depressed sister who always telephoned her at lunchtime to recount her troubles. After these calls my patient always overate. Once she realized what was happening, she asked her sister to make the daily phone call after dinner.

POINT TWO: *Control the stimuli.* Normal-weight people eat when they feel hungry, not just because food is there. From a number of laboratory experiments, we know that with over-weight people, the very availability of food will trigger eating. As food is available at many times and in many places, overweight people eat constantly—at their desks, snack bars, on the street, in front of the TV set, in the bedroom just before going to sleep, and on and on.

Because eating occurs under many different conditions, many different stimuli become associated with the act. These become discriminative stimuli (stimuli that signal conse-quences) that say, "Go ahead—eat!" The TV set may give you the signal or sitting at your desk or reading or riding in a car or maybe just being in your bedroom.

It would take superhuman willpower to resist all the urgings: it is far easier to weaken the signals that these stimuli set off. The first step is the reduction of the number of stimuli you associate with the act of eating. This does not require that you stop eating, but that you control where and when you eat.

(1) At home, you may eat anything you want at any time, but *you must always eat in the same place.* If you choose your dining-room table, that means you never eat in the living room, bedroom, or standing in front of the kitchen sink.

(2) *When you eat, you cannot perform any other act.* You cannot read, sew a patchwork quilt, or watch TV. If you are watching Johnny Carson and feel an overwhelming urge for a chocolate chip cookie, you must turn off television, go get the cookie, eat it at the dining-room table, and when you finish, you can then turn on television.

CASE

When Jane Jones came to me, she confessed, "I'm a chocolate candy bar addict." Single, and in her late twenties, Jane felt her twenty excess pounds impaired her relations with men. "I feel fat and unconfident. I can't be myself, and so I turn men off," she told me sad-eyed. Jane ate normally at mealtime and drank only an occasional cocktail, but her passion for candy bars kept the twenty pounds glued to her hips. Every afternoon at 3 P.M., she would leave her office, go down to the newsstand, purchase six or eight candy bars, and, before work ended, finish them all. Sometimes she would make a return trip, buy more, and put them in her purse to munch on the bus.

When I suggested even a mild cutting down as a beginning, she insisted, "I can't. I have to have them."

Obviously many stimuli signaled to Jane "go eat a candy bar." My goal was to lessen these. I set up a program for Jane. She could eat as many candy bars as she wanted, but only under three conditions: (1) she could buy only one candy bar at a time; (2) she could eat it only in an eating place; (3) she had to keep track of each one she ate.

For example, her firm maintained a company cafeteria that

contained a candy machine. Whenever Jane craved that candy bar, she had to go to the crowded cafeteria (not the newsstand), buy a single candy bar, sit down at a table, make a tally on her record sheet, and eat the candy bar. If she felt the urge for a second candy bar, she had to go back to the machine, buy the bar, and repeat the process. If she felt the craving while traveling on a bus, she must get off, find a cafeteria, go in, buy a candy bar, sit at a table, mark her tally, and devour the bar.

Because Jane really wanted to break her habit, she cooperated fully. Knowing she could have an unlimited number of candy bars took away her fear of deprivation. It took close to two months before Jane became aware that she was eating far fewer candy bars. Then she realized that when she was in the office or traveling, she rarely felt the signal "eat." She started to go to the cafeteria far less often. By narrowing down the stimuli, we established stimulus control over the addiction. It took four months before Jane's addiction disappeared. Should it return, she now knows how to deal with it. If Jane had been unable to stick with her stimulus-control plan, I would have had to use the step-by-step approach of removing just one stimulus at a time, and it would have taken much longer.

(3) *Avoid the purchase of high-calorie foods.* Supermarket shelves bulge with many forbidden and enticing items, high in starch and sugar. Keep those foods out of the house. *Shop from a list, and bring into the store only enough money to buy the food you actually need.* This way you avoid the specials on cake, candy, and pasta. If Sara Lee's chocolate cake is your undoing, *never* buy it. Your husband and kids will usually be willing to forgo it for the sake of your diet. Give them something else that doesn't lure you as much.

(4) *Do your food shopping after you have had a full meal.* Dr. Richard B. Stuart, professor at the University of British Columbia and author of *Slim Chance in a Fat World*, studied behavior among obese women and found that those who shopped after dinner bought 20 percent less than those who shopped before eating.

(5) *Use smaller plates.* Make your portion seem larger than it really is. The identical amount of food looks larger on a salad

plate than it does on a dinner plate. Use a salad plate for your main course. Experiments have proved that overweight people report greater satisfaction with the smaller plate, even when they themselves have measured identical quantities into the two plates.

Or if you crave cookies, do not bring the box to the table. Take two or three, put them on a plate, and eat them at the table. Three cookies on a plate look like more than the same three you grab from a box and munch. You will feel more satisfied with a smaller number of cookies if you eat them from a plate rather than the box.

(6) *Do not serve high-calorie condiments or sauces at meals.* Principle: you keep that stimulus out of the situation. If your children want maple syrup on their pancakes, let them go and get it for themselves.

(7) *Make acceptable foods as decorative as possible.* A beautifully curled radish may tempt you. Use a special mat, a decorative place setting, your nicest crystal.

POINT THREE: *Change your eating behavior.* You want to develop special techniques that will help you gain control over the very act of eating.

(1) *Slow down.*

(a) Take one small bite at a time and put down your fork while you savor it.

(b) As you eat, count each mouthful. After every third mouthful, put your knife and fork on the table until you chew and swallow that mouthful.

(c) At one point during the meal, stop eating completely and take a minute or even two-minute break. Or put down your utensils for five seconds, by the clock, several times during a meal. This will help break the automatic nature of rapid eating. One patient slowed herself up by using chopsticks.

(d) If you find you still eat faster than others, make sure that you are the last to sit down at the table and the first to leave. Try to keep away from the presence of food.

(2) *Always leave some food, even if just a mouthful, on your plate.* This technique begins to break the bad habit of eating just because food is there. Goal: to eat your food if you feel hungry, leave it if you feel sated.

(3) *Make eating of caloric foods just as difficult as possible.* Dr. Stanley Schacter of Columbia University proved that obese persons are less willing to expend energy to secure food than nonobese persons. In one of Dr. Schacter's experiments, only one of twenty obese people ate almonds when they required shelling.

Apply this theory to your own eating behavior. If you like bread, you must always toast it. When you toast it, prepare only one slice at a time. Put the loaf back in the refrigerator before you eat the slice.

While you're at it, make sure any fattening foods you eat require a lot of preparation. For instance, if you want cake, you must make a homemade angel food cake—from scratch, not a mix. The breaking of the automatic eating habit is a bonus: if you have to expend energy, you may not eat.

(4) *Control your snacking.* By taking action on specific behaviors that may seem trivial, you gain control of your eating between meals.

(a) Save allowable foods from meals for snacks. Hoard your allowable piece of bread from breakfast to have at your 10 A.M. coffee break.

(b) Establish behaviors incompatible with eating. If you usually indulge in an English muffin or Danish pastry at 10 A.M., make that the time to wash your hair or write a letter. If you work, make an out-of-the-office appointment for that hour.

(c) Fix your snacks the way you fix your dinner—on a plate. This increases the effort involved and helps establish stimulus control.

(d) Keep a quantity of noncaloric foods, like raw carrots, celery, radishes, and cucumbers, on hand to use as snacks. Have them ready to eat—carrots in curls, celery in sticks, cucumbers in slices—and easy to get at.

(5) *Search out your own eating weakness areas and change them.* Many housewives gain because they eat leftovers from their children's plates. If you do this, scrape leftovers directly into a garbage bag. If your child wants a cookie and you eat one every time he does, let him get his own treat. Again, you are searching for behaviors to change. Many of these appear to be trivial. But control of eating-trivialities encourages an active— and specific, not vague—approach to dieting.

(6) *Monitor yourself.* Naturally, the aim of the change in eating habits is to cut down on caloric intake. Dr. Jean Mayer, professor of nutrition at the Harvard School of Public Health, says, "You can become fat by eating just one percent more than you need every day." That extra slice of bread and butter in the morning can add up to ten pounds in a year.

Set a reasonable goal of the amount of calories you want to consume each day. Many times you cannot go directly to that goal; you may have to reach it in stages. For instance, you consume 3800 calories daily, and your desired goal is 1200. You may have to progress through a series of sub-goals—from 2500, down to 1600, and eventually to 1200. Remember, you want a series of successes.

(a) Keep a calorie record for each day. Every time you eat something, estimate the number of calories in it, and keep a cumulative total for each day on index cards. In that way, at any time of the day you know where you stand in relation to your goal. At the end of the day, enter the total number of calories on a graph which you keep posted in a convenient spot.

(b) Check your weight. This behavioral change program aims at an average weight loss of one to two pounds a week. If after a number of weeks the scales do not show a weight loss, either you have set your calorie level too high and you must lower it or you are underestimating the number of calories in your food intake. Check this out and make needed adjustments.

(7) Take steps to control unhappy or unpleasant feelings that produce eating excess. You may maintain your unwanted eating behavior because you think doing this reduces certain emotional reactions. The notes you made under the heading "How you felt when you ate" in your AT notebook should show if this applies to you. Here are suggestions for controlling some of these feelings.

(a) Deprivation. Always eat three regular, planned meals a day. Overeaters frequently skip breakfast, eat a light lunch or drink it, gorge at night because they're starved and feel they've earned the right to a gargantuan soup-to-nuts dinner and midnight snacking. Almost always this involves much more caloric intake than if they had planned their food intake for the day.

(b) Loneliness, boredom, or depression. When you experience these feelings and the concomitant urge to raid the icebox, be ready with a program of activities that you can easily start to do. Keep a list of friends you can call. Develop another list of chores to perform. My wife goes through her clothes. One patient kept her half-completed afghan in the kitchen on a pot hook. Another developed the houseplant hobby. Your activities can be social, vocational, or traditional hobbies, but they should not be related to food.

(c) Anger. Try pillow pounding instead of eating. Or better still, if at all possible, take assertive measures about whatever set off your angry reaction.

(d) Fatigue. Tired people think they'll gain energy by eating. To keep eating under control, you must have sleep control. Get enough sleep to keep you going comfortably.

It may seem peculiar to discuss sleeping and hobbies in a weight-control program, but clinical experience shows that a great many overeating men and women who build good living habits can more easily change the role of food in their lives.

POINT FOUR: *Change your exercise behavior.* People have strange ideas about exercise. Many think you must perform an enormous amount of walking, running, lifting, pushing, barwork, or whatever to burn up enough calories to do any good. They also believe you have to do it all at once. They reason "it takes fourteen hours of walking to lose a pound, and fourteen hours is just too much." However, if you walk fairly fast for one hour a day, you can lose one pound every two weeks. In one year, this can mean a twenty-five-pound loss.

People also make the assumption that exercise causes an increase in hunger. Not true. Studies have shown that when rats were not allowed to exercise, they ate and grew fat. Allowed exercise, they ate less and remained at normal weight. This finding also applies to humans. In his book *The Thin Book by a Formerly Fat Psychiatrist*, Dr. Theodore Rubin points out, "I have experimented both with myself and with patients, and the rate of weight loss is increased about 10 percent with exercise."

You must make exercise a habit.

(1) *Determine whatever exercise you do now and increase it by an extra 500 calories' worth a day.*

Exercises fall into three classifications: light, moderate, and heavy.

Light exercise burns 4 calories a minute. Into this category fall slow dancing, gardening, golf, Ping-Pong, walking at the rate of 3 miles an hour.

Moderate exercise burns up 7 calories a minute and includes fast dancing, heavy gardening, swimming, singles tennis, walking at 4.5 miles per hour.

Heavy exercise burns up 10 calories a minute and includes going up and down stairs, vigorous calisthenics, cycling at 12 miles an hour, stationary jogging, jogging, squash, skipping rope. Remember 3500 calories equal one pound of fat.

Before you can add the extra 500 calories worth of exercise a day, you must know your current exercise rate.

(a) Make out an index card for each day of the week or use pages in your Assertiveness Training workbook. Divide each card into three sections: light, moderate, and heavy exercise. Every time you estimate you have performed fifteen minutes of that kind of exercise (it does not have to be continuous), put a check in the appropriate section. Each check under "light" equals 60 calories (fifteen minutes multiplied by 4 calories a minute), under "moderate" a check equals 105 calories (fifteen minutes multiplied by 7 calories), and under "heavy" 150 calories (fifteen minutes multiplied by 10 calories).

Monday	Light (each check is 60 calories)	Moderate (each check is 105 calories)	Heavy (each check is 150 calories)

(b) On a separate page of your AT workbook, enter the total number of calories you've used up with exercise for each day.

(c) Keep filling out these daily forms for two weeks to see your exercise pattern—and then add additional exercise.

(2) *Eliminate the stimuli to inactivity.* For example, keep your car in the garage instead of the driveway. That way you may walk the two blocks to the Brown's house instead of driving.

(3) *Strengthen the stimuli to activity.* Take up a new sport. Investigate gym classes and join one. Sign up for things with friends. This will help you to launch and continue an exercise program. Warning: choose an exercise you will enjoy. Remember, you want to succeed.

POINT FIVE: *Set up a system of positive reinforcements. In other words, reward yourself.*

First, you must clearly define the behavior you want to reinforce. It may be the lesser number of calories you've eaten on one day. It may be the number of calories you used up by an hour of exercise. It may be one of several specific acts, such as leaving food on your plate. You may also want to reinforce achievement of specifically set weight goals.

You reinforce any of these behaviors, or others, by using the methods I described in Chapter VIII. Select the rewards that will work for you. Some cautions:

(1) *Again, do not use food as a reward.*

(2) *Do use your friends and family for reinforcement purposes.* Tell them about the various behaviors on which you are working—like eating in the same place, extra exercise—and give them the following instructions:

(a) When you perform the behavior, the friend, child, or spouse should comment on it, encourage it, socially reinforce it. When you do *not* perform the behavior, they should ignore it completely and give no sign of noticing your lapse.

(b) If you live alone with no one to monitor, keep an eating-intake and an exercise chart and show them to a particular friend on a regular basis. The friend reinforces as above.

(c) If married, enlist the help of your spouse—but watch out. He, or she, may not be motivated to help you lose weight. For example, at the University of Michigan, Dr. Richard B. Stuart conducted interviews with fifty husbands who wanted their wives to reduce. However, only twenty-seven were willing to assist the wives' weight-loss program, fearing such consequences for themselves as loss of eating as a shared activity, loss of bargaining position in arguments, divorce, and possible unfaithfulness.

(3) *Remember the principle that you want to make the reinforcers harder and harder to earn.* At first, you promise yourself that if you walk the three miles to your job, you can telephone Bob and arrange a Friday night poker game. Soon, you should do the three-mile stint for three successive days before you win your reward.

(4) *Try the token, or point, system as a reinforcement technique.* For instance, you earn 3 points if you stick with your diet for one meal, or 40 points for following your diet for three successive days, or 150 points for a whole week of diet behavior. You need different numbers of points for different reinforcers—25 points gives you an afternoon out at a movie; 1500 points wins you a weekend trip.

CASE

No matter how hard she tried, twenty-eight year-old Lucille Crandall, a very successful stockbroker, couldn't stick with a diet. This upset her. "I'm a success at everything else; it bothers me that I'm not in command of this part of my life," she told me." Determined to gain this control, Lucille was willing to use her weekend retreat ("the place that renews my spirit") as a reinforcer.

Her daily food intake averaged 3800 calories. Her goal: 1200 calories a day. We set up a point system to help her achieve this in stages.

· Under 3500 calories for one day equaled one point. Under 3000 for a day equaled an additional point.

· In order to spend the weekend at her Colonial saltbox, she had to earn 8 points during the week. Lucille felt she could do this. We set up the total points so that at least once during the week, she had to get below the 3000 calories to get to her country place that weekend. We also arranged it so that if she slipped on one day, she could make up the loss by getting the double point the next day.

Lucille earned her 8 points that first week, and we immediately lowered the calorie count to 3300 and 2800 for her to win the desired points. It took five months of this kind of shaping for Lucille to reach her 1200-calories-a-day goal, and by that time, she felt in control of her food intake. She kept up the reinforcement point schedule for three months and still uses it when she starts to slip.

(5) *Use creative reinforcers.*

(a) Drop a quarter in your piggy bank for each day you stay within the calorie count. The prize should be something you really want.

(b) Give your pounds to a child. Put a dollar away for each pound you drop, and earmark the money for a worthy charity like UNICEF or Save the Children Federation. Take a dollar back for each pound you regain. It will make you feel bad to think you're taking money from starving kids.

(c) Start a "buddy system" with an overweight friend. For each day you do not stay on your diet, put one dollar in a box. Winner takes all at the end of the month.

(d) Dramatize your successes. Be creative. One woman bought two huge plastic sacks. Whenever she lost a pound, she put a pound of flour in her "lost weight" sack. When she gained, she put a pound of flour in the "gain weight" sack. The sight of the "gain weight" sack became so abhorrent to her that she maintained a steady weight loss.

(e) Sometimes life itself may provide the necessary reinforcement.

CASE

Mary Paparella weighed 198 pounds—some 70 too much. While she didn't feel much concern about her extra poundage, her husband did. He refused to be seen with her in public. For five years, he had never accompanied her anywhere, including church on Christmas Eve.

We set up a weight-control program for Mary with the aim of having her family reinforce her when she kept her calorie count to the allotted limit. Mr. Paparella refused to participate in any way in Mary's diet program, but the kids helped with such compliments as "Oh, Mummy, you're wonderful. You left half your spaghetti on your plate."

Mary kept up her regimen. At the end of six months, she was down to 165 pounds, and her husband spontaneously started taking her places. At this, Mary lost her motivation to reduce and started to gain back the weight. At which point, and without any instructions from me, her husband said, "You're getting fat again. I won't take you out." Mary regained control and went back to 165 pounds. Now every time she starts to gain weight, her husband stops their joint social life. Even though Mr. Paparella cooperated only minimally in our program and Mary never went down to 128 pounds, he did exactly the right thing in terms of providing reinforcers.

Behavioral change of your eating habits enables you to *get thin and stay thin.*

Control of eating habits can also make you feel better about yourself. By changing the way you eat, you do more than lose weight. You lose the anger, shame, and self-disgust that make you dislike yourself. One patient told me, "All my life I've been gaining, losing, and gaining. Now I've got my weight under control, and I feel happy with myself."

Chapter XI
The Problems of Sexual Variants

Fearing revelation of his homosexuality will result both in job loss and parental scorn, John stays in the closet. His perpetual nightmare: what if his boss calls him "a screaming queer"?

Chris gets his sexual turn-ons from fantasies about shoes. When he goes to bed with his girl friend, he feels distant, alienated, and unsure of his masculinity. His fantasies about high-heeled pumps come between them.

Bill is a transvestite. Happily married for ten years and a good father, he loves to sport his wife's black dinner dress and parade around the apartment. His horrified wife pleads, "If you love me, why do you do this awful thing?" To save his home, must Bill stop his tv-ism?

Even though John, Chris, and Bill differ in age, political beliefs, tastes, and life-styles, they share one common quality. They are sexual variants. They fear ridicule, humiliation, loss of love from peers, co-workers, and family to such an extent that *they have lost the ability to decide what they want to do about their own behavior.* Instead of asking, "What will make me happiest?" they wonder "To be or not to be?" . . . "To tell or not to tell?" . . . "To change or not to change?"

CHANGING IDEAS ABOUT SEXUAL VARIANTS

To understand the rapidly changing concepts about sexual variants, you must know:

What sexual variant behavior is. By contemporary definition, a sexual variant is an individual whose end goal for sexual activity is something *other than genital union with a person of the opposite sex.* This category includes two major groups: (1) homosexuals, whose goal is sexual relations with members of the same sex, and (2) other variants who direct their sexual interests primarily toward objects, toward sexual acts usually not associated with coitus, or toward coitus performed under bizarre circumstances, such as necrophilia, pedophilia, fetishism, voyeurism, transvestism, and masochism.

The attitude of other societies. For centuries, other societies have freely accepted these forms of sex. For instance, the Koniag in the Alaskan peninsula rear some male children from infancy to occupy the female role. These boys learn female crafts, wear feminine garments, and become skilled in wifely duties. The Siberian Chukchee in the Northeastern peninsula of Asia regard the man who assumes the feminine role as a powerful shaman (a religious specialist believed to possess supernatural power). This individual wears women's clothing, assumes feminine mannerisms, and may become the "wife" of another man. The pair copulate, the shaman always playing the feminine role. In addition to the shaman "wife," the husband usually has another wife with whom he engages in heterosexual coitus.

The Keraki bachelors of New Guinea universally practice sodomy, and the older males initiate each boy into anal intercourse in the course of his puberty rites. Among the Australian Aranda, women stimulate each other's clitoris. In Africa, Mbundu and Namu women use an artificial penis in mutual masturbation.

Changing attitudes. While people in many countries have practiced sexual variant behaviors for hundreds of years, it is only in the last few years that professional and social values have changed in the Western world to accept the idea that *any sexual act as long as it involves consenting adults* (this excludes pedophilia and exhibitionism) *is permissible.* In 1973, the American Psychiatric Association declared that homosexuality is not a mental illness, and a spokesman stated that "homosexuality is neither normal nor abnormal."

The basic problems. Although many people have shed the inherited Victorian thinking in which the only "normal" sex is heterogenital union in one set position, others have not. For variants themselves the problems make themselves felt in two ways: (1) when the variant has no control over his behavior and practices it compulsively, he lacks the freedom to decide whether or not he really wants to perform the act; (2) when he cannot accept his own behavior.

How does the sexual variant know what he wants? In this area, the pressures of society—even a changing one—remain so strong that often the individual responds to societal force rather than his own needs and desires. For instance, in a talk to the Association for the Advancement of Behavior Therapy, Charles Silverstein, director, Institute for Human Identity in New York, raised the point that if a homosexual comes to a therapist and asks to be changed into a heterosexual, the therapist cannot assume this to be the patient's true goal. In order for the homosexual to make an honest choice, the therapist must first remove the tensions and fears created by society.

Therapy goals with variants. Many variants who seek psychological help are so troubled and so fearful that the outside world will ridicule them that usually they think only about how to get rid of the behavior permanently.

This is not the only option.

To know what he really wants to do, the sexual variant must take four actions:

(1) If he performs the behavior compulsively, he must regain deliberate control of it. As he feels self-control over his own behavior, his feelings may crystallize, and he will be able to act out of choice rather than compulsion.

(2) He should deliberately develop alternate behaviors so he can decide which behaviors most satisfy him.

(3) If he decides he wants to keep his variant behavior, he should learn to become comfortable with it and accept his right to it. Within the framework of that behavior, he should learn to act assertively. For instance, if he opts for the homosexual way of life, he may decide to emerge from the closet and let the world know his life-style.

(4) If he decides he does not want the variant behavior, he should eliminate it and establish a more wanted (*by him*) form of behavior.

Master these actions and a lot of goal confusion will disappear.

THE HOMOSEXUAL

How do you know if you should attempt to stop being homosexual?

Despite the new sexual liberality, you may face decisions. Are you really straight and, for one reason or another, have had a gay life thrust upon you? Or is being gay really you and your problem that of learning to handle the pressures of society?

Many kinds of homosexuals exist. The well-adjusted homosexual, whether gay or bisexual, has found a life-style which makes him happy and fulfilled. Many homosexuals have only the ordinary problems of earning a living, paying taxes, and affording a meal that come with living in a troubled world. They have found their way.

Others do have psychological problems:

(1) *The man* (and I use "man" because more male homosexuals seek therapeutic help, and I myself have seen very few women homosexuals who came into treatment because of that) *who is basically straight, but fears he may be homosexual.* He has developed fantasies of sexual relationships with men. Occasionally he feels turned on by a man in the street or even the sight of a magazine centerfold male. Possibly he has tried one or two brief sexual encounters with other men. For him, women have become an anxiety-laden stimulus, often due to assertive problems or feared sexual inadequacy. He tends to avoid the anxiety-provoking situation and begins to gain his sexual turn-ons from fantasies of the same sex. In this group, late maturers form an interesting type. These boys don't develop pubic hair until about the age of sixteen. During adolescence, when peers learn the skills of relating to the opposite sex, they learn the skill of feeling inadequate. One study shows that at age thirty these late maturers have very real problems with assertion and women.

(2) *The man who is basically straight, but whose anxieties about women are so severe that he has forced himself into a homosexual life-style.* This is a highly neurotic extension of type one. He has such symptoms as depression, anxiety, and unhappiness with his unwanted seat on the gay exchange. The situation compares with that of the person who has elected to stay with the wrong kind of job—for instance, the extrovert who spends his nine to five hours as a statistician in a one-man office.

(3) *The man who is basically homosexual and gets forced into the heterosexual way of life.* This is the counterpart of the person forced into the homosexual life. In both instances, there is a great deal of confusion about their own sexual orientation.

(4) *The homosexual who is not sure of what he is or what he wants.* In which camp does he belong or does he belong in both? Does he respond in terms of his own needs or because of pressures of society?

(5) *The homosexual who likes his way of life, but resents staying hidden.* He would like to be open and free about his homosexual actions, but fears possible put-downs from the straight world. This makes him feel lonely and alienated.

A HOMOSEXUAL HOW-TO GUIDE

Purpose: To help you decide what you want.

In attempting to find out what you really want, the first aim is an expansion of your sexual experience. With this amplification, you may be in a better position to make a decision. In doing this, you follow the general rules of Assertiveness Training. Start where you are now. Decide where you want to go. Get there on a step-by-step basis. To execute such a program:

(1) *Don't begin with any set ideas.* You are trying to find out whether you prefer the homosexual, bisexual, or heterosexual way of life. Make no decision before you've tried an expansion of your thinking. Don't start with the aim of becoming exclusively heterosexual.

(2) *Realize that your anxieties may mask the actual pleasures you receive from homosexual relations.* Don't ignore the satisfactions that are there. Make yourself more aware of them. Reminisce

about past delights; fantasize about future excitements. Look to what you have now, and think also about your anxieties that keep you from enjoying your homosexuality and what you can do to make it more fulfilling.

(3) *Expand your sexual experience with the opposite sex.* Often this is easier to say than do. Sometimes the intensive anxiety generates avoidance. The anxiety may be directly related to sex or may take the form of general social anxiety. Point: identify the main anxieties and try to reduce them.

(a) If your homosexual fantasies trouble you, embark on a program to get rid of them. Usually an assertive difficulty with women precipitates the fantasy. Often young men, troubled by homosexual fantasies, have problems asking for dates, carrying on conversations, and with other heterosexual behavior. Even after an Assertiveness Training program during which we change these behaviors, the homosexual thoughts persist because, at this point, they have become a habit, with a life and existence of their own. Or else the fantasies prove so troublesome that they keep the individual from developing the proper assertive behavior. In either case, thought stoppage proves an effective technique for bringing the fantasies under control. This is the device I outlined in Chapter IV where *as soon as* and *every time* you have an obsessive thought you want to control, you say STOP to yourself; then, "Calm," and relax your muscles.

(b) Get involved in a heterosexual relationship. With the right teacher, anxiety about sex can be overcome.

CASE

When Charles Shur, a twenty-eight-year-old college-educated computer programmer, came to me, he said, "I'm a homosexual, but I don't want to be one." Over the years, he had dated a number of girls, but as Charles phrased it, "They're like sisters." They didn't expect him to make a pass. He had not had a real date for years and had never had sex with a woman. He needed a sexual outlet, but did not want a permanent homosexual lover. Once or twice a week Charles would visit a gay bar, pick up a man, go to his apartment (never his own), and have sex. He never got involved with the same man twice.

Not only had Charles never been to bed with a woman but he had never even experienced a sexual fantasy involving one. The core of his anxiety was the feeling that if he dated a girl, she would expect him to go to bed with her, and he would be unable to function. He could not conceive of a man-woman date where the girl wouldn't have sexual expectations by at least the second date.

Here's what we did. I instructed Charles to find a prostitute to work with as a surrogate. He did. Then I designed and monitored a step-by-step program to reduce his sexual tension.

STEP ONE: He should just sit and talk with Jenny, about sexual matters. He did this several times until he felt comfortable.

STEP TWO: Jenny gave him a series of lessons in female anatomy. She served as teacher. She did not touch him. No action was expected of Charles. This relieved some of his tension.

STEP THREE: Following the model of Masters and Johnson, Jenny massaged him, taking care not to touch his genitals. When Charles began to experience pleasure from this process, she then moved on to massage his genitals, but not with the intention of specifically arousing him sexually. At first, Charles felt no sensation at all in his genitals, but soon he began to gain pleasurable feelings and finally erections.

STEP FOUR: Jenny progressed to manual masturbation (she to him), oral sex, and eventually intercourse. During this period, she maintained the teacher attitude in the hope of keeping tension low. She also used her considerable experience to teach him to be a good lover. It took close to a year, but at the end of that time Charles functioned well with Jenny.

STEP FIVE: During the second half of the year, I commenced Assertiveness Training with Charles regarding dates. He learned to converse man-to-woman and to flirt. He then had several dates where he practiced these skills. I made it a rule that he was not to ask these girls for second dates.

STEP SIX: Then Charles moved on to second dates where he was allowed to neck and pet. He felt considerable nervousness about this, but this was relieved by the knowledge that I had set a limit: he was not to go beyond this. Soon he started to enjoy this sexual play.

After a year of treatment, during which I saw Charles once a week and occasionally conferred with the surrogate by phone, Charles gathered his courage and drove off to a singles resort. There, in violation of all my instructions, he went to bed with an attractive blonde. It worked out well. At the moment, Charles leads the life of a bachelor around town, and he never goes to gay bars.

(c) Try to take the feeling of sexual excitement that is stirred up by the same sex (men) and transfer the excitement to the opposite sex (women). You do this by taking the feeling of sexual excitement, however it is aroused, and then associating the feeling with another stimulus. Eventually, this second stimulus will elicit the feeling of sexual arousal. *Remember, to change homosexual behavior, there has to be a satisfactory alternate behavior in the repertory.* To merely repress a homosexual response without providing an alternative response will not work. The homosexuality will return. Two methods exist with proven results for changing the impact of stimuli on homosexuals.

· *Fading.* This requires the presence of a therapist and cannot be self-administered. For example, with a male homosexual the therapist flashes a picture of an attractive man on a screen. The patient has a sexual response. Then the therapist gradually fades the picture of a man into a picture of a woman. If the technique is successful, within a relatively few trials, the patient achieves a sexual response to the female photograph. This response in the therapeutic session carries over to the outside world, and he begins to find women sexually stimulating.

· *Orgasmic retraining.* This can be self-administered. Much of the time the attractiveness of the same sex object is constantly reinforced through masturbation fantasy. In other words, the homosexual masturbates to homosexual fantasies and thus constantly keeps associating pleasure with these fantasies. Or the homosexual fantasies lead to positively reinforcing consequences—orgasm. At this point, fantasies about the same sex may be the only way to achieve sexual arousal. Our goal: to change things so that the stimulus of the opposite sex may also arouse. For orgasmic retraining, take these steps.

STEP ONE: When a climax becomes inevitable as you masturbate, you deliberately change the fantasy to involve a member of the opposite—*not the same*—sex. Use someone you know, a movie star, a popular singer. If you have difficulty evoking an image, keep a *Playboy* pinup girl picture in front of you. Do this a number of times.

STEP TWO: When you have practiced the first step sufficiently, then make a series of deliberate shifts to a heterosexual fantasy earlier in the masturbation process. Switch back and forth. At first you may be able to hold the heterosexual fantasy in your mind only for a very brief period. As you practice, you will be able to maintain it longer and longer. With a good result, you should be able to maintain and become aroused by exclusively heterosexual fantasies, and this will be followed by an increase in sexual responsivity to members of the opposite sex in the life situation.

(d) Learn to be assertive with the opposite sex. This may remove the difficulty that produced your unwanted homosexuality. This happened in the case of Polly Wright, where we took the assertive difficulty that had caused her to avoid men and conquered it.

CASE

Polly just couldn't say no to men, and her fear of promiscuity led her into homosexuality. In her college years, she dated many different men, and every date ended up with Polly in bed. One day she heard a couple of young men refer to her as "that easy lay." This so disturbed her that she began to avoid the opposite sex. She didn't want to be an "easy lay." Her solution: no men at all. In her senior year, she became friendly with another woman student, and again Polly ended up in bed. She had her first lesbian experience out of choice. Desperately seeking warmth and tenderness, Polly found it via a sexual relationship with another woman.

Following graduation, Polly moved to Manhattan, became

friendly with another woman, and soon they became lovers and lived together. But Polly was unhappy. She put it to me, "I do love Sally, but I really want to love a man and have him love me."

I worked out a program for Polly. First, I trained her in the "Saying No" exercises (see Chapter III). In my office, we used behavior rehearsal for situations that might come up. Polly was model-pretty and had no difficulty meeting men at her job as assistant account executive at an advertising agency. So I urged her to get a date and go out once with a man, but instructed "that there should not even be a good night kiss, even though the man insists on it." She accomplished this, and was reinforced by being able to refuse that good night kiss. Step-by-step, Polly got involved with dating minus promiscuity. The most difficult point was when her heterosexual life grew so demanding that Polly decided she must break with Sally. It was a painful decision for both, but Polly felt: "I must do it to get where I want to go." Eventually, Polly married and told me, "I'm happy now, but I have no regrets about my homosexual days."

As Polly gained greater command over herself through AT, she became able to set her life-style through choice—not through the need to avoid anxiety.

(4) *Learn to be assertive about your homosexual life-style.* The difficulty may not be with the opposite sex, but with the assertive problems in the homosexual role. On the one hand, the homosexual fears to reveal his way of life; on the other, he experiences the constant burden of living in hiding and feeling a phony. In his presence, other people make continual quips, voice gay jokes, and use pejorative terms. He lives in a constant state of tension.

One reason for this assertive difficulty: he has the wrong idea of what coming out of the closet is. He thinks the alternative to hiding is to stand on a rooftop and announce to the world: "I'm gay. I'm gay." This is not the case. Most frequently, the question of coming out of the closet emerges from a specific situation, usually involving a close friend or relative.

An Assertive Guide for Homosexuals

Coming out of the closet

(a) Expect the worst and make your decision on that basis. Decide each situation individually. Should you tell your parents . . . a co-worker on the job . . . a close friend? In each case, decide whether you would prefer to stay in hiding or risk rejection, and make your decision on that basis.

For instance, you are a homosexual and have a close friend who is straight. Should you be honest with him? You must pose yourself the question of whether it is better to continue to hide or take the chance of rejection. Sometimes there will be rejection. Or the nature of the friendship will change. Often, however, the friend will respond, "I've suspected it all the time." These days, because of the changing social scene and increasing sexual freedom in our society, very few people will care whether you're gay or not. However, there is always a risk.

Very often, a special problem emerges with telling parents, especially mothers. However, with the impact of the gay liberation movement, more and more homosexuals, especially young ones, are revealing their life-styles to parents. Often greater closeness between son and mother follows the initial upset.

(b) Realize that revelation of your homosexuality on the job may result in job loss. The boss may not fire you directly for your homosexuality, but find another excuse to do so.

(c) Understand that revelation of your homosexuality on the job may not matter. Once they are confronted with the situation, many employers don't really care. For example, one homosexual, an executive in a very stuffy brokerage house, was looking for a new secretary. A senior partner in the firm was peripherally involved in the hiring. From among the series of job applicants, the executive selected a slightly effeminate young man. After meeting him, the partner said to the executive, "We can't hire him. We have a policy against hiring homosexuals." The executive spoke up. "Then you'd better think whether or not you want to keep me. I'm homosexual." A long pause ensued before the partner calmly stated, "Well, if you think he can do the job, take him." Not another word was ever said on the subject.

(d) Know that coming out of the closet may help you to cope with the holiday blues. Many homosexuals depart their big city refuges at holidays to visit their parents back in Podunk. There they feel the need to hide, to pretend. They miss warmth, affection, and sex with their lover. Those who can tell their parents about their homosexuality can bring their lovers with them.

(e) Don't come out of the closet in a superficial relationship if revelation will produce extreme discomfort in another person. This happens most frequently in business situations. For example, Peter Fairmont, a homosexual, works at a rather high-level job where he must entertain out-of-town buyers and executives from other companies. His superiors know of his gayness, but do not wish him to take his lover along on any expense-account entertaining. Peter resents this, reasoning, "If I were married, I would bring my wife to dinner. Why shouldn't I take Phil?" The principle here: don't flaunt matters of a personal nature that might make others uncomfortable. In superficial relationships (and business dinners with comparative strangers certainly fall within this category) the homosexual, or any other person, should not deliberately do anything that would produce embarrassment or strain in other people.

(f) Once you've made the decision to come out of the closet, the next question is how to communicate this to the person you want to tell. No set rules exist. It depends on you, the person involved, the kind of relationship you have with him or her, and the situation. Best way of answering the how question: discuss it and rehearse it with a friend who already knows you're gay. Then make the revelation at the appropriate opportunity.

Handling put-downs about homosexuality

There is one rule: *come on strong.* Many people have the erroneous concept that the homosexual is a passive, defense-

less, weak person. If you come on strong, it is at such variance
with this stereotyped idea and so unexpected that the other
person doesn't know what to say. You can get angry and
attack him in turn, put it back on the other person with a
question retort, or be exceedingly firm. Just remember the
basic technique of answering put-downs: you do not use "I,"
"me," or "because" in the first sentence of your answer. Too
defensive. For instance, if you are a male and a friend who is
putting you down says, "How are you today, *Mary?*" what can
you—a male—say? Perhaps you'll feel good if you respond,
"What are *you* so uptight about?" or "Do *you* feel threatened?"

Most people won't make comments like these, but many gay
people fear they will. If you have assertive difficulties because
you fear homosexual put-downs, rehearse some possible responses to them with a friend, until you feel that when, and if,
the situation occurs, you will be able to cope. This will reduce
general anxiety.

Meeting people

You meet people in the same ways that straight people
do—at parties, on the job, at resorts, bars, clubs. You do not
have to accept someone as a friend merely because he, too, is
gay.

Saying no to requests for sex

For example, you wander into a gay bar and a very
aggressive man comes over to your booth, starts to talk with
you, and eventually suggests, "Let's go over to my apartment."
You don't want to. You feel much more attracted to others in
the bar. But you haven't the assertiveness to say no. To
yourself, you rationalize, "I don't want to hurt his feelings."
You go and have an unsatisfactory experience, losing your
self-respect because you have done something unwillingly.
Practice saying no with a few simple phrases, such as "I really
enjoy talking to you, but I don't want to go over to your
apartment," or "Sorry, I'm taken" (just like the "Saying No"
exercises in Chapter III). This may help resolve your passivity.

Remember, you have the right to live your life the way you want to live it

Put yourself in the position to choose this right and act upon it—but know that at this moment society does not acquiesce completely.

ASSERTIVENESS TRAINING OF HETEROSEXUAL VARIANTS

Unlike homosexuality, which includes many complex behaviors, heterosexual variant (and I use this term rather than deviant because of the latter's pejorative connotation) behavior usually focuses on a single, relatively narrow area and rarely effects an entire life-style. Because of this, the heterosexual variant may have few major problems with holding a job, relating to others, and even in achieving a happy family life.

There are two exceptions to this statement. The first is when the variant behavior is not limited to acts performed alone or between consenting adults, but rather is imposed on other people. A man who publicly exhibits his sexual organs inflicts his behavior on others. A person who involves a child in his sexual activities makes a similar imposition, because the child is in no position to give informed consent. This kind of variant behavior can lead the person practicing it into a great deal of trouble both with the people around him and with the law, as society, quite rightfully, takes action to protect others from the variant's actions.

Secondly, even when limited to something performed in private or to privacy between consenting adults, quite often heterosexual variant behavior sets up problems within the person. Very often, the person with the simple variant behavior believes there is something "wrong" with him, that he is "abnormal" or "monstrous" and will be the object of contempt and ridicule should he ever be found out.

An enormous number of sexual variants exist today, most often identified in terms of the act.

Fetishists are people sexually attracted to objects like shoes, fur coats, pillows, or to nonsexual parts of the body like feet. This is their main sexual interest. They either masturbate to these objects or have sex in the presence of these objects, or even if they have sexual relations with a member of the opposite sex, they fantasize about these objects or parts during the act.

Tranvestites cross-dress. They wear clothing of the opposite sex. It may be a single article or garment, or they may dress from tip to toe like a female, including make-up, jewelry, padded bras, girdles, dresses, high-heeled shoes. Often, they, actually go out into the street looking like a woman; this behavior is not confined to times of sexual action. Usually cross-dressing is associated with masochistic fantasies, most often involving their subjugation by a domineering woman. Except for these behaviors, in all other respects, the large majority of tvs are completely normal heterosexual men.

Exhibitionists expose their genitals in public. In the process, they usually have an erection, and find it extremely exciting. They may masturbate at the same time.

Voyeurs get their excitement out of looking. These are Peeping Toms who look through windows and keyholes, often using binoculars to spy on neighbors. Watching builds up a high state of sexual excitement and very often brings on a sexual climax. Very often they masturbate to what they see.

Pedophiles dig children. They may go after little boys or little girls and try to have sexual relations with them. They may or may not be homosexuals.

Sado-masochists get their sexual excitement in the giving or receiving of pain. They may use whips, spankings, or any of a series of ingenious devices, invented just for this purpose, or make a sexual partner walk with a weight tied to her arms or wearing a tight corset lined with sandpaper, or a similar irritant.

These are just some of a seemingly endless list that includes everything from *bestiality* (sexual relations with animals; according to folklore, sheep are tops on the most-wanted list, but pigs, ponies, and fowl are also popular—the important asset seems to be availability) to *necrophilia* (sexual relations with dead people). Just about anything the human anatomy is capable of doing has been done somewhere at some time.

Except when damaging to others, these behaviors are not necessarily pathological. In his book *Sexual Stimulation*, Dr. S. G. Tuffill tells of the increased trust and sensitivity that occur between partners from using the props of sado-masochism, such as pillories, chains, manacles, and fingerless gloves. He also tells of the warmth, intimacy, and closeness that can develop from sharing a fetish or transvestism (one woman writes about her husband: "I must say he made quite an attractive woman when made-up and quite enjoyed it. And so did I."). This does not mean the behavior is never neurotic. If this single type of behavior is the exclusive mode of sexual satisfaction or if it is compulsive and out of control, then it probably is neurotic.

Psychoanalysis invariably considers these behaviors to be pathological. The psychoanalytic theories of what causes them vary, but most center around the Oedipal situation and usually interpret the different variant behaviors as different modes of coping with unconscious castration anxiety.

For instance, a fetishist sees women don't have penises and interprets this as meaning they have been castrated. He reasons: "If this happened to a woman, it can happen to me—I can be castrated." His solution: to reassure himself that women have not really been castrated. To accomplish this, he takes an object, like a shoe, and in his unconscious thinking, he turns it into a woman's penis. Then his thinking goes: "If women have penises, they have not been castrated—then I don't need to worry about being castrated." At the same time, because the object symbolizes a woman's genitals, he finds it sexually arousing.

Whether the elaborate psychoanalytic theories devised to explain fetishism are right or wrong, the fact is that the psychoanalytic treatment of variant behaviors generally proves unsuccessful. J. R. Ewalt and D. L. Farnsworth in their *Textbook of Psychiatry* recommend psychoanalysis, but state it "will be long, difficult, and often unsuccessful." One survey of all psychoanalytic literature found only three reports of successful treatment of fetishists.

The behavior therapy technique has been outstandingly successful in the treatment of sexual variants. Behavior therapists have little interest in formulating theories about the genesis and maintenance of heterosexual variant behavior. Instead, in treating it, we take the position (as with homosexuality) that anything done between consenting adults is acceptable. Because voyeurism, pedophilia, and exhibitionism do not involve consenting adults, they create special problems.

Our concern is to get the variant behavior *under the person's control so that he can perform or not perform his sexual actions out of choice.* By approaching many of these variant behaviors in self-control terms, many of them can quickly be brought under the individual's control—*provided he has the motivation to do so.* In my experience, most people with compulsive variant behavior want to change, with the exception of transvestites.

To establish self-control over the variant behavior, *you must be certain there is another sexual outlet besides the variant behavior available to you.* If you are a fetishist who does not date and gets sexual kicks only from masturbating to shoes, before you try to stop the fetish you should establish social and possibly sexual relations with women. If you already possess this social behavior in your repertory, then it's there, and you don't have to work to establish it. Whatever your variant behavior, you must establish the desired sexual behavior in other areas so you have freedom to make a choice.

You can use three possible methods to bring compulsive variant behavior under control.

(1) *Thought Stoppage.* This is the technique I outlined in Chapter IV and mentioned earlier in this chapter. I have found it to be extremely effective in training the person to be in command of his variant behavior. For effective use, the patient must possess self-discipline and a strong desire to change. When this method works, the patient can usually attain control of his variant behavior within five sessions or less, and although my follow-up shows that while the behavior may reappear, the patient has a method at his command to use on his own.

Study of the patient's behavior chain shows that there is usually a point where an urge, a fantasy, or an action triggers the variant behavior. This is the point at which to intervene. Every time the patient becomes aware that this specific behavior is present, he disrupts it by firmly saying STOP to himself, then "Calm," and momentarily relaxing his muscles.

Sometimes the patient must say STOP literally hundreds of times during the first few days of using thought stoppage. For instance, I treated a thirty-year-old exhibitionist, who last actually exhibited himself ten years earlier. However, he constantly felt the urge to display his genitals and was terrified that he would do it and thus face the ruin of his marriage and possible arrest. During the first few days of treatment he had to say STOP four hundred times a day. By the end of the first week, he was down to twenty times a day, and by the end of the next week, it was zero. A month later, he encountered a stressful life situation, and the urge reappeared; but by using thought stoppage, he brought it under control in twenty-four hours. For two years he has felt no urge.

In many cases, fantasies trigger deviant behaviors. For example, a transvestite sits at home alone watching television. He begins to think about cross-dressing and fantasizes about being submissive to a woman. The fantasy builds up. Soon he goes to the locked trunk where he keeps his female gear; dresses up in nylon pants, slip, pretty dress, fur coat; and goes out into the street, looking like his idea of a *Vogue* model. Most people do not have trouble identifying the fantasy that sets off their variant sexual response. I tell the variant that *as soon as,* and *every time,* he is aware of having such a fantasy, he should say STOP and relax. By disrupting the chain of behavior at this point, he very often rapidly gets the compulsive nature of the variant act under control.

However, people exist who do *not* experience fantasies. They find themselves confronted by the situation or object that turns them on and their first awareness really is the turned-on feeling. For example, a tv might walk down the street, see a lingerie shop, and suddenly find himself feeling very excited as he stares into the window. There he has to introduce the STOP at the first sign of a turn-on—before he rushes home to cross-dress. The important thing is to say STOP at the right point. Choose the point with care. Usually, it is the beginning of a fantasy, but it may also be the excited response to a stimulus.

CASE

When Roger Kane, a newly, but not happily, married man of twenty-five, came to me, he stated his problem succinctly: "I have a belly fetish." Whenever Roger saw a belly curve— whether on the body of a man, woman, or child—he felt enormously sexually aroused. This fetish was particularly destructive for Roger because he had just begun his medical internship year. Because he put in a great deal of time in the hospital's emergency room and also in doing routine physical exams, he spent most of his days and nights in a constant state of being excited by bellies. This interfered with his marriage because Roger interpreted his reaction as casting doubts on his masculinity. It also interfered with his medical training. Roger asked me, "How can a physician perform properly when he feels in a constant state of physical excitement?"

I taught Roger the STOP method. Every time he experienced that feeling of excitement when he saw a belly, he should firmly command himself STOP and deliberately relax his muscles. Apparently there was something wrong with my instruction because at our next session Roger had made no progress. It turned out he used STOP at the wrong point. Every time Roger noticed he was looking at a belly, he told himself STOP and looked away. This produced two difficulties. He was training himself *not* to look at bellies, an impossibility for a physician. Also, he did not give the feeling of excitement a chance for extinction. The idea was to look at stomachs and not feel excitement or disrupt the feeling of excitement before it could be reinforced.

I told Roger, "Don't use the STOP when you see the belly. Wait until you experience the first sign of a turn-on. The idea is to stop the turn-on feeling, not belly-watching." Within two weeks, Roger gained control of his fetish.

(2) *Covert sensitization.* I outlined this method, in which the patient associates the unwanted act with something unpleasant through *imagery*, in Chapter VII. It proves an important technique in controlling variant behavior.

When the transvestite cross-dresses or the exhibitionist makes public display of his private parts, he gets a turn-on. This strong sexual response maintains and reinforces his variant behavior. You can't remove these feelings; you can override them.

The point of covert sensitization is to introduce into the situation a set of feelings so unpleasant that they change the act from one of pleasure to one of punishment. Using imagery in the therapeutic session, we train the patient to associate something repugnant (like spiders crawling all over his body) with the unwanted act. It may take hundreds of repetitions of this distasteful association until the unpleasant feelings mask and make ineffective the pleasurable sexual reactions and suppress the variant behavior. The patient has to be patient, utilize the imagery technique constantly, and help it along by practicing the sexual behavior he desires.

(3) *Aversive therapy.* While covert sensitization falls within the category of aversive therapy, most people think of aversion as involving some form of physically administered punishment. You punish the "undesired" behavior over and over again, until the behavior and the punishment become so inextricably linked in the subject's mind that he avoids such behavior thereafter. Most commonly used today is the faradic method in which the therapist administers a painful electric shock to some part of the patient's body, and the shock is associated with the unwanted behavior. This technique can be used when the patient actually performs the behavior (for example, a transvestite can be given a series of shocks while he puts on female clothing), or when the patient fantasizes about the act, or in conjunction with stimulus photographs that set off the behavior.

Aversive conditioning has also been used to reorient homosexuals who ask to become heterosexual. In one form of therapy, a male homosexual is hooked up to a shock device and shown slides of nude men alternating with slides of nude women. When he is shown the male slides, he is given a shock until he presses a button which brings on the female slide and relief from the shock. If he changes the slide quickly enough, he can sometimes avoid the shock.

While researchers claim generally good results, I believe aversion therapy is one of the most overdramatized and overestimated treatment techniques in the behavior therapy area. I say this not only because of the "Big Brother" and thought control aspect but because, in actuality, its uses are extremely limited.

· Punishment is a poor technique for changing behavior. Reward works much better.

· Aversive therapy tends to suppress the behavior, and the behavior will return unless a further course of treatment is given as a booster shock.

· Recently, theorists have started to question whether it is the aversive aspect of the treatment that brings about the change from homosexuality to heterosexuality—or whether this stems from some other aspect of the treatment method.

· Most therapists feel uncomfortable administering this technique. We don't like the idea of causing physical pain to patients.

The use of aversive therapy is really limited to conditions where you must have a quick change to avoid a really severe consequence—for example, with exhibitionists and pedophiles—or where the variant behavior itself does not allow the development of an alternate behavior. For example, an individual may be so busy masturbating to shoes that he can't let himself develop an alternate form of sexual satisfaction that he would prefer to have.

In aversion therapy and in the treatment of sexual variants in general, I do not set the *extinction* of the variant behavior as my treatment goal. I seek the removal of its compulsive quality, so that it comes under the patient's control, and he has the freedom to do as he likes. I have also found that between thought stoppage, Assertiveness Training, and the development of alternate forms of behavior, I have no need for aversive therapy. In the Behavior Therapy Unit I established at Payne Whitney Psychiatric Clinic of The New York Hospital, our policy is *not* to use aversive treatment.

THE TRANSSEXUAL

Any change in one behavior effects dramatic changes in other aspects of a person. If a tv stops the compulsive wearing of women's clothes, he will experience many other positive changes. Removal of this one compulsion will reduce his anxiety, enable him to act more freely in expressing his feelings and to develop higher self-esteem. If a homosexual comes out of the closet and reveals his life-style, he may be relieved of a tremendous burden and thus develop an improved social life, perform better on the job and in his close relationships.

Sometimes, to bring about the desired change, it becomes

necessary to take several behaviors and treat them one at a time. These successive behavioral changes may bring about a complete change in a person's life.

A transsexual is different from a homosexual. A male homosexual knows he's a man, and his sex choice is another man. A woman homosexual knows she's a woman, and her sex choice is another woman. To a greater or lesser extent, some homosexuals may identify with members of the opposite sex. However, transsexuals (and there are an estimated ten thousand of these in the United States) carry this identification to an extreme. Born with the anatomy of one sex, they suffer from a total, lifelong identification with the other. The male transsexual believes he is a woman trapped in a man's body. The woman transsexual believes she is a man trapped in a woman's body.

Until recently, sex surgery has been the only possible solution for these sad, desperate people. Transsexuals have been so nonresponsive to traditional treatment methods that theorists started to speculate that this unfortunate condition was caused by something in the actual structure of the brain.

However, using behavioral therapy methods, there have now been several cases of gender identity change in a transsexual. This is the story of a case treated by a team, headed by Dr. David H. Barlow, at the department of psychiatry, University of Mississippi Medical Center.

CASE

The seventeen-year-old male patient was the third boy and the last of five children. For as long as the patient could remember, he thought of himself as a girl (the girl his mother had wanted). At the age of five, he began cross-dressing. He also developed an interest in cooking, crocheting, and embroidering. His older brother scorned him because he didn't like "masculine" activities like hunting. The patient remembered being strongly attracted to a boyfriend in the first grade. In his sexual fantasies, which developed when he was twelve, he pictured himself as a woman having intercourse with a man. In high school, his classmates mocked him because of his extremely effeminate behavior. He had tried suicide. When he first entered treatment, he was attending secretarial school where he was the only boy in the class. He wanted to change his sex.

Because of his youth, sex surgery was not possible. He agreed to enter a treatment program designed to change his gender identity on the premise that it might at least make him more comfortable and that surgery could be performed at a later date. The program went like this.

STEP ONE: The therapists used fading and electric shock to try to increase the patient's heterosexual arousal and decrease his responses to transsexual fantasies and male stimuli. They got no results with either method.

STEP TWO: They decided to change his effeminate motor behaviors—sitting, standing, walking—into more masculine ones. For instance, through modeling and video tape feedback, he learned to sit like a man, crossing his legs with one ankle resting on the opposite knee, instead of like a female, who usually sits with legs crossed closely together with one knee on top of the other. This worked, and the patient reported that with his new male behavior, people did not stare at him or ridicule him.

STEP THREE: The patient learned how to act in social situations. With the therapists, he would enact various scenes —like talking to fellow students during class breaks, discussing football or girls in an all-male bull session, asking a girl to go to the movies, the actual going out on a date. The therapists would model the correct behavior until the patient got it right.

STEP FOUR: They retrained his high voice pitch and feminine inflections. Shortly after completion of this phase, the patient looked and acted like a boy, but still felt like a girl, fantasized himself as a girl sexually and socially, and would still opt to change his sex.

STEP FIVE: In his strongest and most frequent fantasy, the patient imagined having a female body and engaging in intercourse with a man. The therapists initiated an attempt to develop a competing fantasy in which the patient had intercourse with a woman. In this procedure, the patient chose four pictures of a *Playboy* model which were least unattractive to him, and the therapists asked him to fantasize sexual involvement with the woman pictured. If he could hold the fantasy for a specified period of time, a second photograph that he had previously chosen as very pleasant (in this case pictures of food and animals) was shown. This indicated successful completion of a trial, and the therapists lavished praise on the patient. Eventually, they asked him to fantasize having sexual intercourse with young female acquaintances. At the end of this phase, the patient behaved and felt like a man and thought as a man does. But despite the sexual fantasies to women, he had little sexual arousal to women. In other words, he could now be described as homosexual.

STEP SIX: Next the therapists tried to develop heterosexual arousal, using the methods of slides, electric shock, and covert sensitization. Female arousal increased.

At the end of a year, the patient reported he was comfortable and relaxed in most social situations and would like to date and have sexual relations with women. Five months later, he reported orgasm and ejaculation for the first time while imagining intercourse with a girl when masturbating. Nine months after treatment termination he had no gender identity confusion, was doing well in school, and had begun to date. In one year, he had acquired a steady girl friend. Sex surgery is far from his mind.

Treatment of variant behavior doesn't always have such a successful conclusion. Sometimes a life situation can undo all the work of the therapist.

For example, I treated Sal de Falcone, a thirty-eight-year-old married man, father of three, for a variety of problems—philandering, lack of openness, fear of authority figures, and voyeurism. Sal worked hard and made such great progress that he decided to have an utterly open talk with his wife about what had happened in treatment and his hopes for the future. He did, and in this open talk, he learned to his shock that she also had been having extramarital affairs for years, but much more flamboyantly than he—and that her promiscuity had made her the talk of the neighborhood and he the laughing stock. Sal was the only one who hadn't known about it!

The day after the talk, Sal called me. "Doc," he said sadly, "I don't need *you* anymore. I need a priest!"

Chapter XII
Assertion on the Job

Do you awake Monday mornings with the I-can't-bear-to-go-to-the-office feeling?

Do you live in constant terror of losing your job?

Do you perform work that should be done by subordinates?

Even though your output and performance rank high, are you continuously passed over for promotions and raises?

Do you fear success?

Whatever your economic status—blue-collar, middle-income, or upper-echelon strata—if you answer yes to any of these questions, you are unassertive about a major life area: your job. Your lack of assertiveness affects not only the pay check you bring home but the way you feel about yourself.

Of all the tests that reveal your power to be assertive, your handling of love and work reveal the most.

To be assertive in either area, you must possess an active orientation and set goals that enhance your self-esteem. But in the close relationship of love, your aim should be openness, communication, and sharing of your whole emotional being. Feelings come first. In the job, the assertive emphasis reverses. Doing comes first. Feeling comes second. The aim is achievement and accomplishment. Because of this, relations with people at work tend to be superficial rather than intimate. The stress in the feelings you express there is more on appropriateness than openness.

In pursuit of job goals, you remain an individual, relating to, but separate from, others. The work itself becomes an extension of yourself, expressing something of you—your style, your speed, the way you meet on-the-job problems. The more assertive you are in relation to work and the more willing to show "this is me," the more satisfactions you gain. When the structure of the job or your own psychological blocks prevent this, dissatisfactions, resentment, and alienation occurs.

Assertion on the job involves five basic skills:

(1) *An active orientation.* You must think through your work goals, the steps you must take to achieve them, and how, in doing this, you can utilize your talents to the fullest possible extent.

(2) *Ability to do the job.* Interferences, obstacles, and blocks sometimes arise in the work situation because you have not mastered the skills you need for your particular job. In addition, you may have problems with self-control. You may possess bad work habits, lack discipline and the ability to concentrate.

(3) *Control of your anxieties and fears.* Inappropriate emotional reactions interfere with work performance. General tensions can produce fatigue, irritability, and poor judgment. Fear of a specific work situation may lead to avoidance of the very task needed to get your job done—and may keep you from achieving your work goal.

(4) *Good interpersonal relations on the job.* Lillian Roberts, a noted personnel counselor, once told me, "Most people get fired because they can't get along with other people." You must be able to relate to peers, subordinates, and superiors; make requests and ask favors; say no when necessary; handle put-downs.

(5) *The art of negotiating the system.* This requires a knowledge of the job society and the specific skills that will enable you to work within, through, or against it to achieve your particular goals.

THE UNASSERTIVE JOB TYPES—FROM THE PIGEON TO THE EXPLOITED

Within the office framework many personalities exist desk by desk—some lively, some quiet, others efficient or inefficient, lazy or hardworking. One group is linked by the common quality of unassertiveness. I divide those who lack job assertiveness into six basic categories.

(1) *The pigeon.* You're good at your work, liked and respected by all, but get nowhere on the job. No promotions, few raises, more work, but no new responsibilities. You're pigeonholed in the same slot. You don't like the situation. You want to move upwards or at least sideways. You keep waiting for someone to make this movement happen. Occasionally you express your desire, but you put it so tentatively that the message doesn't get through or can easily be ignored. Often you remain a pigeon because *you are assertive for the company, but not for yourself.* You have not thought through your job goals or how to take the next step.

(2) *The man in the background.* You do an excellent job, but nobody knows it. Others take all the credit for your actions, and you emerge as the perennial Indian and never the chief. The problem: you have the potential and ambition to be a chief. But because you are so basically unassertive, you have never learned to call attention to your own accomplishments. Your boss and co-workers pick your brain. You let them—and resent it.

(3) *Your own worst enemy.* You substitute aggression for assertion. Your work is good. But you disrupt the office, create turmoil, disagree with everyone in an unpleasant, hostile way. Others dislike your manner so much that they don't listen to what you say—even though your ideas are excellent.

(4) *Always the bridesmaid.* Because you don't mobilize yourself to work properly, you don't fulfill your potential. You have a problem in self-control behavior. Maybe you procrastinate and turn in work late, or daydream the day away. When you finally get going, your work is first rate; but your poor work habits prevent promotion. People who are aware of your talents wonder why you haven't achieved more. At first, superiors feel disappointment, then they stop expecting a top performance or often become irritated as your lack of discipline creates problems for them. You fear getting fired. Often you are.

(5) *The complainer.* Your problem is passivity. You constantly

gripe about work demands, the office environment, the way people speak to you or act toward you. But you never think of what *you* can do about these situations. You feel "*they* should do something about it." However, you don't discuss the situation with, or make your suggestions to, the right people. Instead, you fuss and grumble in places where your mutterings cannot lead to change.

(6) *The exploited*. Smiling sweetly, you say yes to every request. Not only are you overworked, but you often give up your own time and rarely receive a "thank you" for your efforts. You have not learned to say no to unreasonable requests or even to state: "Look, it's impossible to get all that work done today. What should we do about it?" The results: outbursts of crying or anger at the office, often depression or annoyance at home, and finally an impulsive change of jobs.

Most people realize the economic importance of their jobs. They know the way they earn their daily bread determines where and how they live, the schools their children attend, the clothes they buy, the income that will enable them to purchase a Florida condominium when they retire.

However, they fail to take this knowledge a step further. They *do not think through the role of the job in their lives*, evaluate what they want to give to the job and get from the job. As a result, they do not gain what they really want and feel dissatisfied with what they do get.

Depending on such factors as temperament, age, learned attitudes toward work, available work opportunities, goals in life in general, the job means different things to different people. The decision of the kind of job you want to get and keep and the way you want to behave and perform on the job is one only you can make. Failure to make this decision often leads to unfortunate consequences such as frustration, boredom, unhappiness. Because vocation is such a major life area, these consequences may affect every other aspect of your existence.

Whatever decision you make about the importance of work in your life, whether you work on the assembly line in a Detroit auto plant, as a middleman in a middle-league firm, or earn a six-figure income as an industry head, self-assertion is vital to any job situation. Here is a seven-point guide to help you achieve it.

ASSERTIVENESS TRAINING AND YOUR JOB

I: Think through your job goal

When I began dating the woman who was to become my wife, I quickly observed that she had great responsibility for major projects in her job and a tremendous professional reputation. Yet she earned the salary of a middle-league executive secretary. I couldn't understand the discrepancy between Jean's ability and performance and recognition in terms of pay and status.

As I got to know her better, I learned the reason. On her job Jean was extremely assertive. In her planning, she had two goals: (a) to do what "was best" for the publication on which she held an executive post; (b) to make the boss love her. For herself, she was unassertive, never thinking of her own needs or asking herself: "Where do I want to go in life?" . . . "What do I want from this job?" The result: she remained a pigeon, staying in the same job for years and never receiving the pay or promotions she felt she had earned. When, finally, she started to think in terms of money and prestige for herself, she did it *outside* the job. She began to write books and articles at great personal expense of time and energy, while still carrying on her demanding post at *Seventeen* magazine. The goals there had become a fixed habit. She couldn't leave her pigeon position.

Jean's case is fairly typical. Many people lack assertion because they have not formulated their goals. Many possible job goals and combinations of job goals exist.

Reality Goals

(1) *The job is simply a place where you earn your living.* You put up with your 9:00 to 5:00 stint so that you can collect a paycheck and meet your bills. You will work overtime for extra pay, but you want the right to choose whether you work overtime on any specific occasion. If you enjoy the work, that's gravy. If you don't enjoy the work, you can live with it. Your self-respect comes from the fact that you are working, not the kind of work you do. You derive your satisfactions elsewhere. Your goal is to do what you have to do on the job and have the

job interfere only minimally with the outside activities that really matter to you. You can run into two troublesome situations.

(a) *When you don't get your satisfactions elsewhere.* Pete Sterns was completely disinterested in his low-key, routine civil service job with a government agency, but he liked the security and the pension he would eventually get. However, he felt that the job was deadening and that this deadness had spread to the rest of his life. "I'm depressed," he said in his initial session with me. "I'm forty-three years old and I'm not enjoying life."

Pete felt his only solution was to leave the job which caused the "deadness," but he realized the impracticality of giving up seniority and pension rights. Working with him, I tried to make him see that the choice was not quitting or staying, but to see the job in the right perspective. His "gray job" provided money and security for him, his wife, and his three children, payment on the mortgage, and took up only thirty-five hours a week. What Pete had to do was invest his creative energies in building up his avocational and leisure time activities. This he was able to do.

(b) *When the routine job takes over your life.* Poets, painters, writers often have to spend their days earning money to secure the freedom to do what they really want. Composer Charles Ives spent thirty-two years in the insurance business. The problem occurs when the secondary job assumes too much importance and takes too much time. For instance, when John Brown came to me for therapy, he had lost sight of his goals. He had made a good start as a concert pianist, but he needed money to eat. So he became a piano teacher. Before he knew it, he had a full schedule of pupils, little time to practice, and even had to cancel a recital because he wasn't prepared. Without realizing it, he had switched from the goal he wanted—that of being a concert pianist—to a goal he didn't want, that of being a piano teacher. Our solution: we set aside a reasonable number of hours to spend teaching and termed this his "scholarship fund." Under these circumstances, he was able to switch back to his original goal. Incidentally, on John's first visit, he had thought none of this through. He just said, "I'm depressed."

(2) *You want to make as much money as you can.* For this goal, you will sacrifice pleasure, leisure, relationships. You will accept pressures, worries, and do anything you have to do to earn a huge income. Unlike the first category where the job is secondary, here the job is paramount. But what matters is not the kind of work, but the opportunity for making money. Many people with this goal tend to forget this fact and get sidetracked.

(3) *You want glory, status, prestige.* You willingly undertake responsibilities to get that exalted title. But remember the higher you rise, the more front and center you become, the more people will try to undercut you, and the more tensions you will have.

(4) *You want the work to be rewarding to you, to be in terms of your own interests and skills.* Many people never achieve this goal because they start in the wrong field and never have the guts to leave. Sometimes this is unavoidable. You can't know what a job entails until you do it. Sometimes, basing your thoughts on stereotypes and misinformation, you have a mistaken idea of what the work will be. Nobel laureate Albert Szent-Györgyi writes in *The Crazy Ape*: "Whenever young men come to me saying they want to go into research because they want to help decrease human suffering, I advise them rather to go into charity. Research wants egotists, fascinated by 'useless' problems, willing to sacrifice everything, including their lives, for a solution." You cannot always prevent yourself from starting in the wrong field, but once you discover that you have, shift before it's too late.

(5) *You want personal growth and a feeling of movement through life from the job.* Often this goal involves constant challenge and a high level of anxiety.

(6) *You want to make a social contribution, to do meaningful work.* You yearn to make the world a better place in which to live, help the underprivileged, fulfill a civic obligation by working for the government, or change society by opposing the government. For you, the main thrust of work comes from implementation of a principle.

These are just a few of the possible goals. Some are incompatible. Usually you cannot make a lot of money and have complete job security. Some can be combined. By determining your major goal, you can think through your main job thrust.

But there are also neurotic goals that do not relate to reality.

Neurotic Goals

(1) *The need to be needed.* You have to feel indispensable. If you leave, everything will collapse—a theory that rarely proves true. Often you view yourself as being extremely loyal to your employer. But are you being loyal to yourself? Or do you overwork as a rationalization for not being assertive or happy in other areas of your life?

(2) *The need to be liked rather than respected.* Many unassertive people become very concerned about whether or not people like them. They fear that if they say no to a request (no matter how unreasonable), stand up for themselves, succeed in a difficult project, speak up firmly, other people will not like them. Maybe they won't. But in a work situation, *respect matters far more than liking.* The person who is respected gets a better deal at work. The statement "He's a nice guy, but can he handle responsibility?" is liking—tinged with lack of respect.

(3) *The need to master impossible situations.* Some people reason that if a work situation doesn't come off satisfactorily, it must be their fault. They must remain in the situation until they conquer it; to leave is a cop-out. On her job as an interior decorator, Mary Edwards worked for an older woman whom Mary described as "the complete bitch—demanding, disrespectful of me, exploitative." Mary had been offered a job with another woman decorator who "seemed nice." She hesitated to accept, saying, "The way my boss acts to me must be my fault. If I take the new job, I'm running away from my problem. I should stay until I get Mrs. Marks to respect me. Also, she knows so much. I'm learning a lot." Actually, both bosses, the actual and potential, had equally prestigious reputations. After some sessions with me, Mary did take the other job and was amazed by the change in her own behavior. Her tension disappeared, and she began to enjoy her work. She also admitted, "This woman knows just as much as Mrs. Marks does."

(4) *The need to be the good child, to win approval.* You are

confused between *task orientation*, where you put the emphasis on doing the job well, and *ego orientation*, where you use the job to prove something about the kind of person you are. With the latter approach, you become more vulnerable, more sensitive to stress and disruption, and oriented away from the objective realities of the job itself.

(5) *The need to have the world feel sorry for you.* Without awareness, you set up such impossible job conditions that everyone says, "Poor you." Thus, you gain the reinforcers you want—sympathy and concern—but not the reinforcers that would best serve your professional interests.

Your criteria for choosing job goals should be the same as for other assertive acts. Will the one you choose move you to where you want to go in life? Will it increase your respect for yourself?

Above all, face the fact that as your life situation changes, your goals may shift too.

II: Take the active approach to getting the job that is right for you

Knowing your job goal is not enough. You want to achieve it. Let's assume that having thought through your goal, you decide to look for a new job. You can go about this in two ways.

With the passive approach, you read the want-ad section of the newspaper and send off your resume to the ad that appeals to you and wait for an answer. Or you make the rounds of employment agencies and go off to any interviews they arrange for you. You may get a marvelous, high-salaried job this way, but percentages are against you.

With the active approach, want ads and employment agencies represent only two of the many possible techniques.

(1) *Plan your overall strategy.* Learn the arts of job-hunting and resume-writing. A number of good books exist on this subject. I like *How to Get a Better Job*, by Austin Marshall.

(2) *Gather necessary information.* Use the public library or the library of a trade association to find out about companies where jobs might exist. Talk with friends and friends of friends who have knowledge they can pass on to you.

(3) *Find out where the jobs actually are.* In addition to reading want ads and visiting employment agencies, don't overlook trade associations and professional organizations and employment centers operated by your college or alumni club. These can serve as information sources.

(4) *Master the art of performing well at the interview.* If you feel you will have difficulty with certain questions (like "What do you see yourself doing in twenty-five years?" . . . "How come you left your last job?" or "You've been out of work for six months. Why have you had so much trouble finding a job?"), practice your answers *before* you go for the interview. Use a tape machine, listen to your answers, and try to improve them. Better still, role-play the situation with a friend or spouse. The feedback you get will help you improve your responses.

(5) *Make direct, assertive approaches to possible employers.* Find the right person at the place you'd like to work and try to set up an appointment. It helps if a friend can arrange it, but you don't need that. You can do it on your own. This technique works particularly well for the over-forty. For example, one woman who worked in the public-relations department of a major airline got fired during a company cutback. For eight months, she alternated between feverish job hunting and fits of depression. Then she asked herself, "What do I really want to do?" Her answer: "I want to do public relations for a major auto manufacturer." Some summers before, while on vacation in Mexico, she had met a General Motors executive who had given her his card. Instead of writing him, Grace flew to Detroit, called him at 9 A.M., and saw him at 11 A.M. He provided an introduction to his counterpart in the New York office. It took some months, but Grace now works for GM—and she was in her late forties when she landed the job.

The active approach may enable you to get a better job. More important, this technique makes you feel more in command of yourself. You respect yourself.

III: Make sure you have the skills to maintain your present job

When you start a job, you rarely know everything you need to know. Or you may be skilled in the main part of the job, but not in other subsidiary areas. Active acquisition of any technique needed will improve your morale and the quality of your work. This will prevent the anxiety you feel when you have to do something you realize you can't do well and the tenseness you experience about the consequences—whether the boss's criticism or loss of a customer.

Sometimes lack of skills lead to *avoidance behavior*. Because you cannot perform competently, you procrastinate and feel ashamed.

CASE

Thirty-five-year-old Myron Walters liked his position as an assistant in the personnel department of a large company. Generally, he was conscientious, but he always fell behind on the task of checking employees' vouchers for travel expenses. His superior was furious. In discussing this problem with Myron, I learned that he felt very unsure of his own simple arithmetic. In grade and high school, math had been his poorest subject. I told Myron to buy a grade school arithmetic workbook and to spend a half hour daily practicing simple addition, multiplication, and division. We were both astounded to learn he had never memorized the multiplication table. Once Myron felt sure of his figures, he stopped avoiding checking the travel expenses. By resolving the problem in this trivial, but meaningful, area, he increased his self-esteem— and he got a raise.

(1) *Learn skills that will help you move on to a higher job if that's your aim.* Pick them up on the job, from reading, self-teaching, or courses. Acquiring these—plus letting people know about your new knowledge—makes promotion more probable.

(2) *Take an active orientation to your working environment to make it optimal for you.* Don't be afraid to ask for a chair with a straighter back or a newer typewriter. If people constantly barge into your office, keep the door closed as a do-not-disturb signal. One male patient complained that he was constantly distracted at the office; the simple act of turning his desk to a 45-degree angle cut down his visual distraction and made him less aware of noise.

(3) *Use self-control on bad habits that interfere with work*—like lateness, procrastination, and lack of concentration. I outlined

the self-control techniques very thoroughly in Chapters VII and VIII. Let me just reiterate:

(a) Identify the habit you want to change.

(b) Prepare a specific program for changing this behavior.

(c) Set as your intention something that you can reasonably accomplish—soon. Aim for a series of successes.

(d) Examine the situation to see if you can make the unwanted act harder to perform and the desired act easier to perform.

(e) Establish the desired habit. Positive reinforcers, in terms of praise from friends or giving yourself presents, help.

(f) Monitor yourself. Keep charts. If you see you are performing the wanted behavior more and the unwanted behavior less, you will feel encouraged.

IV: Learn to control general anxiety on the job

In the job situation constant tension produces many effects. It may cause you to have difficulty concentrating on your work, impair judgment so that you make incorrect decisions, make you so unstable and hypersensitive that slight things annoy you to an extraordinary degree. In this way, it interferes both with your output and your relations with co-workers, bosses, and subordinates. Tension consumes energy and can lead to extreme fatigue at the day's end; insomnia at night; physical ills, such as illness stemming from low physical resistance; and can contribute to psychosomatic disorders like high blood pressure or gastric ulcers.

To its victim, tension has even more meaning. Because you cannot control it, you feel helpless and think less of yourself for this helplessness. Often you avoid the stress situations, such as speaking up at a meeting or asking for more challenging assignments, that provoke the tension, thus limiting your work and reducing opportunities for growth and advancement, or you make unreasonable demands of others. Your feeling of helplessness increases.

A few people do possess the ability to relax themselves, but, because of passivity, never think of doing it. I tell them, "Look, when you feel the tension building up, make yourself relax," or "Every hour on the hour tell yourself, 'Relax,' and then do it."

By shifting to the active orientation, they can overcome the tension problem.

It's not that easy for most people. In the 1930s, Dr. Edmund Jacobson, a Chicago physician, showed that just as you can learn to drive a car or swing a tennis racquet, you can acquire the ability to invoke a relaxation technique that works in the time it takes to light a cigarette. But Dr. Jacobson's method, which he carefully stated were not exercises, but rather getting to know your tensions and switching them off, usually required fifty to two hundred training sessions and one hour daily practice.

AT RELAXATION EXERCISES

In Assertiveness Training, we utilize much shorter exercises. The Full Relaxation Exercises take twenty minutes to perform; the Intermediate Relaxation Exercises take seven minutes. You will find these exercises in the appendix. The purpose: to put you in command of tensions on the job as well as elsewhere in life.

LABORATORY EXERCISE IN RELAXATION

Before beginning the Full Relaxation Exercises, you must do and be aware of certain things.

STEP ONE: Estimate your tension level with a sud scale (an acronym for subjective units of disturbance).

0 ——————————————————————————————— 100

Zero signifies that you feel completely relaxed with *no tension whatsoever*. At the far end, 100 means *complete tension*—the most uptight you can imagine yourself. At this moment, you cannot be at either extreme. The very act of holding this book causes some muscle tension so you cannot be zero. If you were at 100, you would be unable to concentrate enough to read these directions. The exercises aim to enable you to be closer to, or at, zero upon completion.

STEP TWO: In the exercise, I ask you to imagine a "pleasant scene," like being at the beach or walking in the country.

Make this a neutral one (neutral in the sense that there are no potentially disturbing elements in it).

If you have difficulty imagining the pleasant scene, just think of the word "Calm." The exercise's aim: to enable you to condition yourself so that whenever you think of your particular pleasant scene, you automatically relax. The scene is the stimulus that triggers your response. When you become fully trained, just thinking of your scene or the word "Calm" should produce some degree of relaxation.

STEP THREE: Use the exercise to study what happens to your tension when you relax. The Full Relaxation Exercises consist of three parts. First, you tighten large groups of muscles. By letting the tension build up, you become more aware of *where* you feel it and what it feels like. You hold the tension for about seven seconds before exploding it out. With this, you experience the relief from tension. In the second part, you check out different parts of your body. Finally, you imagine the pleasant scene or think of the word "Calm" and relax each part of your body systematically.

STEP FOUR: At the beginning of your self-training, perform the Full Relaxation Exercise once a day or even more if you feel the necessity. However, missing a day will not produce catastrophe. The exercises are not a ritual. They are designed to serve as a source of relaxation, not as a spur to compulsion and more pressure. Continue the Full Exercises until you get close to zero each time with fair consistency. Then use the Intermediate Exercise every other day. When this proves effective, you can drop down to two to three times a week for the Intermediate and once a week for the Full. When you eventually feel in control of your tensions, use the exercises only when needed.

STEP FIVE: When you perform the exercises, either from memory or via audio tape, you must be alone. If anyone else is home, close the door. Take the telephone off the hook. Lie down on a comfortable bed or even on the floor. Dim the lights. Turn off the TV. Put the dog in another room. You must be uninterrupted for the necessary period of time.

If you cannot relax with the exercises, do calisthenics just before using them. This physical exercise will facilitate relaxation, and you will begin to associate the feeling with the relaxation training procedures themselves. Eventually, you should be able to discontinue the calisthenics and start directly with the exercises.

If you allow yourself to fall asleep while doing the exercises, you defeat the purpose. The aim is for you to control the situation. Even if you use the exercises to combat insomnia, try to stay awake until you complete them.

STEP SIX: Keep a relaxation record in your AT notebook. Use the sud scale. Each time you complete the exercise, write down the sud level you achieve. Over a period of time, you should be able to lower your sud level, and the written results of accomplishment should encourage you.

The first two exercises in the Appendix are for training. In the life situation at the office, you can employ a much briefer one.

PRACTICAL RELAXATION EXERCISE

Purpose: To allow you to apply your relaxation training on the spot on the job, as well as in other situations.

STEP ONE: Take a deep breath through your mouth. Hold it.

STEP TWO: Say "Hold it" to yourself four times, timing it so that you hold your breath for about seven seconds. Practice with the second hand of a watch until you get the rhythm right.

STEP THREE: Let your breath out slowly.

STEP FOUR: As you let it out think of your pleasant scene and deliberately relax your muscles.

You can train yourself to perform this exercise at your desk or even in a conference room so that no one will notice. I did it myself on a live TV show!

These relaxation exercises prove particularly helpful in three situations that affect on-the-job performance.

Insomnia. You can't turn in a stellar performance at the office if you've spent the previous night tossing, turning, counting sheep, or even having hysterics because you can't fall asleep. Several experiments show that relaxation training proves effective with insomnia victims. The simple procedure: prepare yourself for sleep and go through the Full Relaxation Exercises. Upon completion, *keep imagining* your pleasant scene. Don't let your mind wander, and if it does, bring it back to the pleasant scene or the word "Calm." If you feel tension building up in any part of your body, deliberately relax it. By keeping the state of relaxation, hopefully you will drift off to sleep.

General tensions at work. A general uptightness throughout the working day will impair your judgment and lead to fatigue. As a result of your relaxation training, you should start to lose your passivity about continual tensions and begin to feel a sense of control. Every hour on the hour (or even every half hour) deliberately relax yourself with the short Practical Relaxation Exercise. This takes just a few seconds and you can do it at your desk, in a restaurant over a business lunch, with a customer, or walking down the corridor en route to a meeting with the boss.

Flying. Travel by plane proves a requisite in many jobs today. Yet I have known many people to turn down jobs they wanted because they required flying. Others manage to get on a jet and spend the entire flight shaking. Relaxation may be helpful in conquering this common fear.

Practice the exercises in a lying position until you achieve a good measure of relaxation.

Adapt the exercises to a sitting position and again practice until you feel a sense of control.

Simulate being on a plane. Find a chair that somewhat resembles an airplane seat. Imagine yourself actually in flight. While performing the exercise, practice a minimal tightening of the muscles. Many people feel a sense of inhibition about public performing of the stretching and grimacing that a portion of the Exercises require. For a week before the flight, practice not being obvious about the tightening.

On the plane, go through the Full Relaxation Exercise as soon as you settle into your seat. If, during the flight, you begin to feel rising tension, do it again.

V: Learn to control the specific anxiety you have learned to associate with a specific job task

In addition to the overall tensions you experience on the job, you may also fear certain clearly defined situations. You're an expert copywriter, but you feel nervous writing about food. In person, you can sell anyone anything, but you feel uptight about making the initial telephone call to set up an appointment. The behavior therapist calls these specific fears "phobias," and the word refers not only to fear but to any inappropriate disturbed reaction—such as inordinate tension, depression, irritation, or rage—produced by a specific situation. In the job setting, these fears can lead you to perform poorly, lose your job, and often keep you from ever showing up at the office.

Systematic Desensitization of Phobias

To combat phobias, behavior therapists use the technique of *systematic desensitization.* We know you associate a certain stimulus (whether the closed space of an elevator, the knotting of stomach muscles, the criticism of a superior) with a disturbed reaction. You have learned to react this way. If you can experience the anxiety-provoking stimulus a number of times without feeling disturbed, the conditioned response of anxiety should be replaced with a nonphobic reaction. The fear should disappear.

Systematic desensitization utilizes a step-by-step breaking down of the fears that produce the anxious response. The theory is that relaxation will inhibit the response *because the state of relaxation is incompatible with anxiety.* Eventually, the stimulus loses its ability to provoke your anxiety. (This is Dr. Joseph Wolpe's "reciprocal inhibition principle," which I noted in Chapter I.) Parents often do this with young children, without realizing it. When a three-year-old fears the ocean, his mother will take him by the hand to the fringe of the approaching waves and lift him up when a wave nears. After the child feels comfortable, mother encourages him to dip a foot in the wave, an ankle, and eventually to wade in. Thus, by degrees, the child eventually conquers his fears.

Notice that the mother starts with a situation where her

child feels relatively little anxiety. She approaches the core fear (probably submersion in the water) in stages. At each stage, she helps the child conquer his anxiety. This approach, as observed earlier, is called "constructing a hierarchy."

In office practice, the therapist, using the systematic desensitization method, also constructs a hierarchy. With the patient, he devises scenes of varying degrees of anxiety within the phobic area. (For instance, if the patient is a professional who fears public speaking, the hierarchy might go: speaking to five people . . . ten people . . . twenty people . . . thirty people in a small auditorium . . . one thousand people in a hall.) Then, starting with the lowest anxiety scene, he has the patient *imagine* it. Should the patient feel any increase in disturbance while imagining it, he promptly instructs the patient to relax. Over and over, he has the patient imagine each scene until the patient can do it without any feeling of disturbance. Then they move on to the next step in the anxiety hierarchy.

In this way, the therapist trains the patient to associate nondisturbance with the situation that previously evoked anxiety or fear. Usually, the feeling of decreased disturbance will carry over when the patient encounters the situation in reality.

This is a rather technical procedure, and if not performed correctly, there is some danger that the phobia can get worse. *You can't use it on yourself.* You *can adapt* the technique for your real-life-problem situations.

In Vivo Desensitization

In systematic desensitization in the therapist's office, the patient imagines the stimulus cues that set off the tension. It is also possible to *desensitize yourself in actual life situations.* The principle remains the same: you want a *response that inhibits your anxiety and that occurs in the presence of the anxiety-evoking stimuli.* In less technical words, if *you can actually go through the feared situations while remaining relaxed*, eventually you will cease to be frightened in these situations. This method is known as *systematic desensitization* in vivo *(in life)*. It can be very helpful in job situations.

(1) *Formulate a hierarchy*. First get a starting point. Take your anxiety-producing situation and find a point where your anxiety is minimal and does not produce a rise of more than ten points on your sud scale. It is sometimes difficult to find a series of life situations suitable for self-desensitization procedures. Generally, patients find it simplest with the "thing phobias" like fear of heights, elevators, or trains—all of which have a great influence on the job you take or job you can do. Let's take fear of heights. Determine the starting point for you. It may be looking out of a fifth floor window, a first floor window, or even standing on the lowest rung of a step ladder. Your first step should be a situation where you feel only slight disturbance.

Then determine the cues that bring about your anxiety. You may feel fearful if the window is open and still more fear if you lean out and look straight down. Using these cues, formulate a series of situations which approach the fear of heights in a hierarchical manner.

I treated one young legal secretary who was afraid to go above the third floor of any building. Since most Manhattan law offices are located in skyscrapers, Kathy was eventually forced to take a job selling in a ground floor boutique. When we first started working together, she spent three weeks riding elevators to the third floor, practicing her relaxation. Eventually, she felt comfortable and moved on to the fourth. She went up and up—and now has a job with a law firm on the thirty-second floor.

(2) *You don't have to formulate the entire hierarchy before you begin the* in vivo *process*. In the course of desensitizing yourself, you may find you actually, in life, respond to different cues from the one you originally had supposed. In that case, you may have to revise your hierarchy. Do try to formulate three to four steps ahead.

(3) *Train yourself in the three relaxation methods*. You should have excellent control of the Practical Relaxation Exercise.

(4) *Take the situations one at a time and go and do them*. Before you leave each situation, repeat it over and over until you are completely comfortable in what has been an anxiety-provok-

ing situation. When you feel completely relaxed, you can go on to the next hierarchy item.

CASE

One job-hunting patient experienced enormous anxiety during interviews. His solution *in vivo:* to go on interviews for jobs he definitely did not want or knew he could not get. During these he practiced relaxation. Because he knew no job was at stake, he had a relatively low level of anxiety, and the relaxation proved effective. This procedure markedly reduced his anxiety during subsequent interviews for jobs he really wanted.

CASE

A lawyer had great trouble with dictation. She wrote out all her letters in longhand before she gave them to her secretary because she feared that while dictating, she would say something "silly," and the secretary would feel contemptuous of her. In my discussions with Kay, I learned she felt much less fear with routine letters than with intricate interoffice memos. We grouped her dictation fears into five categories. So, in using desensitization *in vivo,* Kay started by dictating letters from the routine category and kept using the Practical Relaxation Exercise as she did it. Gradually, she moved up the hierarchy. At the interoffice-memo level, she discovered that she needed careful notes before she began dictating and also learned to say to her secretary, "This is just a draft. I had better go over it before you do final copy."

Life itself is not always so cooperative in providing opportunities for desensitization. You may have to simulate the problem through role-playing. To present the disturbing cues, you will need the help of a friend. Remember, each time he presents the cue and you respond with even a slightly disturbed reaction, you should concentrate on relaxation. He should repeat the presentation of each cue until you feel no tension. Then go on to the next step in the hierarchy.

Assume the problem is that of asking for a raise. John Jones fears that if he does this, his boss will fire him. He uses the sentence, "Mr. Smith, I'd like to talk to you about a raise. I think I deserve one." Role-playing the part of the boss, friend Brown can respond in the following hierarchical manner:

· "Well, I'll think it over."
· "I'm not so certain. Keep trying and we'll talk it over again in three months."
· "No raise for you. Actually your work has been falling off, and I've been thinking of letting you go."
· "Raise? You're fired!"

These responses serve merely as illustrations. The actual phrases have to be customed tailored to your particular anxieties. They do not have to be based on actual probabilities. In this instance, Jones knows that little chance exists of his being fired. Yet this irrational fear keeps him from asking for a deserved raise. Use of the "you're fired" phrase in the hierarchy helps to eliminate the fear. When role-playing, make it as real as possible. *The friend should repeat each of the stimulus phrases until you experience no disturbance.*

(5) *Use desensitization to treat fear of symptoms.* Sometimes what you're really afraid of are the anxiety symptoms themselves. You know that certain situations, like presenting a report to the boss, tend to set off trembling, blushing, dizziness, or that knot in your stomach, and that these symptoms will set off a secondary anxiety. The idea is to teach yourself to abort the attack. If you can do this, your confidence will return, your fear diminish, and you will be able to make that speech, address that meeting, or attend that conference.

When you feel the nervousness start during a meeting, use the Practical Relaxation Exercise. This requires only seconds to do and just part of your attention. It need not interfere with your performance. If you reduce your anxiety only slightly, you break the panic pattern.

As you feel the nervousness start, perform various physical and mental actions in an attempt to control it. Move your arms. Shuffle your papers. Look out the window. Imagine the chairman of the meeting streaking across the room. Think of that marlin you caught last summer. Note what—if any— changes each of these activities brings to your anxiety. By doing these things, you have introduced *task orientation to counter the anxiety.* Here the work is that of experimenting with your anxiety reaction.

VI: Master the art of good personal relations on the job

The kind of work you do and your ability to perform it represent only a portion of your professional picture. A major share of your success or failure on the job, plus your own satisfaction, depends on relations with others.

You need the same skills you require in social situations, such as the ability to make requests, ask favors, say no, express appropriately positive and negative feelings. But on the job the aims of assertiveness are different. You want pleasant relations with others to get the job done. You are not seeking deep relationships with others in a job situation. Such relationships may develop, but then they move out of the confines of the work area. Your job aim: to facilitate your work goal. Complications develop because most working situations include hierarchical structures in the forms of subordinates, peers, and superiors. Different criteria for appropriate behavior exist.

Many people misunderstand the meaning of assertion on the job. They do not differentiate between assertion and aggression. But assertion does not signify putting the office in an upheaval or punching a co-worker in the nose; it involves *honest communication at the right moment to achieve mutual job goals.*

A GUIDE TO ASSERTIVENESS ON THE JOB

(1) *Make it easy for people to do what you want them to do.* For example, in asking for a raise, do anything possible that will simplify the situation so the boss can say "yes."

(a) Give your chief the reasons you deserve a salary increase. Don't make him hunt for them. For example, one female bank vice president suspected that her salary was less than that paid to male vice presidents. For years, she endured this inequity. Finally, in desperation, she added up her assets, mustered up her courage, and went to see her boss. She told him she was managing some $25 million in loans, whereas her four male bank colleagues together were handling only $10 million. "Good God," was all the boss said. Shortly afterward she got a big raise.

(b) Make sure you know office policies about raises (they are usually reviewed when the budget for the upcoming year is prepared). If you ask for one when it is not due, you run up against the Standard Operating Procedure barrier.

(c) Do homework. If you can't screw up your courage to make the pitch for more pay, try role-playing with a close friend or spouse.

CASE

Wendy Hilton had learned the AT concept in one of my groups. Her husband, Bob, a lawyer, had started a new job in the legal department of a large company some six months ago and now felt (1) underpaid and (2) that he was being given all the routine work, so that the job had become boring and without challenge. They determined that Bob must talk to his boss and that the time to confront him was when the boss asked his daily question "How are things going?"

Wendy taught Bob to role-play. She played the boss. They worked out Bob's initial statement ("I'm very glad you asked, because I've been here six months, and there are a couple of points I'd like to discuss with you"). They also worked out how he might answer if the boss responded to his raise request with, "We consider raises only after an employee has been here for a year." If this happened, they decided that Bob would ask the boss to evaluate his work so that he could improve it—and be sure of his raise at the end of a year.

What happened in real life differed only slightly from the role-playing. Bob seized his opportunity to state, "I have a couple of things I'd like to discuss with you." He didn't get the raise, but the boss admitted: "I know you're underpaid, and I've been fighting with the upper echelons of the administration for pay increases. This gives me more ammunition. I'm delighted you brought this up." He hadn't realized Bob did such dull work. He immediately assigned him several challenging jobs and arranged for him to attend an especially interesting legal conference that very afternoon.

(2) *Speak up*—to praise others, to keep others from putting you down, when you're right or wrong, and to protect your

own position. Usually these situations involve the use of feeling talk, saying no, and just plain talking up for yourself, and occur in four circumstances:

(a) As a superior, you must give feedback. Employees want to know what you think of their work. You can praise or criticize constructively, but let them know your opinion in a positive way. Don't dwell on what the employee does wrong; tell him how he can do it better.

CASE

I treated one fifty-year-old vice president of an engineering company who had great problems being open with people, so I instructed him in the use of feeling talk. For several weeks, we rehearsed how he might respond at his weekly group conferences where subordinates tossed ideas around. Then Tom put his therapeutic rehearsal into business action. His report to me: "It was the most stimulating conference I've ever had." At the weekly conference, Tom had given his immediate feeling reaction—"I like that," or "I don't like that," when a subordinate presented an idea. This had led to exciting group discussion. Tom admitted, "Now I see what I did before. I didn't react when anyone came up with a thought. Instead, I moved on to the next report. This time, because I gave immediate feedback, the whole group got involved." From there we went on to work on Tom's behavior with peers and superiors, and as he became more open, his fears of showing feelings disappeared.

(b) You must stand up for yourself. When you deal with other people, they either deliberately or inadvertently will do things that affect you, your work, your company standing. By communicating your feelings, you prevent them from putting you down.

For example, if someone repeatedly takes credit for your ideas, you have the right to say "I don't like what you did. You know damn well that the idea you presented at the meeting this morning was mine. Don't let this happen again." Ignore the behavior and you encourage the other person to continue the pattern. Communicating your feeling doesn't mean you'll stop the idea-stealing, but the other person might think twice about doing it the next time. And you feel free to take stronger preventive action. For instance, you do not *tell* this particular person any brilliant thought you have; you *send* it to him in memo form, with a copy to the boss.

You also express your feelings to the office troublemaker. You say, "I feel upset when you steal my copy of *The Times*" . . . "I feel extremely annoyed when you eat your lunch at my desk and leave crumbs" . . . "You've been gossiping about me, and I don't like it." Express your thoughts tactfully, but make sure you communicate them. Then you set limits on the troublemaker—he or she knows you know. If you never say anything, he'll continue to steal your *Times*, eat at your desk, and tell lies about you.

(c) As a subordinate, you can say no to a superior. Yes, you have reason to feel some trepidation at saying no to the boss who has the power over your vacation schedule, promotions, raises. Some people in power positions never want to hear the word "no," but most bosses are human and will respond when you put your negative properly. Your no response must include the reason why. In a social situation, if a friend says, "Let's do such and such," it's quite appropriate to answer, "No, I'm just not in the mood." In the job situation your no answer must relate more to the factual aspects of the matter involved than what you feel.

Let's say a supervisor says, "I'd like you to stay late tonight and finish that job." You might try three types of no responses according to your individual situation.

· "No, I'm sorry, but I can't. I have a long-standing appointment for this evening."

· "No, when I took the job, I told you I would always give up my lunch hour, but I must take the 5:57."

· "No, it's not a good idea. I have that important conference at 9 A.M. tomorrow, and I must be sharp for it. I won't be in good shape if I get home at midnight."

By saying no, you don't always win your case, but the matter becomes open to discussion and negotiation. Whether you win, lose, or draw, your speaking up makes you feel better about yourself. This also applies to bosses. If you have trouble saying no to the people who work for you, your unassertiveness will affect both your own work and self-respect.

(d) As an independent, in business for yourself, you must speak up for the money your services are worth. With goods, you know the cost to you; you add the overhead and a preset rate of profit. But "services" represent your own time and skill. Objectively, you realize what a reasonable fee would be. But then doubts enter. "Am I really worth this?" . . . "What if I lose the client?" . . . "What if the client says my services aren't worth that fee? Is that a reflection of me, a put-down of my professional competence?" Thinking these self-deprecating thoughts, many people ask for a lower fee and then resent it. One designer told me, "I get too hungry and too eager. I bid lower and come out losing financially and emotionally." I have found this to be a fairly common problem among psychotherapists starting their own practice, and it sometimes crops up even among well-established therapists.

Such a problem may threaten your professional enterprise. Yet, you can often overcome it with simple practice. First, set the fee. If you're not sure of what it should be, consult with someone whose judgment you respect. Then practice saying it aloud: "My fee for this job will be ———— dollars." Say it into a tape machine, to your spouse, roommate, a friend. Then say it in the professional situation. The client may accept it. If he does not, you may have another decision to make: "Am I willing to work for a lower fee in this particular instance?" If you make this deliberate decision after having spoken up, the chances are you will not feel resentful.

(3) *Define your problem behaviors in job interpersonal relations and deliberately work to change them.* Try to reduce the anxiety connected with them, or actually change your pattern.

(a) When you must fire an employee. No one likes to do this, but sometimes it must be done. If you are upset about letting an ineffective employee go to the point where you have avoided it, desensitize yourself. Determine the stimulus cues that might make you feel uptight and then role-play them with someone. Usually they fall into two categories:

· You are uptight about saying, "You're fired."
· You are uptight about the potential response that might come from the person you fire.

If it's the former, set up a hierarchy where you use the following phrases:

"Jones, please try to do better work."
"Jones, things are bad, and we might have to let you go."
"You're not working out. We have to let you go."
"Your work is terrible. You're fired."

You may have no intention of using the "you're fired" phrase, but by continuing the desensitization to this point, you make it easier for yourself to say, "We'll have to let you go."

If you are uptight about what the employee might say, you usually fear either an angry or a tearful response. Here is an example of an anger hierarchy where you role-play responses to the following statements:

A crestfallen, "OK, I'm sorry it didn't work out."
An annoyed, "You're being very unfair to me."
An angry, "You're just using me to cover up your own inadequacies."
An anger outburst: "Goddamnit to hell. You're just a no-good bastard."

If you fear tears or that the person will plead poverty, role-play your responses to the following:

"I'm sorry it didn't work out."
"This is a very bad time for you to fire me. I need the money, and the job situation is tight."
"You didn't know it, but my boy is very sick. This means I can't get him the medical treatment he needs."
Complete hysterics or a dead "This was my last chance. I don't know what I'll do now. I guess I'm just no good."

Deliberately relax yourself as you role-play whatever situation applies to you until you can experience each step without anxiety, and then go on to the next step. Then do it in the life situation.

(b) When you know what you want to do, but don't know how to do it in a manner you respect. Women particularly want to stand up for themselves, but they have been brainwashed by society to think that if they make demands, ask for raises, push for promotions, it will be "masculine" or "castrating."

LABORATORY EXERCISE FOR WOMEN

If you are female, know what you want, but don't know how to get it without unfairly criticizing yourself, use a form of the "Idealized Self-Image" technique, devised by Dr. Dorothy J. Susskind of Hunter College.

Imagine the ideal woman you would like to be on the job. What is she like? What are her characteristics?

How would this Idealized Woman act in the situation that you are concerned about? What would she say, do, and how would she go about doing it?

Role-play the situation mentally a couple of times (this is called *covert modeling*). Keep doing this until you are able to act that way in the life situation. I have known people who performed this covert modeling about one hundred times before they could actually do it—but they did it.

Go do it.

The Idealized Self-Image technique should help you select the actual behaviors you want to perform, and the covert modeling should prove of assistance in actually doing them.

(c) Practice problem situations beforehand. Be prepared. Don't expect some divine angel to come to your aid on the spot. Use behavior rehearsal. Competence often decreases anxiety.

For example, Lorna Elman, a social worker, felt tremendous anxiety about presenting cases at her weekly agency conference. Her main fear: that she would be asked some question about a client that she would be unable to answer. I instructed Lorna that as she prepared a case for presentation, she should also make up a list of possible questions that might come up and practice the responses she might give. She did this homework assignment with a twofold result: (1) because she thought through the case more thoroughly, she organized a better report; (2) she gained the confidence that she could answer any question a fellow staff member might ask. This didn't mean she would know the correct answer to every question; it did mean she would give a professionally adequate answer. With her anxiety reduced, Lorna actually began to enjoy her case presentations.

(d) You can't prepare for everything in advance. You must be able to think creatively on your feet and communicate your thoughts so that they get through to others. This ability is particularly important in major business meetings and conferences but also in informal groups and even in one-to-one situations. You can train yourself.

LABORATORY EXERCISE IN THINKING
AND COMMUNICATION

Purpose: To help you develop creative ideas—and communicate them.

For his doctoral thesis at Columbia University, Dr. Michael Brown, a former actor, worked out a method of training people for the creative communication so necessary in business conferences, negotiations, and presentations. The following exercises, adapted from his system, are designed to help you think well on your feet and tell a story in an interesting manner. I use them in Assertiveness Training groups, but you can perform them with the aid of a friend or audio tapes and a mirror.

STEP ONE: Take a subject and talk about it for one minute in as interesting a manner as you can.

STEP TWO: Choose from two kinds of subjects: (1) something that has to do with your own life. For instance, in one minute tell why your piece of stationery is the best on the market or how, after eighteen failures, you solved the paper shortage for your company. Point: to discuss something factual in an interesting way. (2) Talk in a creative way about some completely nonsensical topic. Tell why you believe a full-grown man-eating crocodile makes a perfect household pet or why you believe the Johnny Carson Show is the "most educational program on TV" or how shoe trees got their name. In therapy, the value of this exercise comes from springing the topic suddenly on the patient and training him to think quickly and creatively on his feet, as he must in so many business situations.

STEP THREE: After you make your one-minute presentation, evaluate both content and manner. Could you have given your talk in a more imaginative way? Did you speak loudly and firmly, without pauses? Did you stand with confidence?

In doing this exercise, I have found certain common difficulties. If you don't personalize your story with the pronoun "I," it comes out flat. If you make your story too abstract and general, instead of specific, it won't get attention. Don't get caught in so much detail at the beginning that you never get to the subject.

STEP FOUR: After evaluating, repeat the story, trying to be still more creative. I know one group of business executives who use these exercises as a warm-up before all important meetings.

(4) *Recognize that other people have feelings too.* All the reactions of co-workers do not center around you. They are independent of you, and possess their own thoughts, feelings, problems. A colleague may act irritably with you, not because of anything you've done, but because he has a headache, had a fight with his wife, or is worried about *his* job. Just because you are task-oriented at the moment does not mean he is, too.

For example, one morning one of Jean's bosses telephoned her in a wild fit of temper and ordered her to do something Jean considered "unprofessional and unreasonable." In despair, and wanting either to tell off the editor or quit, Jean called me for advice. "Wait," I counseled. "Maybe she was upset about something." That afternoon, the boss apologized. "When I called you," she told Jean, "I had just learned my favorite niece is dying of cancer. Forget what I told you to do—and please forgive me."

VII: Negotiate the system

Having the behavioral skills is necessary, but not sufficient. You must know where and when to apply them. This means a knowledge of the business system in general and your own job situation in particular. You have to learn to keep abreast of changes within your company and determine whether they provide a threat or opportunity for you. If you're ambitious, you must work in an area where your work shows. Research scientists call this finding a Grade A problem. For example, James D. Watson of *Double Helix* fame knew that if he solved the structure of the DNA molecule, he would win a Nobel Prize. If you want to move up the corporate ladder, you can't remain in an invisible corner. You have to understand the importance of socializing outside the company and the who, what, when, and where of this social interaction. You have to absorb the policies, attitudes, and prejudices within the company. This knowledge of the system will enable you to make the decisions you want to make.

(1) *Keep your job goal in mind.* Just because an opportunity comes up does not mean you have to take it. It may actually lead you away from your goal. Or the opportunity may cause you to see your present situation in a different way.

CASE

I was treating Dick Harris, a black physician, for assertive difficulties in close relationships. During the course of treatment he was offered the position of chairman of the department of pediatrics at a prestigious medical college. Dr. Harris didn't know whether to accept the job or not.

I did two things to help him make the decision. I had him imagine what he would like his professional life to be like five years from now. In addition, I had him describe the professional duties of the department chairman and then to imagine himself performing them. The discrepancy between what he wanted and what he would get became obvious. As department chairman, he would be involved in administrative work instead of the clinical and research work he desired. He decided that the opportunity would take him away from his goals.

When Dr. Harris arrived at my office the next week, he informed me that he had accepted the position. He said, "We didn't consider one point. That medical college has never had a black department chairman before, and it is important to establish the precedent. For the sake of this principle, I am willing to sacrifice my own personal goals." Here, he acted out of deliberate choice, and was sufficiently assertive to reconsider his goals.

(2) *Know how to deal with the prejudices you face.* Sometimes you can discuss them. Sometimes you must fight. This applies particularly to women in business; for despite all the liberation, many men still find it hard to treat a woman boss with respect and others feel it's only right that men earn more.

CASE

Peggy Berke competed with a man in her firm for a job. She won out, and the former peer, now her subordinate, commenced to give her a hard time. He started to hand in work late, and Peggy began to get in trouble with her own job. She knew she must confront him, but was bothered by her own fears. "It's enough that I beat him out. Why do I have to finish the castration and take away what is left of his manhood," she told me. We role-played the situation. Peggy gained control over herself and eventually had her showdown. She began, "We have a problem," laid out the situation, and then asked, "What can we do?" She did this feeling like a boss and knowing that if the man's work did not improve, she had the self-confidence to let him go. After the discussion, there was a great deal more friendliness and a better performance by the male subordinate. Peggy had established her position.

(3) *Know when to quit.* Sometimes the system is too inflexible or lacks the potentiality for fulfilling your goals. One woman, formerly an executive secretary, taught typing at a female junior college. She found the job oppressive, but liked the fact that there were no secretarial duties. In therapy with Dr. Iris Fodor of New York, she thought through what she could do that she would prefer. Her solution: a job at a much higher salary at a suburban night school where there were male and female teachers.

Sometimes, the system doesn't work for you because your goals or the job situation has changed. Twice in my own life I faced this problem. The first time was many years ago when I had a full-time job in a hospital setting and a small office practice in the evenings. The hospital routine was so unstimulating that it began to affect my own work. One day, I was reading a very bad psychological report on a patient and saw my own signature at the bottom of the page. "How could I have allowed myself to do something so bad?" I thought, and I knew I had to leave the job. I decided to take the chance on full-time private practice even though I was married to my first wife, had one small child and another on the way. Within two months of leaving the hospital, I had made up the income.

The second time occurred recently, when I was fifty years old, on the faculty of a medical college, divorced and remarried with extensive financial obligations. Suddenly there was a series of administrative changes at the college. Most of the people I respected left. No one was left to challenge me, and the bureaucrats hampered my work. I knew I had to get out. By that time, I had an excellent professional reputation, and when I cast about for part-time faculty jobs, I found quite a few. Most paid well, but would take me from the main thrust of my professional development. I opted for the one that would give me a chance for professional growth even though it entailed a major cut in income. It did have a side benefit. Because of its growth opportunities, my reputation grew and so did my practice.

I want to stress that I felt enormous fear and anxiety in making these two choices at different times in my life. Both situations might not have worked out. I was lucky. They did.

Was it luck? It worked for me. Would it work for you? I knew my goal: the opportunity for professional development. For the person with the goal of security, these would have been the wrong decisions.

In operating in the business world, always ask yourself two assertive questions:

Where do you want to go?

What do you have to do to get there?

Chapter XIII
The Group

This is the story of an Assertiveness Training group which met last winter in my living room for ten successive weekly hour-and-a-half sessions.

Of the eight-member group, ranging in age from twenty-five to sixty and in occupation from plumber to pediatrician, five had undergone previous analytically oriented therapy. It had worked very well for one, moderately well for another, not well for two, and had, in his own words, made one member go "from bad to worse."

At the end of ten weeks of AT, each participant had changed his life in some way. For some, the changes were major.

The group:

· Tess A., a slim, tense pediatrician in her early forties. Despite her successful analysis, Tess felt she had one problem left to conquer. She couldn't say no—not to the mothers of the kids she treated, her secretary, her husband. As a result, Tess constantly assumed new burdens for which she had neither the time nor the desire.

· Rose W., sixty-year-old director of a settlement house. She presented her problem as one limited to the job situation. "I have no trouble talking to individuals, but groups of people terrify me. When I have to give a speech, I shake, and my work requires a lot of public speaking."

· Dorothy M., an actress who twenty years ago had played second leads in a series of broadway shows, but left the theater for marriage and motherhood. Now, at forty, children away at school, she yearned to return to the stage. But in two decades Dorothy had lost her confidence. She said, "Everyone will have forgotten me. I've lost my looks, and people will reject me. I'm not sure I can act anymore."

· Jill J., a twenty-five-year-old married executive secretary who felt dissatisfied with her lack of friends and wanted to build a social network.

· Willie R., a thirty-five-year-old plumber who entered treatment because his schoolteacher wife insisted on it. As in all things, Willie did what she wanted. On the job, Willie acted very assertively about leaks and clogged kitchen pipes, but at home he never took the initiative. His wife wanted him to be a man of action. So did Willie, but he didn't know how to go about it.

· Lyle S., a computer programmer in his early thirties, had come to me originally because of his marital and sexual difficulties. The problem: Lyle's aggressiveness. A tall, slim man, he seemed quiet; but when he spoke up, it took the form of sharp remarks, sarcasm, and temper outbursts. Unable to express anger appropriately, he also had trouble communicating tender feelings to his wife, whom he really loved very much.

· Ernie K., a thirty-year-old taxi driver (the one who had gone from "bad to worse" in traditional analytically oriented therapy). Like Lyle, Ernie also acted aggressively with people. He felt "furious" at Manhattan traffic, had decided the police were "devils out after me," and constantly engaged in fights with passengers. In addition, Ernie suffered from tremendous tension. This emerged at the initial group session. Although he made eye contact with the seven others, he glared at them so much that he antagonized everyone. Unmarried, Ernie lived in a furnished room, and his experiences with passengers represented virtually his sole social contacts.

· Frank B., a forty-two-year-old accountant in a big firm, who felt he should have advanced much further in his job. His problem: Frank was a homosexual. He believed that if he spoke up on the job in any way, his fellow workers would reject him with disgust.

I used the first session to get the group members to know each other, to formulate the individual goals, and to establish a task-oriented attitude in the group. In successive sessions, I used a variety of Assertiveness Training techniques, ranging from relaxation to role-playing.

For example, with Ernie I had two goals: (1) to reduce his tension. In the group, he had to practice relaxing himself and then carry this same technique over to the life situation while driving and talking with passengers. (2) To shape his behavior so that he could make mannerly conversation with riders in a normal voice and with no threat of violence. I also taught him to handle put-downs. With Ernie, we did a lot of group role-playing as we did with Rose, Willie, Tess, Lyle. With Jill and Dorothy I utilized behavior assignments. I gave Jill exercises in saying hello to neighbors in the elevator, making dates with other couples. I instructed Dorothy to renew her theatrical contacts.

The group interaction proved of tremendous help. For example, Frank feared the group members would find out about his homosexuality and reject him. He particularly feared Ernie's reaction. So I had to see Frank individually and give him role-playing practice in how to speak up to the group. I played Ernie. At the third session, Frank spoke up to the group about his homosexuality, and they accepted it as if they'd known it all the time. I asked Ernie, "How do you feel about it?", and he responded simply, "That's Frank's business." This gave Frank the confidence to practice speaking up on his job, give opinions at meetings, deal with superiors, converse with co-workers.

The following is a capsule account of what had happened with each participant at the end of ten weeks.

Using my tapes and exercises in the group, plus in-life practice with mothers and her secretary, Tess had learned to say no. She had also started saying no to her very demanding husband. This crystallized Tess's decision to break up her marriage. She told us, "I don't know if it's for good or bad, but it's something that has to be done."

Rose had discovered that her problems in dealing with people weren't limited to the job. Her newly acquired openness and ability to communicate her thoughts and feelings had affected her marriage. She reported, "My husband told me, 'You've changed more in ten weeks than in twenty-five years of marriage.' " For Rose, the turning point had come midpoint in the ten sessions. For the fourth session, I asked every group member to come in prepared to tell a two-minute story about a meaningful emotional experience before the age of twenty. The point of this story-telling was to increase openness. Rose related a moving story of how, during her childhood, an older boy neighbor, whom she adored, was killed in a hunting accident. Although she told the story well, Rose confessed to enormous nervousness. So I asked her to prepare another story for the next session. When she entered the room, Rose looked so terrified that I commanded, "Take control. Relax yourself." She was able to do this. Later she told me, "This was the point of change. From then on I could control my anxiety."

Young Jill had started socializing with a whole group of people and had established a solid beginning for a social network. One of her new friends was Rose.

Dorothy was ecstatic. By the tenth session she had reestablished a circle of acquaintances within the theatrical world and was being considered for a forthcoming Broadway production. At the initial session, she gave long lists of reasons why she wouldn't be considered for any part, so she "shouldn't even apply." As she described a recent tryout at the last session, she stated firmly, "This part's for me."

Lyle seemed to be on his way. Through extensive role-playing of fights within the group, he had learned to tell his angry feelings in an open way, without tantrums. Now Lyle spoke assertively rather than aggressively. He had also learned to reveal tenderness. For the group, he played a tape made by his wife in which she told of the changes in his relationship with her.

Willie was only a partial success. He had assumed more responsibility in making marital decisions. For instance, he had planned the next vacation he and his wife would take. He was also doing more things on his own, such as going to hockey games with friends. He still had a long way to go, and more AT was indicated.

Frank had told a co-worker (one he had known for fifteen years) about his homosexuality. The colleague had responded just as the group members had, saying "Everyone knows it and nobody cares." By the end of treatment, Frank had achieved no job advance; but six months later, he switched to a much better position with another firm.

Ernie felt much calmer, had ceased fighting with passengers, and had almost doubled his tips. But his treatment wasn't finished. Because of his bad manners, he had never built a social life, so I placed him in another AT group with the goal of a social network.

In concluding this book, I would like to take the two most frequent questions I am asked—one practical, one personal.

Q. *How do you find a behavior therapist who can do Assertiveness Training?*

A. I recommend two ways:

(1) If you want a roster of behavior therapists, write for a list of Clinical Fellows of the Behavior Therapy and Research Society, c/o Eastern Pennsylvania Psychiatric Institute, 3300 Henry Avenue, Philadelphia, Pennsylvania 19129.

(2) Write the Association for the Advancement of Behavior Therapy, 475 Park Avenue South, New York, New York 10016, for a list of members in your area. This organization is an interest organization, not a competence organization, and will not recommend behavior therapists. However, its members are professionals interested in behavior therapy, and should know a therapist in your area.

Q. *Do you think doing so much Assertiveness Training has made you more assertive?*

A. Yes. I find myself constantly doing all the things I teach my patients to do. In social and work situations, I encourage myself to speak up. In talking with patients about goals, I reevaluate my own goals. Thus, I changed my professional affiliation, my wife, and my entire life-style.

It worked for me. It can work for you.

Appendix

FULL RELAXATION EXERCISE

The following is the text of a tape recording made during a relaxation session and given to patients to take home. Readers who wish to record it for their own use should have it read by a person whose voice can on demand assume a lulling quality. The passages referring to the tensing of the muscles should be read briskly. Those calling for relaxation are read in a slow, soothing, almost musical cadence that carries some element of hypnotism.*

Lie down. Your eyes are closed. Your arms are at your sides, your fingers open. Get yourself good and comfortable. If stray thoughts enter your mind, say to yourself, STOP. Push them away and concentrate on what we are doing—

The first thing to do is tighten the muscles in the lower part of your body. Turn your feet inward, pigeon-toed, heels slightly apart. Curl your toes tightly, bend your feet downward away from you—now upward toward you—this tightens the muscles along your shins and in your calves—At the same time, tighten up your thighs, tighten up the muscles of your buttocks, and the muscles around your anus—not so tight that they are strained, but tight enough to feel the tension—Study it, study the tension—Tense, tense, tense—*(Five-second pause)*.

---

* From *Help Without Psychoanalysis,* Herbert Fensterheim, Ph.D. New York, Stein and Day, 1971.

Now relax—Just feel the tension flow out—Concentrate on relaxing the muscles of your toes—Relax the muscles of your legs—Relax the muscles of your thighs—Relax your buttocks, the muscles around your anus—Now concentrate on each part of your body as I name it—Toes relaxed—legs relaxed—thighs relaxed—muscles of your buttocks—relaxed—All the tension out—*(Ten-second pause)*

Now tighten up the muscles of your abdomen. Make the muscles of your abdomen as taut as if a child were going to shove a football into your stomach—Get them good and tight—Study the tension—Feel where the tension is—Hold it for ten seconds—Hold it—Tense—tense—tense—

And now relax—Relax the muscles of your abdomen—Let them go—Try to relax the muscles deep inside your abdomen —the muscles of your gut—Let them go—You are more and more and more relaxed—*(Ten-second pause)*

And now the muscles of your back—Arch your back—arch the small of your back until you feel the tension build—Try to locate the tension—There are two long muscle columns alongside your spine—You may feel the tension there—Wherever it is get to know the feel of tension—Your back is tense—tense—tense—

And now relax—Relax the muscles of your back—Let them go—Let all the tension out—Your back feels limp and heavy—Let it stay that way—More and more and more relaxed—*(Ten-second pause)*

And now the muscles of your chest—Take a deep breath and hold it—Just keep on holding it—Five seconds—Notice as you hold your breath the tension begins to build up—Note the tension in your chest muscles—Study where it is—Ten seconds—Keep holding your breath—Recognize the feeling of tension—Fifteen seconds—Now slowly, as slowly as you can, let your breath out—Slowly—Now breathe easily and comfortably, as in a deep sleep—*(Pause)*—Keep on relaxing the muscles of your chest—Let them go—Let the tension out—*(Ten-second pause)*

Now concentrate on each part as I mention it—Abdomen relaxed—Back relaxed—Chest relaxed—All the tension out—*(Pause)*

And now the muscles of your fingers, arms, and shoulders—

Make a tight fist with each hand—Keep your elbows stiff and straight—Elbows stiff and straight as rods—Raise your arms from the shoulders to a forty-five degree angle—The angle of your arms is halfway between the couch and vertical—Now feel the tension—Study the tension—Study the tension in your fingers—in your forearms—in your arms and your shoulders—Hold the tension for ten seconds—Hold it—Hold it—Tense—tense—tense—

And now relax—Fingers open—Arms down to sides—Just relax—Relax the muscles of your fingers—Let them go—Relax the muscles of your upper arms—Let them go—And now the muscles of your shoulders—Let them go—*(Pause)*—Fingers relaxed—arms relaxed—shoulders relaxed—Let your arms feel limp and heavy—Just keep letting go—*(Ten-second pause)*

And now the muscles between the shoulder blades and the muscles of your neck—Pull your shoulders back until your shoulder blades are almost touching—At the same time arch your neck until your chin points to the ceiling—These are areas very sensitive to nervous tension—Many people feel most of their tension here—Feel the tension—Not so tight that it hurts—Study the tension—Let it build up—

Now relax—Relax the muscles between your shoulder blades—Let the tension flow out—Let it go—And relax the muscles of your neck—Let them go—Your neck muscles are not supporting your head—Your head is falling limply against the pillow—All the tension out—Feel it flowing out—*(Ten-second pause)*

And now the muscles of the upper part of your face—Make a grimace with the top part of your face—Squeeze your eyes tight shut—Wrinkle your nose—Frown—Notice where you feel the tension—Study it—Note that you feel the tension in the forehead, between the eyebrows, in the cheeks below the eyes—

Now relax—let all the tension out—Just concentrate on relaxing the muscles of your forehead—Let them go—Relax your eyelids—As they relax, you note they begin to feel heavy—They make you feel drowsy, but you're not going to sleep—You must stay alert—Relax the muscles at the bridge of your nose—Let them go—Relax the muscles of your

cheeks—Remember where they felt tight—Let them go—
(Ten-second pause)

And now the muscles of your jaws and tongue—Bite hard
with your back teeth, press them together until your jaws are
tight—Feel the tension at your temples, by your ears—Wherever you feel the tension, study it—Push your tongue against
the back of your lower front teeth—Your jaws are tight—Your
tongue is tight—Study the tension—Get to know it—Learn
the feel of the tension—Hold it, hold it—

Now relax. Relax the muscles of your jaws—Let them
go—Relax your tongue—Your teeth should be slightly parted
—Your jaw is hanging slack—More and more relaxed—*(Ten-
second pause)*

Now the muscles around the lower part of your face—Tense
the muscles around your mouth and chin—The best way to
make them tense is to grin—A big grin, a grimace—Draw
back your lips to show your teeth, upper and lower teeth—
Draw the corners of your mouth wide, pull them back and
down—Feel the tension in your lips, around your mouth, in
your chin—Let the tension build up—Hold it—feel it—study
it—Tense—tense—tense—

Now relax—Relax the muscles around your mouth and
chin—Let them go—Get all the tension out—*(Ten-second
pause)*—Now try to relax the muscles of your throat—Relax
the soft part of your throat—Relax the soft part of your throat
where you swallow—Relax the muscles of your voice box—
Just try to get all the tension out of there—*(Ten-second pause)*
That's the end of the first part of the exercise—Keep your eyes
closed; you're still relaxing.

Now for the second part. Just ask yourself: Is there any
tension in my legs, in my thighs, in my buttocks? If there is, let
it go—Try to get all the tension out—More and more
relaxed—*(Ten-second pause)* Then ask yourself: Is there any
tension in my abdomen, my back, or my chest? If there is, let it
go—Breathe easily and comfortably, the way you do in a deep
sleep—All the tension out—*(Ten-second pause)* And now ask
yourself: Is there any tension in my fingers, my arms, or my
shoulders?—If there is, let it go—Let your arms get limp and
heavy—*(Ten-second pause)* Now ask yourself: Is there any
tension between my shoulder blades or in my neck? If there is,

let it go—Your head is falling limply back to the pillow—
(Pause)—And now ask yourself: Is there any tension in my
face, my jaws, or my throat? If there is let it go—All the
tension out—Just keep letting go. *(Pause)*

And now the third part of the exercise.* Picture your
pleasant scene, the scene we discussed before, or if you have
trouble with that, picture the word CALM—Get a good clear
picture, not just the sight, but the sounds, the smells, and the
feel—If your mind wanders, always bring it back to the
pleasant scene. And while you hold that picture in mind,
concentrate on relaxing the muscles of your toes—Let them
go—*(Pause)*—Relax the muscles of your thighs—Let them go
—*(Pause)*—Relax the muscles of your buttocks—Let them
go—*(Pause)*—Keep picturing your pleasant scene. If stray
thoughts come into your mind, just tell yourself STOP. Put
them away—Just concentrate on the muscles of your abdomen—Let them go—Relax—*(Pause)*—Relax the muscles of
your back *(Pause)*—Relax the muscles of your chest—Breathe
easily and comfortably—Keep picturing your pleasant scene
—*(Pause)*—Relax the muscles of your fingers—Let them
go—*(Pause)*—Relax your forearms—*(Pause)*—Relax the muscles of your shoulders—Let them go—*(Pause)*—Relax the
muscles of your shoulder blades—Let them go—*(Pause)*—
Relax the muscles of your neck—Let them go—*(Pause)*—
Keep picturing the pleasant scene—Relax the muscles of your
forehead—Let them go—*(Pause)*—Relax your eyelids—
(Pause)—Relax the muscles at the bridge of your nose—Let
them go—*(Pause)*—Relax your jaw muscles—Relax your
tongue—Relax the muscles around your mouth and chin—Let
them go—*(Pause)*—Relax the muscles of your throat—All the
tension out—Let yourself feel limp and heavy all over—Now
keep picturing the pleasant scene—Calm and relaxed—Calm
and relaxed—*(Ten-second pause)*—If you feel tension anywhere,
just let it go—*(Thirty-second pause)*—Now I'm going to count
from three to one. At the count of one, you will sit up and open
your eyes. You'll be alert and wide awake and very refreshed
—Three—two—one.

INTERMEDIATE RELAXATION EXERCISE

This takes thirteen minutes less than the Full Relaxation Exercise. Instead of tightening each part of the body separately, you tighten your whole body all at once, hold the tension about seven seconds, and then explode it out. Next step: take a deep breath, hold it for about twenty seconds, and then slowly release it. This permits the carbon dioxide in your blood to build up. Finally you imagine your pleasant scene or the word "Calm" and relax your body as in the Full Relaxation Exercise.

Lie down. Make yourself comfortable. Arms at sides. Fingers open. Eyes closed. Throughout these exercises if stray thoughts come to you, you tell yourself "Stop," push them away, and concentrate on whatever you're doing.

First part of exercise: tighten your whole body all at once. Not so tight that it is strained, but tight enough so that you can feel the tension build up. Your job is to study the tension, to get to know where you feel tight.

Put your toes together pigeon-toed, heels slightly apart, and push your toes down away from you. That tightens your leg muscles. Tighten your thighs—tighten your buttocks—tighten your abdomen. Raise your arms from your shoulders, fists clenched, elbows stiff. Squeeze your eyes tight shut—clench your teeth—keeping your face all tight, arch your neck, point your chin to ceiling. Just hold it. Hold it (about seven seconds). Let it explode out. Arms back to your sides, chin down. Concentrate on feeling of tension flowing out (about ten seconds).

Now check out the muscles of legs and thighs. Any tension? Take it a spot at a time and let it go. (About five-second pause). Relax the muscles of your abdomen and back. (five-second pause). The muscles of fingers and arms, let them feel pleasantly heavy (five-second pause), the muscles of your face and jaws, relax those (five seconds).

Now take deep breath through mouth and hold it. Just keep holding it. (Fifteen- to twenty-second pause.) Now slowly let it out (pause), and at the end breathe easily and comfortably the way you do in a deep sleep.

And now picture your pleasant scene* (continue from paragraph 1 page 263) to end of that exercise.

Bibliography

Agras, W. Stewart. *Behavior Modification*. Boston: Little, Brown and Company, 1972.

Alberti, Robert E., and Emmons, Michael L. *Your Perfect Right*. San Luis Obispo, California: Impact, 1970.

Aldrich, Elizabeth Perkins. *As William James Said*. New York: The Vanguard Press, 1942.

American Psychiatric Association. *Behavior Therapy in Psychiatry: Task Force Report 5*. Washington, D.C.: American Psychiatric Association, July 1973.

Bach, George R., and Wyden, Peter. *The Intimate Enemy*. New York: William Morrow & Company, 1968.

Bandura, Albert. "Modeling Approaches to the Modification of Phobic Disorders." In *The Role of Learning in Psychotherapy*, A Ciba Foundation Symposium, edited by Ruth Porter. Boston: Little, Brown and Company, 1968.

————. *Principles of Behavior Modification*. New York: Holt, Rinehart and Winston, Inc., 1969.

Barlow, David H.; Reynolds, Joyce; and Agras, W. Stewart. "Gender Identity Change in a Transsexual." *Archives General Psychiatry*, Vol. 28, April 1973.

Beck, Aaron T. *Depression*. Philadelphia: University of Pennsylvania Press, 1967.

Bergin, Allen E., and Garfield, Sol L. *Handbook of Psychotherapy and Behavior Change*. New York: John Wiley & Sons, Inc., 1971.

Bibring, Edward. "The Mechanism of Depression." In *Affective Disorders*, edited by P. Greenacre. New York: International University Press, 1953.

Block, Jeanne Humphrey. "Conceptions of Sex Role." *American Psychologist*, Vol. 28, no. 6, June 1973.

Cautela, Joseph R., and Kastenbaum, R. "A Reinforcement Survey Schedule for Use in Therapy Training and Research." *Psychological Reports* 20 (1967): 1115–1130.

————. "Covert Conditioning of Addictive Behaviors." In *Behavior Modifica-*

tion with the Individual Patient, edited by Upper, Dennis, and Goodenough, David S. Proceedings of the Third Annual Brockton Symposium on Behavior Therapy. Nutley, New Jersey: Roche Laboratories, 1972.

——. "Covert Reinforcement." *Behavior Therapy* 1 (1970): 33–50.

Chirico, Anna-Marie, and Stunkard, Albert J. "Physical Inactivity and Human Obesity." *New England Journal of Medicine* 263 (1960): 935–940.

Edwards, Neil B. "Case Conference: Assertive Training in a Case of Homosexual Pedophilia." *Journal of Behavior Therapy and Experimental Psychiatry*, Vol. 3, no. 1, March 1972.

Eisler, Richard M.; Herson, Michel; and Miller, Peter M. "Effects of Modeling on Components of Assertive Behavior." *Journal of Behavior Therapy and Experimental Psychiatry*, Vol. 4, no. 1, March 1973. New York: Pergamon Press.

Eisler, Richard M.; Miller, Peter M.; and Herson, Michel. "Components of Assertive Behavior." *Journal of Clinical Psychology*, Vol. 23, no. 3 (1973), pp. 295–299.

Ellis, Albert, and Harper, Robert A. *A Guide to Rational Living*. North Hollywood, California: Wilshire Book Company, 1960.

Ellis, Albert. "Rational-Emotive Therapy." *Direct Psychotherapy*, edited by Jurjevich, Ratibor-Ray M. Coral Gables, Florida: University of Miami Press, Vol. 1, 1973.

Eysenck, H. J., and Rachman, S. *The Causes and Cures of Neurosis*. San Diego, California: Robert R. Knapp, 1965.

Fensterheim, Herbert. "Assertive Methods and Marital Problems." *Advances in Behavior Therapy*, edited by Rubin, Richard P.; Fensterheim, Herbert; Henderson, John; Ullmann, Leonard P. New York: Academic Press, 1972.

——. "Behavior Therapy: Assertive Training in Groups." *Progress in Group and Family Therapy*, edited by Sager, Clifford J., and Kaplan, Helen S. New York: Brunner/Mazel, Inc., 1972.

——. *Help Without Psychoanalysis*. New York: Stein and Day, 1971.

——. "The Behavior Therapy of Sexual Variants." *The Journal of Sex and Marital Therapy*, Nov. 1974.

——. "The Initial Interview." *Clinical Behavior Therapy*, edited by Lazarus, Arnold A. New York: Brunner/Mazel, Inc., 1972.

Ferster, C. B. "A Functional Analysis of Depression." *American Psychologist*, Vol. 28 (Oct. 1973): 857–870.

Ford, Clellan S., and Beach, Frank A. *Patterns of Sexual Behavior*. New York: Harper & Brothers and Paul B. Hoeber, Inc. Medical Books, 1951.

Franks, Cyril M., and Wilson, G. Terence, eds. *Annual Review of Behavior Therapy and Practice*. New York: Brunner/Mazel, Inc., 1973.

Freedman, Alfred M., and Kaplan, Harold L. *Comprehensive Textbook of Psychiatry*. Baltimore: The Williams and Wilkins Company, 1967.

Freud, Sigmund. *An Outline of Psychoanalysis*. New York: W. W. Norton, 1949.

——. "Mourning and Melancholia." *Standard Edition of the Complete Psychological Works of Sigmund Freud*. London: Hogarth Press, 1957.

Friedman, Philip H. "The Effects of Modeling and Role-Playing on Assertive Behavior." *Advances in Behavior Therapy*, edited by Rubin,

Richard D.; Fensterheim, Herbert; Lazarus, Arnold A.; Franks, Cyril M. New York: Academic Press, 1971.

Gazda, George M. *Basic Approaches to Group Psychotherapy and Group Counseling.* Springfield, Illinois: Charles C. Thomas, 1968.

Gordon, Thomas. *P.E.T.: Parent Effectiveness Training.* New York: Peter H. Wyden, Inc., 1970.

Gornick, Vivian. "Why Radcliffe Women Are Afraid of Success." *The New York Times,* January 14, 1973.

Gutride, Martin E., and Goldstein, Arnold P. "The Use of Modeling and Role-Playing to Increase Social Interaction Among Asocial Psychiatric Patients." *Journal of Consulting and Clinical Psychology,* Vol. 40, no. 3, June 1973.

Herson, Michel; Eisler, Richard M.; Miller, Peter M.; "Development of Assertive Responses: Clinical, Measurement and Research Considerations." *Behavior Research and Therapy* 11 (1973): 505–521.

Hilgard, Ernest R., and Bower, Gordon H. *Theories of Learning.* 3rd ed. New York: Appleton-Century-Crofts, 1966.

Horney, Karen. *Neurosis and Human Growth.* New York: W. W. Norton & Company, Inc., 1950.

Jacobson, Edmund. *Self-Operations Control.* Philadelphia: J. P. Lippincott Company, 1964.

Jakubowski-Spector, Patricia. "Facilitating the Growth of Women Through Assertive Training." *The Counseling Psychologist,* Vol. 4, no. 1 (1973), pp. 75–86.

James, William. *The Principles of Psychology.* New York: Henry Holt & Company, 1890. Reprint. New York: Dover Publications, Inc., 1950.

———. *Psychology, Briefer Course.* New York: Collier Books, 1962.

———. *Selected Papers on Philosophy.* London: J. M. Dent & Sons, 1917.

Kanfer, Frederick Y., and Karoly, Paul. "Self-Regulation and Its Clinical Application: Some Additional Conceptualizations." In *Conscience and Social Reality,* edited by Johnson, R. C.; Dobecki, P. R.; and Mowrer, O. H. New York: Holt, Rinehart and Winston, 1972.

Kanfer, Frederick H., and Phillips, Jeanne S. *Learning Foundations of Behavior Therapy.* New York: John S. Wiley & Sons, 1970.

Kaplan, Helen S. *The New Sex Therapy.* New York: Brunner/Mazel, Inc., 1974.

Knox, David. *Marriage Happiness.* Champaign, Illinois: Research Press, 1971.

Lake, Alice. "Get Thin/Stay Thin." *McCall's,* January 1973.

Lazarus, Arnold A. "Learning Theory and the Treatment of Depression." *Behavior Research and Therapy* 6 (1968): 83–89.

———. *Behavior Therapy and Beyond.* New York: McGraw-Hill Book Company, 1971.

———. *Clinical Behavior Therapy.* New York: Brunner/Mazel, Inc., 1972.

———. "On Assertive Behavior: A Brief Note." *Behavior Therapy,* Vol. 4, no. 5 (October 1973), pp. 697–699.

Lehrman, Daniel S. "Behavioral Science, Engineering and Poetry." In *The Biopsychology of Development,* edited by Tobach, Ethel; Aronson, Lester R.; and Shaw, Evelyn. New York: Academic Press, 1971.

Lyons, Richard D. "Psychiatrists, in a Shift, Declare Homosexuality, No Mental Illness." *The New York Times*, December 16, 1973.

Maliver, Bruce L. *The Encounter Game.* New York: Stein and Day, 1973.

Marlatt, G. A., and Kaplan, B. E. "Self-Initiated Attempts to Change Behavior: A Study of New Year's Resolutions." *Psychological Reports* 30 (1972): 123–131.

Marshall, Austin. *How to Get a Better Job.* New York: Appleton-Century, 1964.

Maslow, Abraham H. *New Knowledge in Human Values.* New York: Harper and Brothers, 1959.

————. *The Farther Reaches of Human Nature.* New York: The Viking Press, 1971.

Masters, William H., and Johnson, Virginia E. *Human Sexual Inadequacy.* Boston: Little, Brown and Company, 1970.

————. *Human Sexual Response.* Boston: Little, Brown and Company, 1966.

McFall, Richard M., and Lillesand, Diane V. Bridges. "Behavior Rehearsal with Modeling and Coaching in Assertion Training." *Journal of Abnormal Psychology*, no. 3, June 1971.

McFall, Richard M., and Twentyman, Craig T. "Four Experiments on the Relative Contributions of Rehearsal Modeling and Coaching to Assertion Training." *Journal of Abnormal* Psychology, Vol. 81, no. 3, June 1973.

Neuman, Donald, "Using Assertive Training." In *Behavioral Counseling*, edited by Krumboltz, John D., and Thoresen, Carl E. New York: Holt, Rinehart and Winston, Inc., 1969.

Patterson, Gerald R. *Applications of Social Learning to Family Life.* Champaign, Illinois: Research Press Company, 1971.

Patterson, Gerald R., and Gullion, Elizabeth M. *Living with Children.* Champaign, Illinois: Research Press Company, 1968.

Pavlov, I. P. *Conditioned Reflexes.* New York: Dover Publications, Inc., 1960 (an unaltered republication of the translation first published in 1927 by the Oxford University Press).

Penick, Sydner B.; Filion, Ross; Fox, Sonja; and Stunkard, Albert J. "Behavior Modification in the Treatment of Obesity." *Psychosomatic Medicine*, Vol. XXXIII, no. 1, January-February. New York: Harper & Row, Publishers, Inc., 1971.

Razran, Gregory. *Mind in Evolution: An East-West Synthesis of Learned Behavior and Cognition.* Boston: Houghton Mifflin, 1971.

Reese, Ellen P. *The Analysis of Human Operant Behavior.* Dubuque, Iowa: William C. Brown Co., 1966.

Robbins, Jhan, and Fisher, Dave. *How to Make and Break Habits.* New York: Peter H. Wyden, Inc., 1973.

Ross, Dorothy M.; Ross, Sheila A.; and Evans, Thomas A. "The Modification of Extreme Social Withdrawal by Modeling with Guided Participation." *Journal of Behavior Therapy and Experimental Psychiatry*, Vol. 2, no. 4, Dec. 1971. New York: Pergamon Press.

Rubin, Theodore Isaac. *The Thin Book by a Formerly Fat Psychiatrist.* New York: Pinnacle Books, 1972.

Sager, Clifford J., and Kaplan, Helen S. *Progress in Group and Family Therapy.* New York: Brunner/Mazel, Inc., 1972.

Salter, Andrew. *Conditioned Reflex Therapy.* New York: Farrar, Straus & Giroux, Inc., 1949; Capricorn Books Edition, 1961.

Sansweet, Stephen J. "Aversion Therapy: Punishing of People to Change Behavior Gains Use, Controversy." *Wall Street Journal*, 3 January 1974.

Serber, Michael. "Teaching the NonVerbal Components of Assertive Training." *Journal of Behavior Therapy and Experimental Psychology*, Vol. 3, no. 3, Sept. 1972. New York: Pergamon Press.

Skinner, B. F. *Beyond Freedom and Dignity.* New York: Alfred A. Knopf, 1971.

———. *Science and Human Behavior.* New York: Macmillan, 1953.

Stuart, Richard B., and Davis, Barbara. *Slim Chance in a Fat World.* Champaign, Illinois: Research Press Company, 1972.

Stuart, Richard B., and Stuart, Freida. *Marital Pre-Counseling Inventory.* Rev. ed. Champaign, Illinois: Research Press Company, 1973.

Stuart, Richard B. "Operant-Interpersonal Treatment for Marital Discord," *Journal of Consulting and Clinical Psychology*, Vol. 33, no. 6, Dec. 1969.

Stunkard, Albert J. "Obesity." In *Comprehensive Textbook of Psychiatry*, edited by Freedman, Alfred M., and Kaplan, Harold L. Baltimore, Maryland: The Williams and Wilkins Company, 1967.

———. "New Therapies for the Eating Disorders." *Archives of General Psychiatry*, Vol. 26, May 1972.

Stunkard, Albert J., Levine, Harold; and Fox, Sonja. "The *Management of Obesity.*" *Archives of Internal Medicine*, Vol. 125, June 1970.

Susskind, Dorothy J., "The Idealized Self-Image (ISI): A New Technique in Confidence Training." *Behavior Therapy*, Vol. 1., no. 4, Nov. 1970.

Szent-Györgyi, Albert. *The Crazy Ape.* New York: Grosset & Dunlap, 1971.

Tuffill, S. G. *Sexual Stimulation: Games Lovers Play.* New York: Grove Press, Inc., 1973.

Ubell, Earl. *How to Save Your Life.* New York: Harcourt, Brace Jovanovich, Inc., 1973.

Ullmann, Leonard P., and Krasner, Leonard. *Case Studies in Behavior Modification.* New York: Holt, Rinehart and Winston, Inc., 1966.

———. *A Psychological Approach to Abnormal Behavior.* Englewood Cliffs, New Jersey: Prentice-Hall, Inc., 1969.

Upper, Dennis, and Goodenough, David S. *Behavior Modification with the Individual Patient.* Proceedings of the Third Annual Brockton Symposium on Behavior Therapy. Nutley, New Jersey: Roche Laboratories, 1972.

Voltaire. *Philosophical Dictionary.* New York: Basic Books, 1962.

Wolpe, Joseph. *The Practice of Behavior Therapy.* Elmsford, New York: Pergamon Press, Inc., 1969.

———. *The Practice of Behavior Therapy.* 2nd ed. Elmsford, New York: Pergamon Press, Inc., 1973.

———. "Supervision Transcript: V—Mainly About Assertive Training." *Journal of Behavior Therapy and Experimental Psychiatry*, Vol. 4, no. 2 (1973), pp. 141–148.

Wolpe, Joseph, and Lazarus, Arnold A. *Behavior Therapy Techniques.* Long Island City, New York: Pergamon Press, Inc., 1966.

Index